[8—0a]
Peaches

[8—0]
Plums

[8—0b]
Pears

[8—0c]
Apples

[8—1]
Peonies and Daylilies

NEW *ILLUSTRATED*

ENCYCLOPEDIA

OF GARDENING

UNABRIDGED

EDITED BY T. H. Everett

Assistant Director (Horticulture) and Curator of Education
The New York Botanical Garden

WITH CONTRIBUTIONS FROM

TWENTY HORTICULTURISTS AND AUTHORITIES
IN THE UNITED STATES AND CANADA

Growers, Breeders, Exhibitors, Plantsmen, Writers, Lecturers, Professors, Editors and Superintendents of Famous Estates, who are Experts in all Fields of Horticulture, including Pests and Their Control.

VOLUME EIGHT—Ora-Pic

 GREYSTONE PRESS · NEW YORK

ORCHARD: PLANNING, PLANTING AND MANAGEMENT
Basic Advice for Obtaining Successful Crops

An orchard is a plot of land chiefly used for fruit growing. The land may be cultivated in preparation for planting and grassed down as soon as the orchard trees are well established, or the trees may be planted in grassland without further cultivation. In many orchards the trees are planted in arable land which is kept permanently cultivated, bush fruits being planted as "fillers" among the permanent trees for the first few years, or permanently.

If properly cared for, the home orchard produces an abundance of high-quality fruit.

The commercial orchard established solely for profit and conducted throughout on marketing lines hardly falls within the scope of this article; chief attention will be given to the garden or home orchard. This may form a part of the amateur's garden or estate, and is planted mainly for the purpose of supplying the home with fruit.

How to Ensure Quick Returns. To hasten returns from the orchard, it is now a general practice to plant the permanent trees in well-prepared ground, and interplant quick-cropping "filler" trees and bush fruits to provide fruit in the early years. The temporary "filler" trees and bushes must be ruthlessly removed as soon as they begin to crowd the permanent trees, which they will begin to do in 8-15 years, depending upon the distances of planting.

Alternatively, as stated above, the orchard ground may be cultivated permanently, permanent fruit trees being set far enough apart to permit intercropping with bush fruits throughout the existence of the orchard. The grower must give these matters careful consideration before planting if disappointing results are to be avoided. Mistakes in planning and planting the home orchard are easily made and may prove almost impossible to correct except at considerable cost and inconvenience.

An important consideration is the suitability of the district for particular kinds of fruit. Certain localities are much more favorably situated for the cultivation of some kinds of fruits than of others. Particularly is this the case with the "stone" fruits, as Plums and Cherries, and with Pears.

The prospective planter should make a careful survey of neighboring orchards and gardens, and be guided by the kinds of fruit known to succeed in the district. Those kinds and varieties which local conditions obviously do not favor should be avoided; failure to pay due attention to peculiarities of soil and situation has led many amateur planters to disaster. It is quite

An Apple orchard in bloom is one of the prettiest of garden scenes.

In fall, well-tended Apple trees bear abundant crops of choice fruit.

In this Peach orchard the trees are just coming into bloom.

Cherry trees are favorite orchard trees in regions where climatic conditions suit them.

advisable to consult the State Agricultural Experiment Station (See State Agricultural Experiment Stations) and the local County Agricultural Agent before planning an orchard.

Ideal Position for an Orchard. In low-lying situations and valleys, late spring frosts may be so prevalent and severe as to destroy all prospects of fruit trees' setting and maturing good crops. Well-nigh ideal conditions are provided when the site is somewhat high in relation to the surrounding country, yet sheltered from cold winds, and where the ground slopes slightly to the south or southwest. Such favorable conditions cannot be available to all, nor are they essential to success; though bleak, low-lying land should be avoided if good results are to be obtained with the minimum of disappointment and serious effort.

The ideal soil for an orchard is deep loam with well-drained subsoil. Very light, sandy soil and heavy clay land both have serious disadvantages and tend to predispose many fruit trees to disease. In general, many types of soil are suitable for orchard planting but, when at all possible, extremes should be avoided.

Good Drainage Is Most Important. Many failures can be traced to planting in waterlogged and sour land, a condition which must be improved before the trees are planted. In heavy clay, tile drains should be laid 2 ft. or 2 ft., 6 in. deep, and about 30 ft. apart, and leading to a suitable discharge point or outlet.

The preparation of the soil for orchard planting is most important, and has considerable bearing upon the future welfare of the trees. If the land has been previously well cultivated for ordinary garden crops, no special preparation should be required, beyond cleaning and deep digging or plowing. When farm land is being prepared for fruit, an important cultural item is to break up the hardpan of subsoil formed by the shallow plowing carried out for many years past. This hardpan may be broken up with a special subsoil plow or by a deep-working mechanical cultivator.

When the orchard is to be devoted entirely to trees, planted wide apart in cultivated ground or grassland, it will be sufficient to prepare deeply a space some 5-6 ft. in diameter where each tree is to be set. If small bush (low-headed) trees are to be interplanted among the tall trees, however, the whole area should be deeply cultivated.

In every instance the ground must be thoroughly cleaned of all deep-rooting perennial weeds. To plant in ground overrun with these is a mistake not easily remedied later. When planting in grassland even, the grass should be brought into good condition before the trees are set, such perennial weeds as thistles and docks being eradicated. Before planting fruit trees, it is advisable to devote a whole season to proper tilling and cleaning of the land.

In the arable orchard, or orchard to be grassed down later on, Potatoes may be planted as a cleaning crop, the ground being well manured for these. The repeated cultivating and earthing-up tills the soil thoroughly and destroys troublesome weeds; when the potato crop is

Part of a demonstration home orchard at the Berkshire Garden Center, Stockbridge, Massachusetts.

lifted, a further cleaning and cultivating will leave the ground in good condition for the fruit-tree planting during late autumn and early spring months.

If the orchard land is poor and light, a dressing of manure should be applied when the ground is being prepared. Cow or horse manure should be put on at the rate of 15-30 tons per acre, according to the nature and condition of the soil. Good land will not need this, for it is unwise to make the ground so rich that young trees are excessively vigorous in growth; rank, coarse growth delays fruiting and encourages disease. If manure is not obtainable, a heavy application of compost will help.

Green manures, such as Mustard, Rye, Vetches, Lupines and so on, may be sown in summer and plowed under during autumn, just previous to planting, and are especially beneficial on light land. Fertilizers (see the article under this heading) are best applied after the trees are well established.

Experience and experiment show clearly that when grass is allowed to grow over the roots of newly planted fruit trees, it has a most detrimental—sometimes even fatal—effect upon the trees. When you plant trees in grassland, a circle 4-5 ft. in diameter should be kept cultivated or mulched for the first three or four years.

Land that is acid should be well limed before planting. Particularly is this necessary where Plum and Cherry trees are to be planted.

If the orchard is very exposed and open to strong winds, it is advisable to plant a windbreak or shelter belt of tall trees on the windward side and at some little distance away. Quick-growing trees should be chosen for this.

Protection from rabbits, deer and other animals, including straying stock, will be necessary in many districts and should be provided before any trees are planted. In a single night rabbits may damage the trees so severely as to ruin them entirely. The cheapest and best protection is afforded by erecting a chicken-wire fence round the orchard. Galvanized wire netting, 4-5 ft. wide, 1½-in. mesh, and 18 gauge, should be used, and supported by stout posts driven in at intervals of 12-15 ft. or so apart. The bottom 6 in. of the netting should be let into the ground and

bent outwards, so that animals such as woodchucks, approaching close to the fence and attempting to burrow beneath, are foiled by the part of the netting underground.

The wire netting will be held taut and prevented from sagging if it is secured along the top to a single straining wire of about 14 gauge, stretched tightly between the tops of the supporting posts.

How to Prevent Damage by Rabbits. If the orchard is not fenced against rabbits the young trees may be protected from damage by smearing the stems with paste or liquid distasteful to them. Special rabbit deterrents can be bought, or a homemade smear may be prepared from this recipe:

Take 1 lb. of salt, 2 lb. of painters' or paper-hangers' size, a little less than ½ pint of kerosene and 10 lb. of good clay. Mix the lot together thoroughly; puddling it with sufficient water to make a creamy paint. Brush this on the tree stems in winter, for 2 ft. or more up from the ground.

How Far Apart to Plant. Orchard trees should be widely and regularly spaced. It must be remembered that many make big spreading branches when mature and need ample space for proper development. Too-close planting is a common error. The best distances to plant vary with the general arrangement of the orchard and are indicated in this work in the articles dealing specifically with each of the various kinds of fruit. (See Apple, Pear, Plum, Cherry, Peach, etc.)

How to Estimate the Number of Trees Required. When preparing to plant an area of land with fruit trees, the grower must estimate closely the number of trees he will require to fill the allotted space. Knowing the distance apart at which the trees are to be set and the size of the piece of land to be planted, this number can be easily ascertained. As an example, take an acre of land to be planted with trees 10 ft. apart each way. To ascertain the number of trees required, multiply the distance in feet between the rows (10 ft.) by the distance in feet the trees are to be apart in the rows (10 ft.), and that gives the area each tree requires. This number divided into the number of sq. ft. in an acre, which is 43,560, gives the number of trees required to plant the acre—43,560 divided by 100=435 trees. Work any other example on the same lines. Ascertain the number of sq. ft. each tree requires, then divide that figure into the number of sq. ft. covered by the area of land to be planted—which gives the number of trees needed. Failure to estimate the exact number of trees needed may lead to unnecessary expenditure, or delay in completing the planting.

How to Arrange the Trees. Many systems of arranging the trees in the orchard are practiced: for example, the Square system, the Quincunx, the Triangular and Hexagonal; probably the simplest plan is to plant the trees on the Square system. Here the trees are equal distances apart each way, so that each tree stands at the corner of a square. This system is well adapted for interplanting and for the removal of temporary or alternate trees when permanent trees are mature and need more space, or when drastic thinning becomes necessary.

Autumn is the best time for planting most orchard trees; planting should in any case be completed before the trees commence growth in spring. The ground should be carefully marked out and the position for each row or tree marked with a peg or cane, in readiness for planting.

A hole at least 3 ft. across should be dug out for each average-size nursery tree, though a hole half that size would be sufficient for each "maiden" tree. When planting in grassland, make the planting hole at least 5 ft. across. The holes should rarely be dug out more than 9-12 in. deep, but the bottom of each must be well broken up with the fork. Turf pared off the surface may be chopped up and thrown into the bottom of the holes. It is a mistake to dig out the holes for the trees a long time before the actual planting date; if wet weather follows, water collects in them, making the soil waterlogged and unfit to receive the trees.

All broken and damaged roots should be pruned off, and coarse or deep-striking taproots should be shortened by half their length before the tree is placed in position in the hole.

Too-deep Planting Is a Common Error. In heavy land the topmost roots should be covered by not more than 3 in. of fine soil, and even in

very light ground they should be not more than 5-6 in. below the surface. Roots must be spread out evenly in natural tiers and good topsoil packed around and among them, each tree being tested for exact alignment in the rows before the roots are covered with soil.

The use of a planting board and long line, together with sighting posts, is necessary to ensure correct alignment when long rows of trees are being planted. When the roots are just lightly covered with soil, this should be trodden down firmly before the planting hole is quite filled up. A layer of well-rotted manure may be placed in and covered with the remainder of the soil.

Staking the Trees. Young trees should be staked at planting time. For high-headed trees in grassland the double stake and crosspiece afford most serviceable support. Drive in a stout stake on each side of the tree and about 6 in. from the stem, the top of the stakes reaching to about a foot below the lowest branches. Near the top of these stakes nail a crosspiece of wood and, after binding the stem with a thickness of burlap or rubber hose, tie it securely to the crosspiece.

For low-headed trees the single upright stake tied close to the main stem, and planted with the tree, is often sufficient, but the oblique stake is considered by many growers to be best. Drive the stake well into the ground about a couple of feet from the tree stem and slantwise, so that the top comes against the stem of the tree at a point just below the lowest branch.

Bind rubber or burlap around the stem, then tie it securely to the stake with strong twine or soft cord. The top of the oblique stake should point in the direction from which the strongest and most frequent winds are to be expected.

The trees should be pruned after planting and before growth commences in spring. All growths bruised or broken during lifting or transit should be cut back, and further cutting is directed to the shaping of the small branches to build up a well-balanced head. The newly planted trees should be given a mulch of manure or compost in spring, this being spread in a circle all around the tree and left to decay. Applications of fertilizers may also be made as described in our articles on the various fruits.

The cultivation and general management of

the orchard are carried out in the manner described for the different fruits under the separate headings of Apple, Plum, Cherry, etc. In particular, the young trees planted in the grass orchard will need to be generously fertilized until well established, and subsequently. If growth is stunted and weakly, the area clear of grass around each tree should be increased in size and the cultivated circle liberally mulched with manure each spring. If the grass orchard is cut for hay, the land must be heavily manured to compensate for the plant foods removed from the soil by the hay crop. Generally, it is advisable to cut the grass and leave it to rot on the ground around the trees, rotting being accelerated by dressings of sulphate of ammonia and ground limestone.

When the orchard ground is cultivated, the surface soil must be kept continuously stirred during spring and summer months to prevent the soil from caking hard, to destroy weeds, and to arrest the excessive loss of water during dry spells.

The trees must be pruned each winter, and spraying operations must be carried out as thoroughly as with garden trees, each winter and spring. When the permanent orchard trees are temporarily interplanted with bush fruits and "filler" trees, the removal of these must on no account be delayed unduly. When the removal of the close-planted temporary trees is delayed long after the permanent trees have reached good bearing age and require the full space for proper development, the big trees may suffer a serious handicap, not easily overcome in after years.

Renovating a Neglected Orchard. Many amateur gardeners have to deal with a neglected orchard filled with old, unprofitable trees, so crippled by age and years of neglect as to present a serious problem. When the trees are aged and badly infested with disease and pests, it is very difficult to restore them to health and fruitfulness without considerable labor and cost. Trees obviously badly diseased should be grubbed up and burned, root and branch.

Thinning Out the Trees. Old orchards are often unproductive and unhealthy owing to close planting, the trees presenting a thicket of entangled branches which deprive each other of light and air sufficient to permit healthy and normal development. Drastic thinning out and hard pruning will effect improvement in most such cases. It may be necessary to grub up alternate trees and drastically to reduce the number of branches in the remaining trees. Crossing and crowded branches in the middle of the trees and dead and unhealthy growths should be cleanly amputated, and the tree brought into balanced and shapely form by judicious trimming of straggling branches. Thinning the crowded parts is more beneficial than cutting back big branches all over the tree, which encourages further rank growth.

The cutting should be sufficiently severe to allow sunlight and air to penetrate to every part of the tree, even during the summer months, so that the wood will ripen satisfactorily and the crops color and mature normally. All large pruning cuts made during this renovation must be at once sealed over with a coating of tree-wound paint to prevent the entry of disease germs through the exposed tissues.

A Common Cause of Failure. A very common cause of old established orchards' falling into ill-health and unproductiveness is insufficient fertilizing. It is certain that many old orchards are practically starved, having long since exhausted the soil of natural supplies which have not been replaced. In the cultivated orchard, manure should be applied in autumn, followed by sulphate of potash at the rate of about 300 lb. to the acre in late winter, and sulphate of ammonia at the rate of 100-200 lb. per acre in early spring. If the trees are very weak and make little or no new growth, the fertilizing program should be repeated for two or three seasons in succession.

Spraying will play an important part in the renovation of neglected trees. The greatest improvement will be effected by spraying according to schedules recommended by your State Agricultural Experiment Station. Dormant sprays (sprays applied in late winter before new growth begins) are usually of the utmost importance in renovating neglected orchards.

The spraying must be done very thoroughly and the spray applied with the maximum pressure. Amateur gardeners often attempt it with equipment poorly designed for the purpose.

ORCHID: IT ADDS BEAUTY
TO THE GREENHOUSE AND GARDEN
A Guide to the Cultivation of These Fascinating Plants

The orchids are a group of plants consisting of many genera and containing about 15,000 different species or wild types distributed throughout the world, except in the coldest regions. They are classed, according to their manner of growth, as epiphytal (those which grow naturally perched on trees, etc.) or terrestrial (those which grow in soil). In addition to the wild species, many thousands of hybrid kinds have been raised and each year their number increases.

The Orchids comprise the family Orchidaceae. The flowers are often quite showy, possessing a corolla of three petals, one of which, the lip (labellum), may be spurred. The name Orchid comes from the Greek word *orchis,* testis.

Probably no other family contains so great a variety of plants and flowers. The beauty, the strange shapes, and the longevity of many Orchid flowers, together with the comparative ease with which many kinds can be grown, have drawn increasing attention to these plants, particularly the epiphytal kinds, which mostly have larger flowers than the terrestrial kinds. In Cypripedium, Cymbidium, Cattleya and Odontoglossum, the hybrids artificially raised far exceed the species or wild types in number and in many instances surpass them in size and floral coloring.

Orchids from different countries, and the hybrids which have been raised from them, can be grown in the same greenhouse, for many kinds need similar conditions. Details of cultivation concerning the various kinds of orchids will be found under their respective names.

Environments for Tender Orchids. In the warmest parts of the United States considerable success is had with the cultivation of certain groups of tender Orchids out of doors. In southern California, for instance, Cymbidiums are grown in garden beds filled with specially

Among the best-known Orchids are the highly decorative Cattleyas, Laelias and Laeliocattleyas. This is a Laeliocattleya.

prepared soil, in southern Florida various epiphytal kinds including Dendrobiums, Epidendrums, Laelias, Oncidiums and Vandas are grown on trees out of doors with, usually, provision made to protect them from extremely low temperatures by covering them on nights when such conditions are expected with hoods of heavy cloth. Although outdoor cultivation is possible in favored regions, over most of the United States and Canada the only practicable way of cultivating tender Orchids is to grow them indoors, and even in the warmest parts of the United States this is the method chiefly followed.

In recent years considerable attention has been directed towards the possibilities of cultivating Orchids as house plants. While some skilled amateurs have undoubtedly had measures of success in growing these plants in their homes the needs of most Orchids, especially with regards to atmospheric humidity, temperatures and observance of their resting seasons, are too exacting for them to succeed under the environmental conditions and care that can be afforded them in most houses and apartments. The best success is to be expected when Orchids grown as house plants are accommodated in terrariums. It must be remembered that Orchid plants are tenacious to life and that even under adverse circumstances it usually takes a long time to kill them; but keeping alive slowly deteriorating specimens in the house and successfully growing Orchids are two very different things.

For best success tender Orchids must be grown in greenhouses. For convenience they may be divided into three groups, those that prefer tropical greenhouse conditions, those that thrive in moderately warm greenhouses and those that definitely need cool greenhouses for their best development. Examples of kinds that require each of these environments are given below.

In all cases high relative humidity of the atmosphere is necessary; relative humidities of 60-80 per cent are favorable. Care must be taken not to permit the air to become dank and stagnant; careful attention to damping down, syringing and ventilating will prevent this.

Orchids need shade, but not so much as most people believe. Except in the deep South and Southwest no shading is needed from late fall until February. Many popular Orchids, including Cattleyas, Laelias, Dendrobiums, Oncidiums, Vandas and Epidendrums flower most freely if

A greenhouse devoted to the cultivation of Cattleyas and Orchids requiring similar cultural conditions.

in summer they receive 20-30 per cent of the outdoor light, Aerides, Calanthes, Cymbidiums and Lycastes prosper if they receive 15-20 per cent of outdoor summer light, Coelogynes, Miltonias, Odontoglossums, Cypripediums and Phalenopsis give the best results if they are subjected to 10-15 per cent of outdoor light in summer. Plants grown in excessive shade develop rich green foliage but tend to be soft and do not bloom freely. If given optimum light the foliage usually is slightly yellowish and the pseudobulbs yellowish or reddish. Too much sun causes excessive yellowing and burning (browning) of the foliage.

Orchid greenhouses may be shaded with roller blinds which can be raised or lowered as light conditions change or by painting or spraying the outside of the glass with a mixture of gasoline and white lead, whitewash, cold water paint or one of the special compounds that are sold for the purpose.

Because epiphytic Orchids require a free circulation of air about their roots as well as their tops it is advisable to stand those growing in pots and pans on a lattice made of wood slats spaced 1-1½ in. apart or on a framework covered with stout hardware cloth. The greenhouse bench should be covered with a layer of pieces of coke, coarse cinders, gravel or charcoal and the lattice or hardware cloth should be raised a few inches above the surface of this. The purpose of the layer of coke or other materials is to hold moisture which is evaporated into the air, thus humidifying the atmosphere.

Some epiphytic Orchids thrive best when they are grown in pots, pans or baskets, on orchid rafts or simply attached to pieces of bark, wood or sections of stems of Tree Ferns, and suspended from the greenhouse roof so that they are fairly close to the glass.

Potting. Orchids are grown in a number of media. Traditionally, the favorite compost in which to grow the epiphytic kinds is osmunda fiber (known also as orchid peat and osmundine). This material is sometimes modified by the addition of other ingredients. In recent years other potting media have been employed with increasing frequency, but osmunda fiber is still by far the most commonly used potting compost for epiphytic Orchids. Chopped live sphagnum moss is mixed with the osmunda fiber for some

An Orchid greenhouse in which Odontoglossums, Miltonias and Cymbidiums are grown.

Orchids by some growers. Other, equally successful cultivators prefer to use osmunda without the admixture of sphagnum moss.

One of the most practical substitutes for osmunda fiber for potting is shredded tree bark. The barks of Douglas Fir, Redwood and some other trees have been used successfully. Yet another satisfactory potting medium is the fiber of the trunks of Tree Ferns.

Orchids are also grown in inert materials such as gravel and are fed with nutrient solutions. This, of course, is a hydroponic practice; it has been successfully used with Phalenopsis and three or four other kinds of Orchids but is still somewhat experimental and is not well suited for the average amateur. Orchids potted in tree bark and those potted in Tree Fern fiber also require regular applications of very dilute fertilizers. No fertilizing is necessary when osmunda fiber is used as a potting medium.

The technique of potting in osmunda fiber and in mixtures of osmunda and sphagnum moss differs from that of potting in other media. The chief difference is that instead of the material being rammed into the pot from the top with the potting stick it is stuck in from the top and then is pressed in to the center from the sides. The procedure is as follows: after the plant has been prepared for potting by taking out any stakes, removing it from its pot, cutting away unwanted parts, picking out the old crocks and all old decayed compost, and after the plant has been carefully examined for and cleaned of, scales and any other insects, it is placed in a clean

Here are three interesting Orchids that are comparatively easy to grow. Coelogyne pandurata. A Hybrid Cattleya. Bulbophyllum Medusae.

pot filled with crocks to about one third the depth of the pot and of a size just sufficient to easily accommodate it.

If it is an Orchid of a kind that grows chiefly in one direction laterally over the surface of the compost by extending a rhizome from which it sends up new growths or pseudobulbs, as do Cattleyas, Laelias and many other kinds, the plant should be set with the growing end of the rhizome (the end which gives rise to the new growth or pseudobulbs) towards the center of the pot and with the oldest pseudobulb touching one side of the pot, if it is of a kind that does not have rhizomes but produces more or less erect stems that extend themselves upward (here belong Vandas, certain kinds of Epidendrums and Vanillas) the plant is set in the center of the pot. Kinds which extend themselves over the surface in all directions, as do Coelogynes, are also centered in their new pots.

Pieces of osmunda fiber (the osmunda fiber is thoroughly soaked in water before it is cut into pieces and is allowed to dry to the extent that when used it is fairly pliable but not wet) about as large as an egg (smaller for pots less than 5 in. in diameter) are placed under and among the roots and, with the plant held in position with one hand, other pieces are stuck between the roots and the sides of the pot. A tapered potting stick is then pressed between the fiber and the pot and, using its lower end as a fulcrum against the side of the pot, the fiber is levered towards the center. More and more fiber is added in the same manner and in the same way is forced towards the center. Only when it is virtually impossible to make way for more fiber is the potting firm enough.

The surface of the fiber should be mounded slightly from sides to center, with the sides a little below the rim of the pot and the center about level with it. Care must be taken not to break the roots and also to keep the rhizome on top of the fiber and not to bury it. A neat finish is obtained by trimming the surface of the osmunda fiber with shears. A well-potted Orchid should be so secure in its pot that it is possible to pick the plant up by its leaves without the pot dropping off or the plant seeming loose.

Newly potted Orchids do not need watering for a week or two and great care should be taken not to over water them after that. Light overhead spraying of the plants is beneficial.

When Orchids are potted in shredded bark, gravel and the like, the compost is simply worked among and around the roots and made firm as the work proceeds.

Terrestrial Orchids, such as Cymbidiums and Cypripediums are potted in the same manner as any ordinary plant grown in soil but the compost is not packed very firm. Soil mixtures for them are given in the cultural directions for each kind.

Vegetative Propagation. The propagation of Orchids from seeds is a highly specialized procedure and is undertaken chiefly for the production of new hybrids. Most Orchids can, however, easily be increased by division and some by offsets, cuttings or air layering. Division of large plants is done just before or as new growth starts

(at potting time). With few exceptions (a few terrestrial kinds such as Calanthe and Phaius) it is unwise to let each division consist of less than four or five growths or pseudobulbs. Dividing Orchid plants into fractions that are too small results in weak plants.

When Orchids of many types, for example Cattleyas, are divided, either for propagating purposes or at potting time, there remain some "backbulbs." These are the pseudobulbs attached to the piece of rhizome that is left when the forward portion that includes the youngest four or five pseudobulbs is removed for potting as an individual plant. The backbulbs have no eyes or growing buds and hence, unlike the forward portions of the rhizome, do not soon develop new growths. But if they are stood closely together on a bed of sphagnum moss or shredded bark kept constantly moist, in a warm, well-shaded place and if they are syringed lightly two or three times a day they will, after several months, develop good eyes and can then be potted individually. At potting time backbulbs have few or no roots, hence they must be secured in place with hairpinlike loops of wire pushed over the rhizome into the compost and by tying the pseudobulbs to wire stakes pushed vertically into the compost.

Some Orchids, such as Dendrobiums and the tall-growing Epidendrums, produce young plants or offsets freely from near the tops of their canelike shoots. When they have completed a season's growth these offsets may be carefully removed and potted individually as young plants.

Dendrobiums and Epidendrums that form canelike stems can also be increased by stem cuttings. The mature canes are cut into sections and laid horizontally on a bed of moist sphagnum moss, shredded bark or sand in a shaded moist place. The flower stems of Phaius, cut after the blooms have faded and treated as cuttings in the same manner as the stems of Dendroniums and Epidendrums, will give rise to young plants if they are treated in the same way.

Vandas, Vanillas and other erect-growing Orchids that produce aerial roots are easily propagated by air layering.

Orchids from Seeds. Raising Orchids from seeds requires special apparatus and the

A Cattleya Orchid plant in need of potting.

Note that the end of the rhizome has reached the edge of the old pot and new roots are beginning to grow over the side.

In preparation for repotting, the growths are untied from the stakes and the stakes are removed from the pot.

Dead scales are removed from the bases of the pseudobulbs and the plants are carefully inspected to make sure they are free of scale insects.

The pot is then inverted and the rim tapped sharply on the edge of a bench to remove the plant.

The plant is divided with a sharp knife. The forward part of the rhizome, containing 4 or 5 pseudobulbs, is retained as the new plant. The back bulbs may be kept for propagation.

A clean pot is crocked by first placing a large piece of crock concave side downward in the bottom.

Then the pot is filled to one-third its depth with smaller crocks.

Orchid peat (osmunda fiber) is cut into egg-sized pieces after first being well moistened.

A cone of fiber is placed over the crocks.

The plant is placed with its new growth towards the center of the pot and pieces of fiber are pushed down around it.

The fiber is made firm with a potting stick by levering it from the sides towards the center of the plant.

A wire stake is then pushed down among the fiber and the pseudobulb is tied to it.

The surface of the fiber is cut smooth with a pair of shears.

Potting finished, the plant is ready for returning to the greenhouse.

employment of special techniques. Briefly, it is necessary first to sterilize the seeds then to sow them under strictly aseptic conditions on an agar jelly which contains certain nutrients in carefully weighed proportions. The jelly is held in glass flasks and after the seeds are sown these are kept in a place where light and temperature can be carefully controlled. Those interested in raising Orchids from seeds should consult one of the specialist books devoted to the culture of Orchids. There are special laboratories which, for a fee, will germinate Orchid seed sent to them by growers.

Watering. Good judgment in watering Orchids is of first importance to their successful cultivation. Carelessness in this spells poor results or failure. Many amateurs ruin their plants by applying water too often. This results in excessively rapid decay of the potting compost and rotting of the roots among other troubles. The chief danger of overwatering occurs in winter, during spells of dull, moist weather at other times and during those seasons when the plants are partially or completely dormant. In summer when days are long, good light abundant and temperatures high Orchids in active growth require generous supplies of water. When a plant is watered sufficient should be given to wet the entire mass of roots and compost. Generally, it is advisable to complete watering during the forenoon rather than later in the day. Water applied at about the same temperature as the atmosphere is better than water that is much colder. Rainwater is to be preferred to water from other sources and this is especially true if the other water is alkaline. The water should be neutral or slightly acid in reaction, never strongly alkaline.

Syringing and Damping Down. To maintain the necessary atmospheric humidity and promote healthy growth it is necessary to syringe the foliage of Orchids one or more times a day whenever the weather is favorable and to damp down (wet) all such surfaces as paths, walls and beneath the benches in greenhouses so that they are always moist. In warm, sunny weather more frequent syringing is needed than at other times.

When to Pot. Orchids may need repotting because they are outgrowing their containers, because the osmunda fiber or other compost in which they are planted has rotted and is becoming sour or because they are in a compost that does not suit their needs. Osmunda and shredded bark normally remain in acceptable condition for 2 and sometimes 3 years, after that repotting is necessary. Sometimes, in the case of Orchids such as Coelogynes which resent disturbance of their roots, the need for repotting can be delayed by picking out from the centers of the pots (where the fiber decays most rapidly) decayed portions of the osmunda and replacing it with fresh. If pressure of work or other reason prevents repotting Orchids that grow in the manner of Cattleyas before their newest growth pushes over the side of the pot it is a good plan to tie under the new growth when it is developing a sizable wad of osmunda fiber and let a part of this rest between the rim of the pot and the new growth. The new growth will root into this added fiber and this

Orchid plant potted in bark.

will make it easier to keep the roots intact next time the Orchid is potted.

Orchids Which Need a Tropical Temperature. The greenhouse in which tropical Orchids are grown should have a winter temperature of 65 degrees by night, rising to 70 degrees or more by day. It suits the needs of most kinds of Vanda, Phalaenopsis, Renanthera, Dendrobium, Oncidium, a few of the Cattleyas, Anoectochilus, Catasetum, Cirrhopetalum, Bulbophyllum and Cypripedium.

Orchids for a Warm Greenhouse. The intermediate house, often called the Cattleya house, should have a minimum winter temperature of 60 degrees with a rise to 65 degrees by day; in very cold weather, the temperature may fall to 55 degrees at night. Most kinds of Cattleya, Laelia, Brassavola, Stanhopea, Sobralia, Zygopetalum, Bulbophyllum, Cirrhopetalum, Cypripedium, and Epidendrum can be grown there.

Orchids for a Cool Greenhouse. In a cool greenhouse several beautiful Orchids can be grown. The minimum temperature in winter should be 45 degrees, but a temperature of 50-55 degrees is more suitable. Orchids which are dormant during the winter, and make their growth during the summer, give the best results in the cool greenhouse; such, for instance, as Odontoglossum grande, O. pendulum, O. Rossii, Oncidium Marshalianum. O. Forbesii, O. crispum, Vanda Amesiana, Cymbidiums, some kinds of Coelogyne, Lycaste, Epidendrum vitellinum, Cypripedium insigne, several Dendrobiums, Maxillaria, Laelia, and, with care in watering, Sophronitis coccinea.

Dormant plants withstand a low temperature better than others.

The cool greenhouse should be kept at as even a temperature as possible; never force it above 55 degrees by artificial warmth, but keep it as near 60 degrees as weather conditions allow.

Hardy Orchids. Many kinds of Orchids can be grown outdoors. In the far South some epiphytic kinds (kinds which grow on trees), including certain Epidendrums, are natives, and these as well as a selection of exotic epiphytic Orchids can there be grown outdoors. Further north, epiphytic Orchids will not live over winter outdoors but there are many terrestrial

Orchids (kinds that grow in soil) that can be grown. Many of these are native Americans, others are natives of Europe and Asia. Most are rather difficult to establish in the garden and to propagate. An attempt should be made to duplicate, as closely as possible, the conditions under which they grow in nature. Hardy Orchids are found in the genera Bletia, Cypripedium, Habenaria, Liparis, Ophrys, Orchis, Pogonia and Spiranthes.

Hints on the Management of Orchids. All the greenhouses in which Orchids are grown require shading from early March until autumn by painting the glass, or by wooden shades, the latter being preferable. A moist but not dank atmosphere and ventilation without drafts or undue falls in temperature are necessary.

The best time to repot an Orchid is just as new roots are seen, which may be before young growths appear or at the same time as they are first noticed.

ORCHIDANTHA (Orchidan'tha). Two tropical perennial herbaceous plants that are natives of Malaya and are suitable for cultivating in greeenhouses. They are sometimes named Lowea. The name is derived from Orchid and from *anthos,* a flower, and refers to the likeness of the flowers to those of certain Orchids. Orchidantha belongs in the Banana family, the Musaceae.

Orchidanthas require a well-drained soil that contains an abundance of organic matter. The plants should be watered sufficiently often to keep the soil always evenly moist but not constantly saturated. A humid atmosphere is necessary and shade from strong sun should be provided. A night temperature of 60-70 degrees is satisfactory and the daytime temperature may exceed this by 5-10 degrees, or even more when outdoor temperatures are higher. Established specimens that have filled their pots with healthy roots benefit from weekly applications of dilute liquid fertilizer.

Propagation may be effected by seeds and by division. Division is best done in late winter or spring, and the divisions, after they are potted, should be kept in a warm propagating case until they have rooted freely into the new soil in which they are planted.

Kinds. O. borneensis, 12 in., pale yellow and purple; O. maxillarioides, 15 in., green and purple.

ORCHID BASKET. Orchid baskets are composed of strips of hardwood such as teak, cypress or redwood, from one-half to three-quarters of an inch square in section. Holes are bored in the ends of the wood, copper wire is passed through them, and the free ends are brought together and twisted into a hook. Similar strips of wood are used to form a base. Pieces of flowerpots, rather flat and large, are placed in the bottom of the baskets to keep in the compost.

An Orchid basket.

The advantage of baskets is that they can be suspended, and when it is necessary to renew the orchid peat or other compost in which the Orchids are growing the old compost can be easily removed from the roots by pricking it out with a sharp-pointed stick without disturbing the roots. Their disadvantage is that, when they are decayed, they are troublesome to renew without damaging the roots of the plants.

ORCHID, BUCKET. See Coryanthes.

ORCHID, BUTTERFLY. See Oncidium Papilio.

ORCHID, CHAIN. Dendrochilum, which see.

ORCHID, FRINGED. See Habenaria.

ORCHID, GOLDEN CHAIN. See Dendrochilum.

ORCHID, HELMET. See Coryanthes.

ORCHID, JEWEL. See Anoectochilus.

ORCHID, LADY SLIPPER. See Cypripedium.

ORCHID, MOTH. Phalaenopsis, which see.

ORCHID PEAT. This is a material used in place of soil for potting epiphytic Orchids. It consists of the roots of certain Ferns, chiefly Osmunda cinnamomea and O. Claytoniana. It is also called osmunda fiber.

ORCHID, PUNCH AND JUDY. Gongora, which see.

ORCHID RAFT. See Raft.

ORCHID, SPIDER. See Brassia.

ORCHID, SWAN. See Cycnoches.

ORCHID TREE. See Bauhinia.

ORCHID, TULIP. See Anguloa.

ORCHID, WOMAN'S CAP. See Thelymitra.

ORCHIS (Or'chis). A large group of terrestrial, leaf-losing (deciduous) Orchids, found in North America, Europe, the temperate parts of Asia, and northern Africa. All are tuberous-rooted and have erect, leafy stems and dense spikes of flowers.

Though these Orchids are small, some of them have attractive flowers; others are more interesting than showy. The flower formation varies considerably but in the greater number the sepals are equal in size, the upper one, with the petals, being arched over the column. The lip is three-lobed and is inclined downward, its base being protracted into a spur, usually rather short. They belong to the family Orchidaceae, and their name comes from the Greek word *orchis,* a testis.

The American kinds are more easily managed than many other native Orchids. They will thrive in rich, woodsy soil and partial shade in the wild garden or rock garden. They dislike hot, dry positions and should be set where the soil does not dry out in summer.

Native American Kinds. Two species occur in the United States and Canada and a third in Alaska. The best known of these is the Showy Orchid, O. spectabilis, which is found wild in rich woods from New Brunswick to Minnesota

and Nebraska and southward to Georgia and Arkansas. It grows about 1 ft. high and bears white and pink or white and pale purple flowers, 2-7 in each spike, in May or June. In cultivation it needs rich, moist soil and partial shade.

O. rotundifolia enjoys a natural range from Greenland to Yukon and southward to Quebec, northern New York, Michigan, Minnesota and British Columbia. It grows to nearly 1 ft. tall and has few-flowered, short spikes of blooms that are predominantly magenta but have a white lip, magenta-spotted.

European kinds include the Madeira Orchis, Orchis foliosa; it is of vigorous growth, the stems reaching a height of about 2 ft. The rose-

The Madeira Orchis, O. maderensis (foliosa), a handsome plant producing dense spikes of purple flowers on stems 2 ft. tall.

[8—2]
Palms in Florida

[8—2a]
Cinnamon Fern
(Osmunda cinnamomea)

[8—3]
Odontoglossum

[8—3a]
Oncidium varicosum

[8—3c]
Ornithogalum lacteum

[8—3b]
Osmanthus fragrans

purple blooms are in full beauty in May. This kind, like the others referred to below; thrives best in deep, loamy soil which remains moist in hot, dry weather.

O. mascula, the early Purple Orchis, flowers in spring. The leaves are deep green, spotted with brown, and the flowers are purplish.

O. Morio, the Green-winged Orchis, which has green veins on the petals, also flowers early.

O. maculata, the Spotted Orchis, like O. mascula, has deep purple-brown blotches on its leaves; the flowers are set closely together and are pale purple or lilac. The stem sometimes reaches 2 ft. in height.

O. latifolia, the Marsh Orchis, is very similar to O. maculata, but the flowers are darker in color, often purple, and the leaves are broader.

The Military Orchis, O. militaris, has flowers set closely together and variable in color, purplish or reddish.

ORCHIS, BEE. Ophrys apifera, which see.

ORCHIS, FLY. Ophrys muscifera, which see.

ORCHIS, SPIDER. Ophrys sphegodes, which see.

ORDEAL BEAN. A name given to the seed of Physostigma venenosum, a large woody climber common in western Africa, particularly in Nigeria. The beans are very poisonous, and they were at one period used for trial by ordeal in the detection of crime, under native law. Seeds were administered to the accused. If he lived after eating them, he was discharged as innocent; if he died, he was considered to have deserved his end. As trials of this character were frequent in Old Calabar, the seeds became known by the second name of Calabar Beans.

OREGANO. This name, of Spanish origin, is applied to several distinct fragrant plants, including Origanum, Lippia, Lantana and Coleus amboinicus. See Coleus amboinicus.

OREGON, GARDENING IN. See Regional Gardening.

OREGON GRAPE. Mahonia nervosa, which see.

OREGON LAUREL. See Arbutus.

OREOCEREUS (Oreoce'reus). Cacti from Bolivia, Chile and Peru, of the family Cactaceae. The plants form clusters of spiny stems which are thickly covered with hairs. For details of cultiva-tion see Cacti. The name is derived from oreos, mountain, and Cereus, an allied genus of Cacti.

The chief kinds are O. Celsianus, white hairs, yellow spines; O. Hendriksenianus, golden-yellow hairs, red spines; O. Trollii, silvery hairs, red to white spines. All have brown-red flowers.

OREODOXA. See Roystonea

OREOPANAX (Oreo'panax; Oreopan'ax). A group of tropical American evergreen trees and shrubs of the Aralia or Ginseng family, Araliaceae, that are chiefly natives of the Andean region. The name is derived from oreos, mountain, and Panax, an allied genus of plants. These plants can be grown in the open in the warmer parts of the United States, but their bold, handsome foliage renders them well worthy of cultivation in pots and tubs in greenhouses, as decorative specimens. They succeed in any average garden soil that is not excessively dry, and thrive well in partial shade. They are propagated by seeds, cuttings, and by air layering.

When grown indoors, Oreopanax succeeds best in well-drained containers in rich, fertile soil. Old plants should be repotted or top-dressed in spring. From spring through fall, they require an abundance of water; less is required during the winter season, but at no time should they be permitted to suffer from dryness. Plants that have filled their pots with roots benefit greatly from weekly applications of dilute liquid fertilizer. Spraying the foliage on all bright days with clear water is a beneficial practice.

During the warm summer months the plants may be stood outdoors in partial shade or their pots or tubs may be sunk outdoors, nearly to their rims, in a bed of ashes or coarse sand. At other seasons they succeed in a night temperature of 50-60 degrees.

Kinds. O. xalapense, from Mexico, is a shrub or small tree with long-stalked leaves, each composed of 5-10 more or less drooping leaflets. It is of handsome appearance. O. reticulatus, probably a native of South America, has undivided leaves, 2 ft. or so long, and short-stalked. The leaves are dark green with a paler midvein and a netting of paler secondary veins. Other kinds are O. Andreanus, a very ornamental species that is a native of Ecuador, and O. Sanderianus, which has mostly three-lobed leaves and hails from Guatemala. Many others are known to botanists.

ORGANIC GARDENING. In recent years this term has been applied to a system of growing plants which involves the use of natural materials only, as opposed to chemical fertilizers, to enrich the soil. While much benefit is to be derived from using manures, composts, and other organic sources of the nutrient elements required by plants (few soil scientists or practical gardeners will disclaim this), it seems equally certain that chemical fertilizers are also of immense value when used with intelligence and discretion.

To its most enthusiastic devotees, organic gardening is something of a cult, and extraordinary and often completely unproved claims have been made for it. The breeding and introduction into the soil of earthworms, the application of rock dust to the soil and of preparations of herbs to compost piles are practices recommended by some of the more extreme followers of the organic gardening method.

The publicity given to the organic gardening method has yielded at least one important benefit. It has focused attention on the importance of the soil, and created renewed awareness of its value to the whole human race. Serious investigators now patiently examine the claims and counterclaims made on behalf of organic gardeners and of those who hold opposing views; there can be no doubt that out of such investigations will come a better understanding of the soil and of the part it plays in plant and crop production.

In the meantime, amateur gardeners will be well advised to steer a middle course and neither hitch their wagons to the star of the "chemical" gardener who would grow everything in chemical solutions in sand, gravel and similar cultures, nor to make a fetish of relying upon organic materials alone as soil improvers. By using as much organic matter as can conveniently be obtained at moderate cost, and by supplementing this with chemical fertilizers, the gardener can obtain results the equal of, or better than, those obtained by the followers of one extreme or the other.

ORGAN-PIPE CACTUS. Lemaireocereus marginatus, which see.

ORIENTAL BELLFLOWER. Ostrowskia magnifica, which see.

ORIENTAL POPPY. See Papaver orientale.

ORIGANUM (Ori'ganum; Origa'num). Hardy herbaceous or shrubby plants with aromatic leaves. Origanum belongs to the Mint family, Labiatae; the name comes from *oreos,* a mountain, and *ganos,* joy, and refers to the plant's favored surroundings. The herbs Pot Marjoram and Sweet Marjoram were at one time included in Origanum but are not included in Majorana, which see.

The Dittany of Crete (O. Dictamnus) is found wild in southern Europe, and is cultivated in herb gardens and as a pot plant for its showy flowers. It forms a procumbent plant, 12 in. or less in height, with slender wiry stems and small, woolly, ovate leaves, and bears a spike of pink flowers in hoplike heads.

Dittany of Crete as a Pot Plant. This requires a minimum winter temperature of 45 degrees and a soil compost of two parts of sandy loam and one part leaf mold, with sand added freely. Repotting is done in March. The shoots are first shortened to one third and syringed daily to assist them to break into growth. The plants are then removed from the pots, the ball of soil being slightly reduced, and they are repotted in slightly larger pots.

After potting, they are shaded from bright sunlight and no water is given until the soil becomes quite dry; it is then thoroughly saturated. When well rooted, the plants are exposed to full sunlight. As the flower shoots elongate, they are lightly fastened to a thin cane inserted in the center of the pot. After flowering, water is gradually withheld from the soil, and during the winter sufficient only is given to prevent the leaves from shriveling.

Propagation Is by Cuttings. Small side shoots are removed in spring. The lower leaves are cut off and a clean cut is made just below the bottom joint. The shoots are inserted in sand and are covered with a bell jar. This is wiped inside each morning to prevent the condensed moisture from falling on the cuttings and setting up decay.

When roots are formed, the cuttings are potted separately in 2-in. or 2½-in. pots, or

Origanum hybridum, with pink flowers and glistening bracts, one of the Marjorams, makes an attractive pot plant.

three are placed in a 3-in. pot, to obtain bushy plants more speedily. When the shoots are established, their points are removed and the resulting side branches are similarly treated. The plants are then given the treatment detailed above.

For the Rock Garden. Two kinds, O. hybridum and O. pulchellum, which grow about 9 in. in height and bear spikes of rosy-pink flowers with glistening bracts, are excellent plants for the rock garden in regions where winters are not excessively severe.

The plants require a sunny position and a soil of sandy loam. They are planted out in March or April, and are increased by division in March, or by cuttings in summer. The shoots are inserted in a cold frame and covered with a bell jar. When rooted, they are potted separately in small pots, and planted in their permanent positions in the following spring.

ORIXA JAPONICA (Orix'a). The only species of the genus Orixa, this is a hardy Japanese and Chinese shrub that belongs to the Rue family, Rutaceae. Its name is from the Japanese.

This shrub attains a height of 6-10 ft. and is of spreading habit of growth. Its foliage is aromatic, its flowers small, green and of no decorative value. It lives outdoors without protection as far north as southern New England.

Orixa thrives in any fairly good soil in sun or part shade. It is readily propagated by seeds, summer cuttings, layers, air layering and root cuttings. It is notoriously free of disease and insect pests.

ORLEANESIA AMAZONICA (Orleane'sia). An epiphytal greenhouse Orchid found wild in Brazil; it has stemlike pseudobulbs, about 2 ft. high, with a few evergreen leaves on the upper portions. The green flowers are small and on such short stalks as to appear clustered. This plant belongs to the Orchid family, Orchidaceae. Its name honors the Duc d'Orleans.

This Orchid blooms in summer and autumn; its flowers are long-lasting. It should be grown in a compost of osmunda fiber or of Fir bark, Redwood bark or Tree Fern fiber. Repotting should be done, if necessary, in early spring when the young growths appear. During summer it needs a moist, warm atmosphere, and in winter must be carefully watered and kept in a temperature which does not fall below 60 degrees.

A bronze statue.

Carved stone basket of fruits.

Japanese lantern.

A well head.

An armillary sphere used as a garden ornament.

ORNAMENT. A garden ornament generally looks best when so placed as to form a focal point, as at the end of a garden path, on a corner of a lawn, where paths meet, at the end of a pergola or series of arches, in the middle of a little paved garden, near a garden pool, or in such a position that it seems well placed when seen from the house windows. It should not be placed merely for the purpose of displaying or exhibiting it, but should add charm to the garden.

The presence of stone in a garden, whether it be in the form of a sundial, seat, fountain or birdbath, is satisfying, for if the ornaments are of pleasing design they are in themselves attractive and they associate admirably with the flowers, particularly those of rose, pink, lavender or mauve coloring. A sundial set amidst China

Roses, Lavender, mauve Catmint or purple Aubrieta, Heuchera or Rose Mallow makes a charming garden picture.

Garden ornaments are displayed to advantage on a lawn or when surrounded by paving. It is a mistake to place them among shrubs or closely set flowering plants, where they are scarcely visible. To set up an attractive garden ornament and then to hide it by luxuriant plants is wrong.

In a small formal garden, probably the best place for a sundial or birdbath is in the center. The ornaments mentioned look particularly well if raised and surrounded by paving stone. Low-growing plants, such as Thyme, Pinks and others, may be planted around the base.

Miniature ornaments in the form of animals, birds and gnomes are sometimes used for placing in the rock garden, woodland, or by the side of a garden pool, but have little to commend them; neither do gazing globes.

ORNITHIDIUM (Ornithid'ium). Evergreen epiphytal greenhouse Orchids with curious rather than showy flowers, which are found wild in the tropics of America. Many have ascending, stem-like rhizomes bearing numerous comparatively small, ovoid pseudobulbs; the small flowers are produced in bundles from the bases of the bulbs. Other kinds are cushion-like in growth. The name is from *ornithos,* a bird, and *eidos,* like—the upper edge of the stigma is beaklike. The plants belong to the Orchid family, Orchidaceae.

The most attractive kind is O. sophronitis, from Venezuela. This is of cushion-like growth, with small dark green bulbs and leaves, and bears solitary scarlet flowers very freely in winter and early spring. The plant should be grown in a flower pan, which may be either suspended or placed on the benches in a moist greenhouse having a winter temperature of 50 degrees. In summer the temperature should be kept as near 60 degrees as possible.

Repotting should be done in early spring. Large plants may then be divided, if necessary. Provided a little fresh compost, consisting of cut osmunda or of Fir bark or Redwood bark, is occasionally inserted, the plants need not be repotted for two or three years.

O. coccineum is very similar to O. sophronitis,

but has much longer leaves and taller flower stems. O. confertum and O. densum have dull-colored flowers; they require a moderately warm greenhouse with a minimum winter temperature of 55 degrees.

ORNITHOCEPHALUS (Ornithoceph'alus). Attractive small evergreen, epiphytal (tree-growing) Orchids, which are found wild in Central America. In some kinds the leaves are arranged in the form of an open fan, the pseudobulbs being small, like thickened leaf bases. The flowers are small, but produced in considerable numbers on short, arching spikes from the axils of the leaves. They are white, or white shaded with green. The name is from *ornithos,* a bird, and *kephale,* a head, and refers to the long slender rostellum, which resembles a bird's beak.

All these Orchids require a warm greenhouse with a semitropical atmosphere in summer; the temperature should not fall below 55 degrees in winter. Small flower pans rather than pots should be used for their cultivation. A suitable potting compost consists of finely cut osmunda fiber or of Fir bark or Redwood bark. They do not like being disturbed at the roots, but, if necessary, repotting should be done early in the spring. The smaller kinds may be grown on suspended pieces of wood. Water must be given throughout the year, but very carefully in the winter.

The most popular kind is O. grandiflorus, a Brazilian Orchid with broad leaves and many-flowered arching spikes of white flowers, marked with green, in early summer.

ORNITHOCHILUS FUSCUS (Ornithochi'-lus; Ornithoch'ilus). An Orchid which grows wild in Burma, and must be grown in a warm greenhouse. It has a short stem, with fleshy, oblong, opposite leaves and arching flower stems. The flowers, which open in summer or autumn, are small, yellow, streaked with red; the lip is often fringed and spurlike at the base. The plant has also been known as Aerides difforme. The name Ornithochilus is derived from *ornithos,* a bird, and *cheilos,* a lip and refers to the shape of the lip of the flower.

This Orchid should be grown in a basket in a potting compost of cut osmunda fiber or of Fir bark, Redwood bark or Tree Fern fiber. The compost may be replenished when necessary, but the plants resent frequent root disturbance. When a new or larger basket is required, the plants should be carefully placed in it in early March.

The atmosphere of the greenhouse should be tropical during the summer, and the temperature not less than 60 degrees in the winter. Water must be given throughout the year—freely in summer but sparingly in winter, when particular care should be taken not to allow moisture to lodge on the leaves.

ORNITHOGALUM — *Star-of-Bethlehem, Chincherinchee* (Ornithog'alum). Hardy and tender bulbous plants with star-shaped flowers in spring and early summer. They are found wild in Africa and Europe, and belong to the Lily family, Liliaceae. Their roundish bulbs vary

The exquisitely fragrant Ornithogalum arabicum has large heads of creamy white flowers, each with a black center.

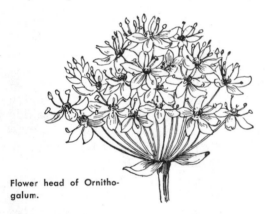

Flower head of Ornitho-galum.

from ¾-4 in. in diameter and give rise to linear (long and narrow) or, in some cases, lanceolate (lance-shaped) green leaves. The flowers are borne in umbels (spreading clusters on the tops of the stems), or in the form of a spike. They are white or yellowish white, star-shaped and six-petaled, and the undersides of the petals of some kinds are striped with a center band of green.

The hardy kinds are grown either in the rock garden or herbaceous border, or are naturalized in grass or under trees. The name Ornithogalum is derived from *ornithos,* a bird, and *gala,* milk; but the application of these terms is not obvious.

Treatment of Tender Kinds. Kinds of Ornithogalums that are not generally hardy in the North may be grown in greenhouses, window gardens and well-protected cold frames and, in mild climates, out of doors as recommended below for the hardy kinds.

Treatment of Hardy Kinds. These will flourish in a sunny or semishaded position in ordinary well-drained soil. The bulbs are planted in early autumn, the smaller kinds being set 2 in., and the larger kinds 4 in., deep. They require very little attention, and need only to be lifted and divided when they show signs of deterioration or become overcrowded. When planted in the wild garden or woodland, they may be allowed to spread in irregular drifts.

The Star-of-Bethlehem, O. umbellatum, is a fine plant for setting in large masses on the edge of a woodland or wild garden, where it will form a carpet of starry white flowers in early summer, but, as it tends to spread rapidly, it should not be admitted to choice parts of the rock garden. O. nutans, the Nodding Star-of-Bethlehem, is also useful for the same purpose. Its drooping spikes of green and white flowers, which have a silver-gray appearance, are 15 in. in height and are useful for cutting. It prefers light shade.

For the perennial border, O. pyramidale is suitable. It grows 3 ft. in height and has slender, upright spikes of white flowers. O. pyrenaicum, sometimes known as the French or Bath Asparagus, has small, greenish-white flowers in May and June, and may be used for naturalizing.

Treatment in Greenhouses. When grown in greenhouses, Ornithogalums require a night temperature of 45 degrees (for O. thyrsoides aureum, 55 degrees) and a soil compost of two

The Chincherinchee, Ornithogalum thyrsoides, is a native of South Africa.

greenhouse kinds are raised in a window or greenhouse and the hardy kinds in a cold frame.

The seedlings of the hardy kinds are pricked off, 2 in. apart, into flats, and grown in a frame until large enough to plant out of doors in their permanent positions. Those for the house or greenhouse are pricked out into flats or seed-pans, and, when large enough, are potted in small pots and subsequently in larger ones. New plants may also be obtained by division at planting and repotting time.

Hardy Kinds. O. umbellatum, Star-of-Bethlehem, 9 in., green and white, May; O. pyramidale, 3 ft., white, summer; O. nutans, 12 in., green and white, spring; O. pyrenaicum, 1-2 ft., greenish white, May and June.

Tender Kinds. O. arabicum, 2 ft., white, fragrant, summer; O. caudatum, 3 ft., green and white, spring or summer; O. longibracteatum, 24 in., white; O. thyrsoides (Chincherinchee), white, 18 in., winter.

The Chincherinchee (O. thyrsoides) grows 18 in. high, and bears white flowers. The flowers of this kind are imported in large quantities into the United States from South Africa. Although they are a long time in transit, they open when

parts of sandy loam, one part of leaf mold and a free sprinkling of sand. Repotting is done at the beginning of the growing season in September and October for most, early spring for a few. The bulbs are taken out of their pots, the crocks and loose soil are removed; they are then repotted in slightly larger pots. The new pots must be well drained. The bulbs are buried so that their tops are just covered with soil, which is made firm with a potting stick.

After repotting, the soil is not moistened until it becomes fairly dry, and the same procedure is adopted until the bulbs are well rooted. When growth is well begun, they are given water more liberally, and throughout the growing and flowering season the soil is kept moist. When the leaves begin to turn yellow, water is gradually withheld and the bulbs are kept dry until the time for repotting. These plants do well in a sunny window or greenhouse. Shading is not required.

Propagation. Seeds are sown in well-drained pots of sandy soil in spring or summer. The

The Star-of-Bethlehem, Ornithogalum umbellatum.

placed in water and last in flower for many weeks. This bulbous plant can be grown as advised for the other greenhouse kinds. Good varieties are aureum, golden-yellow; and flavescens, saffron-yellow.

OROBUS. The Bitter Vetches, previously named Orobus, are now included in the genera Lathyrus and Vicia, which see.

ORONTIUM AQUATICUM—*Golden Club* (Oron'tium). A hardy aquatic flowering plant, native to eastern North America, which belongs to the Arum family, Araceae. It grows about 18 in. in height and is suitable for shallow pools or the margins of large ponds or lakes. The leaves, which arise directly from the rootstock in the mud, have round, smooth petioles 9 in. in

The Golden Club, Orontium aquaticum, is a native American aquatic well suited for growing in water gardens.

length, light green marked with dark green. The leaf blades are lanceolate (lance-shaped), 9 in. long, 3 in. wide, and deep green. While developing, the leaves stand erect, but when they are mature they float on the surface of the water. In early summer the flowers are produced on a slender stem which rises above the water; they are light yellow, minute, and tightly packed to form a clublike head which resembles the spadix in the Arum Lily.

A Plant for Small Pools. This is a suitable plant for small ornamental pools, as it does not require a great depth of water and forms a compact clump. In pools made of concrete which

have not a layer of soil in the bottom, this plant should be grown in a large flowerpot or wooden tub. No drainage is required in the pot and a compost of loam and leaf mold is used.

The crowns (tops of the rootstocks) are covered with a thin layer of soil, which in turn is covered with an inch of sand, and the pot is set with its soil surface 12-18 in. below the surface of the water.

When planted in ponds, with soil at the bottom, the roots are either set in a small wicker basket or enclosed in a piece of burlap with compost around the roots. They are then sunk to the bottom of the water and held in place with large stones until the roots penetrate the soil in the pond. Very little attention is required; the plants will flourish for many years in the same soil.

Propagation is by dividing the rootstocks at planting time in April.

ORPINE. Sedum Telephium, which see.

ORRIS ROOT. The dried rhizomes of Iris florentina, widely grown in Italy, particularly in Tuscany, for the sake of their violet-like scent.

ORYCHOPHRAGMUS (Orychophrag'mus). A small group of eastern Asiatic herbaceous plants one of which is sometimes cultivated as a biennial or annual. These plants belong in the Mustard family, the Cruciferae. The name is derived from *oryche,* a pit, and *phragmos,* a septum or dividing wall, and refers to the fact that the septum in the seed pod is pitted.

Orychophragmus violaceus (which is sometimes called Moricandia sonchifolia) grows to a height of 1-2 ft., has coarsely lobed or pinnatisect foliage, leafy stems and an abundance of attractive lavender-blue flowers each measuring about 1 in. across. It is easily raised from seeds and succeeds in any reasonably fertile, well-drained soil. This plant is not hardy enough to live over winter outdoors in the vicinity of New York City but it may be carried through the winter in a well protected cold frame; in milder climates it winters outdoors without difficulty. It is about as hardy as the English Wallflower. From seeds sown the previous summer plants are obtained that bloom in spring.

In addition to its usefulness as an outdoor plant this Orychophragmus forms an attractive pot plant for cultivating in a cool greenhouse. Specimens raised from seeds sown in late summer may be grown on to occupy 5 in. or 6 in. pots in which they bloom freely in March and April. They succeed in any fairly good potting soil, respond to feeding with dilute liquid fertilizers when their final pots are well filled with roots and need full sun and a night temperature of about 50 degrees with daytime temperatures a few degrees higher.

Orychophragmus violaceus is reported to be used as a vegetable in China.

OSAGE ORANGE. See Maclura.

OSCULARIA (Oscular'ia). Small, succulent perennials from South Africa which at one time were included in the genus Mesembryanthemum and require the same cultural treatment. They belong to the Carpetweed family, the Aizoaceae. The name is derived from *osculum,* meaning a little mouth.

Kinds are O. caulescens (Mesembryanthemum caulescens), which grows to 1 ft. tall and has fragrant, rose-colored flowers, and O. deltoides (Mesembryanthemum deltoides), which also has rose-colored blooms, but slightly smaller than those of O. caulescens. O. deltoides variety muricata (Mesembryanthemum muricatum) is blue-green and smaller.

OSIER. A name used for one group of basket-making Willows, or for all the cultivated forms of Salix viminalis, one of the Willows found wild in Europe and Asia, and also in North America, where it has escaped from gardens.

OSMANTHUS (Osmanth'us). Tender, ever-

Osmanthus Delavayi, a very lovely evergreen with small, dark green leathery leaves and deliciously fragrant white flowers produced freely in spring.

The small white flowers of the handsome evergreen Osmanthus ilicifolius. The flowers are fragrant and are produced in fall and winter.

green shrubs of considerable decorative value, with thick leathery leaves and usually fragrant, white flowers. They are natives of eastern and southern Asia, and one is a native of the southern United States. Although they are useful for planting outdoors in mild climates, they are not hardy in the North. They are sometimes grown in greenhouses and window gardens. Some of them bear a striking resemblance to certain of the Hollies, but one difference is that the leaves are arranged in opposite pairs, whereas in the Hollies they are alternate.

Osmanthus belongs to the Olive family, Oleaceae, and the name is taken from the Greek *osme,* fragrance, and *anthos,* a flower, in allusion to the fragrant flowers.

Raising Plants from Cuttings. Cuttings of half-ripe shoots, 3-4 in. long, may be taken in July and dibbled in a bed of sand in a propagating frame. Cuttings can also be rooted in fall in a greenhouse.

Planting and Pruning. The young plants should be planted or potted in spring. During summer the tips of the shoots should be removed now and then to induce a bushy habit of growth. They should be set in well-drained loamy soil, to which a little peat or compost has been added. Plants that have had care while young, and have formed a good foundation of branches, grow into shapely bushes with little or no subsequent pruning. However, if plants become straggling, they may be pruned as soon as the flowers fade.

In the Greenhouse. Osmanthus, when grown in pots, thrives in sun or light shade. A winter night temperature of 50 degrees suits these plants. They may be stood outdoors in summer. Water freely in summer, moderately in winter.

Evergreen Shrubs with Fragrant Flowers. A very useful kind for general cultivation is O. ilicifolius, sometimes called O. Aquifolium by reason of its holly-like leaves. It is a native of Japan, where it sometimes grows 20-30 ft. high. The glossy green leaves are $1\frac{1}{2}$-$2\frac{1}{2}$ in. long and 1-$1\frac{1}{2}$ in. wide, with spiny margins on the lower parts of the bush, the spines giving place to smooth-margined leaves on the upper parts. The white, fragrant flowers are borne during summer and fall, when comparatively few other hardy shrubs are in full beauty.

A number of varieties have been given distinct names. Of these, specially desirable ones are purpureus, with dark-purple leaves; myrtifolius, a dwarf shrub with elliptical, often spineless leaves; rotundifolius, another dwarf kind with broadly elliptical leaves; and variegatus, with green and white, spine-margined leaves.

O. americanus, the Devilwood, is native from North Carolina to Florida and Mississippi. It grows to 45 ft. tall and has greenish, fragrant flowers.

O. armatus is a bush or small tree with very stiff branchlets bearing leaves up to 6 in. long and $1\frac{1}{2}$ in. wide; the margins are divided into spiny teeth. The flowers are borne in autumn. It does better with some shade from hot sun.

O. fragrans is more tender. It bears very fragrant white flowers which are used in China for scenting tea. In mild climates it attains a height of 20-30 ft. It is an old favorite for growing in pots in greenhouses and sun porches.

O. Fortunei, regarded as a hybrid between O. fragrans and O. ilicifolius, is an evergreen bush reaching a height of 15-20 ft. It bears white flowers in autumn.

For the plant grown in gardens as Osmanthus Delavayi, see Siphonosmanthus Delavayi.

OSMAREA BURKWOODII (Osmar'ea). An evergreen shrub which grows 5 ft. or more high, has glossy green leaves, and in spring bears clusters of fragrant, ivory-white flowers. Ordinary soil suits it, and propagation is by cuttings of young side shoots inserted in sandy soil in a cold frame during July–September. It is hardy in sheltered places as far north as New Jersey.

This shrub is of particular interest because it is a bigeneric hybrid—that is, it was produced by crossing two genera. Its parents are Osmanthus Delavayi and Phillyrea decora.

OSMARONIA—Osoberry (Osmaro'nia). The only member of this genus is Osmaronia cerasiformis, often known as Nuttallia cerasiformis, a leaf-losing (deciduous) shrub that is a native of western North America and belongs to the family Rosaceae. It is hardy as far north as New York.

Osmaronia thrives in ordinary well-cultivated soil which has been enriched with decayed manure or rich compost; a mulch or top-dressing of this material in early summer is beneficial. It prefers a moderately moist soil. Planting can be done in early fall or spring. Pruning should be done about mid-April, after flowering; it consists in thinning out the branches, removing the oldest entirely when necessary.

Under favorable conditions the bushes grow freely and spread rapidly by means of suckers. When space is limited, it is advisable, each year, after flowering, to trim the bushes, sometimes severely.

Methods of Propagation. Seeds, cuttings and suckers, or division of the bushes, provides easy means of propagation. The seeds should be sown as soon as ripe, in cold frame, or in a sheltered position outside. Cuttings, 3 or 4 in. long, made of the side shoots, can be rooted in sandy soil in a cold frame in August. Cuttings made of the mature shoots, 12 to 18 in. long, the thin tops having been cut off, will root on a border out of doors in mild climates if inserted in October or November. Fall is the best time to remove suckers from the outsides of the clumps and to lift, divide, and replant.

Osmaronia cerasiformis is 6-10 ft. in height. The branches are mostly upright in growth and become a thicket in a few years unless thinned freely. The bright green leaves are oblong-lanceolate. The small, white, almond-scented flowers are freely borne in early spring. Male and female flowers are usually on different bushes, and the female bushes bear plum-shaped, purple fruits.

OSMUNDA—*Cinnamon Fern, Royal Fern, Interrupted Fern* (Osmun'da). Evergreen or leaf-losing (deciduous) Ferns which are wild in Japan, North America, the West Indies, northern Asia, and Europe. Those cultivated in North America are all hardy. They grow from 18 in. to 8 ft. in height, and have pinnate (feathery) fronds; the spores are borne on separate leafless spikes, or on spikes on the ends of the fronds.

The best kind is O. regalis, the Royal Fern. This is found growing wild in many parts of the world, as well as in North America. It grows in swampy places and, under favorable conditions, reaches 8 ft. in height. Other hardy kinds are O. cinnamomea, 2-5 ft., and O. Claytoniana, 3-6 ft.; both are natives of North America. Their roots provide the Osmunda fiber which is used for potting epiphytic orchids. The name Osmunda is derived from Osmunder, one of the names of Thor.

Garden Treatment. Osmundas will grow in a sunny or partially shaded position, and require abundance of moisture at the roots. These Ferns do best on the margins of a stream or pond, or in a bog garden, but can be grown in beds or borders provided the soil is kept moist in summer.

Deep, Moist Soil Is Necessary. When planting on the edge of a pond or stream, very little preparation is necessary, as the roots are abundantly supplied with water. In drier situations, however, success can only be assured by taking precautions to keep the soil moist. Take out the soil to a depth of 2 ft. and 2 ft. in diameter, for a single plant, or correspondingly larger for more plants. Puddle the bottom and sides with clay or make them watertight with cement and fill the hole with a mixture of equal parts of loam, leaf mold and peat. Planting is done in early spring, and the crowns of the plants are set just above the level of the soil.

A native American Fern, Osmunda Claytoniana.

The Royal Fern, Osmunda regalis.

Once planted, they need very little attention, so long as they have access to sufficient moisture. A top-dressing of rich compost in April is beneficial, and the dead fronds should be removed at the same time. It is unwise to remove these fronds in the autumn as they form a natural protection for the crowns.

Propagation is principally by spores. The plants may be increased by division, but they take a long time to recover from the disturbance. The spores may be sown as soon as they are ripe or they may be stored and sown at a later date. The spore-bearing spike is gathered when the spores are fully developed. The spores of Osmunda regalis and its varieties are green when they are ripe. The spike is placed in a paper bag, which is hung in a dry, airy room or shed for 48 hours; the ripe spores will then be at the bottom of the bag.

Sowing Spores. The spores are sown in 5-in. pots; or in shallow seed pans, if large quantities of plants are required. They are well drained and filled with finely sifted compost, and a little charcoal dust is sprinkled on the surface. The soil is moistened by immersing the vessel in water until bubbling ceases; then it is placed aside to drain and the spores are sprinkled thinly on the surface. The spores are not covered with soil, but a pane of glass is laid over the pot or seed pan, which is set in a saucer, and this is kept filled with water.

The spores take several weeks to germinate. When the young plants appear on the surface, they form a green mosslike growth made up of thin green, heart-shaped structures, which eventually attain to $\frac{1}{2}$ in. in diameter. When these are fully grown, the fronds commence to develop. At this stage, or before, if they are overcrowded, they are pricked off, 1 in. apart, into seed pans filled with finely sifted compost. The soil is moistened, and they are shaded from sunlight. When large enough, they are potted in 3-in. pots, and subsequently in larger ones.

The Chief Kinds. Among these are O. regalis (Royal Fern), 8 ft., and its varieties—cristata, with crested fronds; gracilis, a slender form with bronze-tinted fronds; and palustris, 3 ft., young fronds light green, older fronds, reddish. Also, O. cinnamomea (Cinnamon Fern), 4 ft.; and O. Claytoniana (Interrupted Fern), 3 ft. The measurements refer to the length of the fronds.

OSMUNDA FIBER. The roots of Osmunda ferns, used in potting Orchids. The fiber comes in more or less thick "mats" and has to be chopped and cut to pieces. For small plants it should be cut rather fine. Sphagnum moss is added to it in preparing the compost for some Orchids. Osmunda fiber is also called orchid peat.

OSOBERRY. See Osmaronia.

OSTEOMELES (Osteome'les; Osteom'eles). Evergreen shrubs from South America, Asia, and New Zealand. They are closely related to the Hawthorn (Crataegus) and belong to the Rose family, Rosaceae. They have slender branches clothed with small, pinnate leaves, and bear small, terminal clusters of white flowers in summer; these are followed by bluish-black, hawthorn-like fruits. The name Osteomeles is derived from *osteon*, bone, and *meles*, apple, and refers to the berries.

For Mild Climates. These shrubs can only be generally cultivated out of doors in mild districts, although in sheltered locations O. anthyllidifolia will live outdoors in New Jersey. They prefer a soil of sandy loam; very light or clayey soils are unsuitable.

Planting is done in spring, the soil being afterwards well soaked with water if it is very dry.

Osteomeles Schweriniae, a beautiful tender shrub. Its white flowers are followed by blue-black fruits.

Sowing Seeds. Propagation is by seeds or cuttings. Seeds are sown in autumn. Deep seed pans or pots are used; these are well drained and filled with a compost of sandy loam. The seeds are sown 1 in. apart and ½ in. deep, and the pots placed in a cold frame. The seeds are slow in germinating, but, as soon as the seedlings are large enough, they are potted separately in 3-in. pots and subsequently in 5-in. pots, from which they are planted in their permanent quarters. They should be kept in a cold frame until they are large enough to plant out.

Taking Cuttings. Cuttings are made, in August, of well-ripened shoots of the current year's growth. The leaves from the lower half of the cuttings are removed and a cut is made below the bottom node (joint). The cuttings are then inserted in a cold frame which is kept close, or in a greenhouse propagating bench. After they have rooted, they are potted and treated as advised for seedlings.

In very cold climates these shrubs may be grown in a greenhouse. They need a minimum winter temperature of 45 degrees, and the best compost consists of two parts of loam and one part of sand. Repotting is done in March, when the plants are removed from the pots and set in slightly larger ones.

The chief kinds are O. Schweriniae, 10 ft.; O. Schweriniae microphylla, 5 ft.; and O. subrotunda, a dwarf, slow-growing species of somewhat contorted growth.

OSTRICH FERN. Pteretis Struthiopteris, which see.

OSTROWSKIA MAGNIFICA—*Oriental Bellflower* (Ostrow'skia). A hardy perennial flowering plant from central Asia, which belongs to the Bellflower family, Campanulaceae. It grows about 5 ft. in height, has tuberous roots, from which rise stout stems with ovate leaves, 5 in. in length, produced in whorls at intervals up the stems. The flowers, which are campanulate (bell-shaped), are lilac in color and open in late summer in the axils of the leaves at the tops of the stems. The name Ostrowskia commemorates N. Ostrowsky, a Russian patron of botany.

Requires a Sunny, Sheltered Spot. The rootstocks are planted in April. The position se-

Ostrowskia magnifica, the Oriental Bell-flower, a herbaceous perennial of rare beauty. Its flowers, of clear lilac color, are carried on stems 5 ft. tall in late summer.

lected must be sheltered from cold winds, but open to full sunlight. Deep, well-drained, sandy, loamy soil, enriched with decayed manure, is required; it must be kept moist in summer. It should be sufficiently well drained to carry away the surplus water in winter; otherwise, the roots will decay. This plant is not easy to grow, and is probably adapted only for gardens in specially favored climates, as on parts of the Pacific Coast.

Propagation Is Principally by Seeds. These are sown in pots of sandy soil in April. The pots are well drained with crocks, which are covered with a little of the rough siftings from the soil compost. The compost is then put in and the surface is made smooth and even. The soil is moistened by immersing the pot to its rim in a pail of water. The seeds are scattered thinly on the surface and covered with a little fine soil. A pane of glass is laid over the pot, which is placed in a cold frame.

After the seedlings appear, they are exposed to the light, and, when large enough, are pricked off separately into 3-in. pots. When well rooted, they are transferred to 5-in. pots, and from these they are planted in their permanent quarters. Seedlings take four or five years to reach flowering stage.

OSTRYA—*Hop Hornbeam* (Os'trya). Hardy leaf-losing (deciduous) trees of medium dimensions, with short trunks covered with scaling bark, and carrying rather dense heads of stout branches with slender branchlets. The ovate or oblong-ovate, long-pointed leaves are marked with prominent parallel veins and have deeply toothed margins.

The flowers are small and produced in slender catkins in late spring. The catkins of male flowers are pendulous, 1½-3 in. or so long, and the female flowers are also in catkins that eventually become pendent. The small fruits are hard and nutlike, each one enclosed by a flattish, thin, scalelike body, several of which collectively make up a fruit rather like that of the Hop. The few species in cultivation are natives of Europe, Asia and North America. Ostrya is the ancient Greek name for a very hard wood. The trees belong to the Birch family, Betulaceae.

Raising Seedlings. Seeds should be sown as soon as ripe, in a compost of 3 parts loam to one part each of leaf mold and sand. Small quantities may be sown in pots or flats, but large quantities should be sown in prepared beds out of doors in early spring, after being stored in slightly moist sand for the winter.

Those sown in pots or flats should be plunged in ashes out of doors or in a cold frame for the winter, and should be taken into a greenhouse, if possible, in March. As soon as the seedlings are large enough to handle, they should be planted in a bed of prepared soil in the nursery.

From then on, transplanting will be necessary every second year until the trees are large enough for permanent places. During this period attention should be paid to the encouragement of a single leading shoot to each tree, and to the restriction of side branches. The trees may be planted in any good garden soil.

Species are O. carpinifolia, the European Hop Hornbeam, a tree 50-60 ft. high, native to southern Europe and Asia Minor; O. japonica, the Japanese Hop Hornbeam, which in Japan grows 80 ft. high; O. virginiana, the American Hop Hornbeam or Ironwood of eastern North America; and O. Knowltonii, 30-35 ft. high, native to northern Arizona. The wood of these trees is very hard, and is used for agricultural implements and other purposes.

OSTRYOPSIS DAVIDIANA (Ostryop'sis). A leaf-losing (deciduous) shrub, 3-10 ft. high, native to northern China and Mongolia. It is allied to the Hornbeam and Hop Hornbeam and is rather like a small-leaved Hazel. The flowers appear in late spring at the same time as the leaves. They are small and in slender catkins, and each nutlike fruit is enclosed in a bract, several being produced together at the ends of the shoots. Cultivation is the same as for Ostrya, except that this plant develops as a bush, not as a tree, and a central trunk cannot be encouraged.

Ostryopsis belongs to the Birch family, Betulaceae, and the name is taken from Ostrya and the Greek *opsis,* appearance.

OSWEGO TEA. See Monarda.

OTAHEITE GOOSEBERRY. See Phyllanthus.

OTAHEITE LEMON. See Lemon variety Otaheite under Citrus.

OTAHEITE ORANGE. See Lemon variety Otaheite under Citrus.

OTHONNA (Othon'na). Tender annual and perennial flowering plants, from South Africa, which belong to the Daisy family, Compositae. The chief kind, O. crassifolia, is a perennial, shrubby at the base and having trailing or drooping stems, clothed with small, fleshy, oval leaves 1 in. in length, and bearing yellow, daisylike flowers, ½ in. in diameter, in summer. The name Othonna is derived from *othone,* linen, a reference to the downy covering of the plant originally called by this name. Othonna crassifolia is sometimes called Little Pickles.

This interesting South African plant blooms almost throughout the year in a sunny greenhouse or window. It is Othonna crassifolia.

For a Sunny Greenhouse or Window. These plants require a minimum winter temperature of 45 degrees and a soil compost of two parts of loam, with a little leaf mold and sand added.

Repotting is done in March. The plants are taken out of the pots and the crocks and all loose soil removed from the roots; then the plants are repotted in slightly larger pots. No shade is required. After potting, the soil is not watered until it becomes quite dry. When the plants are established in the new pots, the soil is, however, kept moist throughout the summer. During the winter comparatively little water is required; the plants are then watered only when the soil becomes quite dry, just enough water being given to prevent the stems from shriveling.

O. crassifolia is an excellent subject for hanging baskets in the greenhouse as well as a fine plant for a sunny window. In mild, dry climates such as that of southern California it is a useful ground cover for the outdoor garden.

When to Take Cuttings. Propagation is principally by cuttings; small side shoots are removed at almost any time, but preferably in spring and early fall, and inserted in pots, which are well drained and filled with equal parts of sand and loam. The pots of cuttings are placed in the open benches or on a windowsill and no water is given to the soil until it becomes dry; it is then thoroughly soaked.

This procedure is continued until roots are formed, when the rooted cuttings are potted separately in 3-in. pots and, later, into larger pots.

Raising Seedlings. Seeds are sown in pots of sandy soil in spring or summer. Well-drained pots are filled with finely sifted compost. The seeds are scattered thinly on the surface and lightly covered with soil. A pane of glass is laid on the pot after the soil has been thoroughly moistened.

When the seeds have germinated the glass is removed and the seedlings are exposed to full light. They are eventually pricked off, 2 in. apart, into a seed pan, and, when large enough, are potted separately in 3-in. pots.

The chief kind is O. crassifolia (capensis), Little Pickles, trailing stem, yellow flowers. Other kinds are O. amplexifolia, 18 in., shrubby, yellow; O. carnosa, 12 in., subshrubby, yellow; and O. tuberosa, 2 ft., tuberous-rooted, yellow.

OTHONNOPSIS CHEIRIFOLIA (Othonnop'sis). An herbaceous, flowering plant from Algeria, which belongs to the Daisy family, Compositae. The only kind in cultivation, O. cheirifolia, grows about 15 in. in height; it is woody at the base, but the young shoots are round and fleshy and about the thickness of a lead pencil. The leaves somewhat resemble those of the Wallflower (hence the name cheirifolia); they are 1-2 in. in length, oval, smooth and glaucous (bluish-gray). The flowers, which appear in early summer, are yellow and daisy-like. The name Othonnopsis is derived from Othonna, and *opsis,* like, a reference to the plant's similarity to the Othonna, with which it is often confused.

For a Sunny Rock Garden or Border. This plant requires a sunny, well-drained position and light, sandy soil. In heavy soil or an exposed situation it is liable to die off in the winter. Planting is done in April, the plants being set 12 in. apart, and the soil is made firm around the roots. Very little attention is required, as they are not affected by drought and usually flower more profusely in dry weather. A topdressing of fresh soil in spring is beneficial when the plants show signs of deterioration. Some of the older shoots may with advantage be pruned to within a few inches of the base in spring.

Propagation Is Chiefly by Cuttings. Firm shoots, about 3 in. in length, are taken off in spring or summer. The lower leaves are removed and a cut is made just below the bottom node; the shoots are then inserted in a cold frame.

When roots have formed, the plants are potted separately in 3-in. pots, and returned to the frame, where they remain until established. They are planted out in the rock garden or on a sunny border in early autumn or spring.

This plant is not likely to be hardy except in mild climates.

OTOCHILUS (Otoch'ilus). Epiphytic (tree-inhabiting) Orchids, natives of northern India and Burma. The pseudobulbs are 2-3 in. long, almost oblong, two-leaved, and produced one above the other. The flowers appear at various times of the year. Otochilus is from *otos,* an ear, and *cheilos,* a lip, and refers to two earlike formations at the base of the lip.

These Orchids are grown on flat pieces of wood, a layer of two parts of osmunda fiber cut into suitably sized pieces being placed between the plant and the board. The boards may be lengthened as needed or, if the Orchids outgrow them, a portion of each plant can be severed in early spring and treated as a new plant. The portion left will often produce fresh growth.

Otochilus may be wintered in a greenhouse with a temperature of 55-60 degrees at night. In summer the atmosphere should approach the tropical. Shading is essential, particularly when the growths are young, but it should be gradually removed as autumn advances; full exposure to light is then required. The plants may be watered freely in summer, but should be kept moderately dry in winter.

The two chief kinds are O. fusca, with white, pink-flushed flowers, and O. porrecta, which is very similar, but the flowers are more fragrant.

OURATEA—*Button Flower* (Oura'tea). Tropical, ornamental foliage and flowering shrubs, from South America, which belong to the family Ochnaceae, and were previously called Gomphia. They grow about 15 ft. in height, have ovate, evergreen, glossy leaves about 6 in. long, with serrated margins, and bear dense terminal racemes of yellow flowers, about ½ in. across, in spring. Ouratea is the native name in Guiana.

For the Greenhouse. These shrubs should be grown in pots in a greenhouse having a minimum winter temperature of 50 degrees; the best potting compost consists of equal parts of loam and peat, with sand freely added. After flowering, the plants are lightly pruned into shape, and are repotted in larger pots when new shoots are formed. Plants in large pots are kept growing vigorously by top-dressing with fresh compost in spring, a little of the old soil having been removed previously. They are watered moderately from October until April, but freely for the remainder of the year.

Propagation is by inserting cuttings of young shoots, 3 in. in length, in a mixture of peat moss and sand in April. The chief kind is O. olivaeformis (decorans), 15 ft., yellow.

Oxalis variabilis.

OURISIA (Ouris'ia). A small group of ornamental hardy perennials, natives of New Zealand and Antarctic South America. They belong to the Snapdragon family, Scrophulariaceae. Ourisia was named in honor of Governor Ouris of the Falkland Islands. Ourisias are not hardy in cold sections. They are most likely to succeed in the Pacific Northwest.

The Ourisias have slowly creeping rhizomatous roots, and should be grown in the rock garden in a shady or half-shady position sheltered from the full power of the sun; they thrive best in a soil mixture of fibrous loam, leaf soil and sand. They can be propagated by seeds sown in pots in spring and kept shaded in a cold frame, or, more readily, by division of the roots in spring.

Ourisia coccinea (elegans) is the best known and most beautiful. It has broad, crinkled, glossy green leaves and loose heads of tubular scarlet flowers. A native of southern Chile, it is a choice plant for a cool position in the lower, shadier parts of the rock garden. It grows 9-12 in. high, and flowers from May to September.

Ourisia macrocarpa, from New Zealand, 9-12 in., is a handsome kind with fine leaves and heads of large, white flowers. Ourisia macrophylla is not unlike the last, but smaller; it flowers in late summer.

OUVIRANDRA. Aponogeton, which see.

OVATE. A botanical term used in describing a leaf which is egg-shaped, with the broadest part below the middle. See Leaf.

OXALIS: WOOD SORREL

Especially Recommended for the Window Garden and Greenhouse

Oxalis (Ox'alis) includes about 200 kinds of hardy and tender plants. Most of them are found wild in South Africa and tropical and subtropical America, but the group is widely distributed and has representatives in many parts of the world, including North America. They belong to the family Oxalidaceae. The name is from *oxys,* acid, the leaves being acid to the taste.

Oxalis enneaphylla.

Several of the hardy kinds are beautiful plants for the rock garden, one or two are showy enough for the flower border, and many are excellent window-garden and greenhouse plants. They are propagated by seeds sown in spring, by offsets, or by division at the beginning of their growing season (September for most).

Hardy Kinds of Oxalis

The Wood Sorrel. Oxalis montana, the American Wood Sorrel, is a charming wild plant with green "Shamrock" leaves and white flowers veined with lilac. It is well worthy of a place in the garden. Being a woodland plant, it thrives best in cool half-shady situations, and makes a pretty ground covering under trees and among shrubs. It may also find a place in the rougher

Oxalis adenophylla is a very choice and lovely plant for the rock garden, forming tufts of blue-gray leaves and producing, just clear of the foliage, glistening pink flowers of waxlike texture in May and June.

parts of the rock garden, though care must be taken that it does not get out of hand and become a tiresome weed. A perennial, it grows only 2-3 in. high and occurs as a native in cool, rich woods in North America.

Oxalis violacea is another native American kind that is worthy of a modest place in the rock garden and wild garden. It occurs naturally from Massachusetts to Florida and westward to the Rocky Mountains. It grows 3-6 in. tall and has rose-purple flowers in summer. Like O. montana, it thrives best in a woodsy soil in light shade.

Attractive Hardy Annuals. Oxalis corniculata is a hardy annual with creeping stems. It forms a pretty, fresh green carpet, very dwarf and close, and bears bright yellow flowers in summer. There is a handsome purple-leaved variety, O. corniculata rubra, in which the golden blossoms contrast very effectively with the dark foliage.

Both these plants, the green and the purple variety, spread rapidly, throwing their seeds far and wide; they should therefore be introduced into the garden, and especially the rock garden, with the utmost caution, for they soon become troublesome weeds.

For filling the crevices in flagstone paths from which they cannot escape and spread, these two little Wood Sorrels are extremely pretty and useful, especially when grown together to contrast with one another.

Oxalis valdiviensis is a handsome and easily grown annual from Chile, 6-9 in. tall, with fresh green clover-like foliage, and heads of golden-yellow flowers. It may be sown in the open in April to flower the same summer.

For Dry Places Under Trees. Oxalis rosea is a beautiful annual from southern Chile. It grows 6-9 in. tall, is fleshy-stemmed, has bright green leaves, and bears quantities of pale lilac-pink flowers all summer. The great value of this plant is that it will grow in the very driest places under trees where scarcely anything else will exist. The plant often mistakenly grown as O. rosea is O. rubra.

For the Rock Garden. Oxalis lobata, from Chile, is an extremely pretty plant for the rock garden where winters are not excessively cold. The bulblike roots should be planted in spring in the moraine or in very light, well-drained soil in full sun. In early summer a crop of small fresh green leaves will appear, but these soon die down and disappear. A second growth will come up in late summer, accompanied by the flowers, which are a rich golden-yellow. The height of the plant is 2-3 in.

A Most Beautiful Kind. Oxalis enneaphylla, a native of the Falkland Islands and the Strait of Magellan region, is the most beautiful of all rock-garden Wood Sorrels and one of the choicest of all rock-garden plants. The root system is a fleshy, scaly rhizome (rootlike stem) about the size of a hazelnut. The leaves, consisting of nine leaflets, more or less, are glaucous blue-green, are folded in such a way as to give a crinkled appearance, and are carried on pinkish, erect stems 3-4 in. high. The flowers are large

This plant, commonly called Firefern, is a new kind which has tentatively been identified as Oxalis hedysaroides rubra. It has rich red foliage and yellow flowers.

for the size of the plant, being 1-1½ in. across; they are trumpet-shaped and white, and of a lovely waxy appearance. They are deliciously fragrant with a scent of almonds. The plant flowers in May and June.

Oxalis enneaphylla is not easy to grow in most American gardens. It is most likely to thrive in the Pacific Northwest. For its best development it needs an especially cool, well-drained loam with plenty of leaf mold added. A fairly cool, well-drained position should be chosen, shaded from full sun during the hot hours of the day. The plant is very lovely when grown in a pan of the soil recommended, in the alpine house.

Propagation of O. enneaphylla is carried out by breaking up the roots, which form themselves into strings of bulblike, scaly masses. The best time to do this is in spring, just as the plant, which is deciduous, begins to show signs of growth. The whole mass should be lifted, split up at every joint, and replanted at once.

Seed is sometimes obtainable, and this should be sown as soon after gathering as possible, in a pot of sandy loam and leaf mold, and kept shaded in a cold frame. Germination may be slow, and the pot should not be discarded under eighteen months or two years.

Oxalis enneaphylla was formerly used in the Falkland Islands for making a cooling, refreshing drink, and this was popular among sailors as a cure for scurvy in the old sailing-ship days.

There is a very beautiful variety, O. enneaphylla rosea, with pale pink flowers, which is a charming companion for the white-flowered type.

Oxalis adenophylla, from the Chilean Andes, is an extremely beautiful rock-garden plant, the leaves and flowers of which much resemble those of O. enneaphylla. The leaves are rather larger, however, but of the same attractive blue-green shade. The numerous large, trumpet-shaped flowers, each carried erect and singly on a 2-3 in. stem, are pale pink, with a crimson spot at the base of each petal. Although so beautiful, the flowers lack the fine waxlike quality and generous rounded petals of the best forms of O. enneaphylla rosea.

The root consists of a large globular bulb composed of innumerable narrow, scaly segments, and it differs from that of O. enneaphylla in making a number of side offsets around the base of the main bulb, instead of making necklace-like strings of bulbs.

Oxalis adenophylla is hardy perhaps as far north as Philadelphia but it is difficult to grow except in the Pacific Northwest. It needs a light, well-drained soil, in a sunny position in the rock garden. It flowers in early summer, and loses its leaves and becomes dormant in winter. It is easily propagated by division of the bulbs in spring, an operation which may be performed every three or four years.

For a Flagstone Path. Oxalis magellanica is a charming perennial, of close, creeping habit. Only half an inch tall, it has comparatively large, cup-shaped, pure white flowers. It is valuable for clothing the crevices in flagstone paths and as cover for choice small bulbous flowers in the rock garden, but, unfortunately, is not hardy in regions of severe winters. It is easily propagated by simple division of the plant in spring. The root system is creeping and wiry.

Tender Tuberous Kinds of Oxalis

Tender kinds of Oxalis that are not hardy in the North can be grown outdoors in mild regions; many kinds are also splendid for growing in greenhouses and in window gardens. They fall into two groups: those that have bulbs or tubers, and the nontuberous kinds.

When grown indoors, the tuberous kinds thrive in a light, well-drained, nourishing soil in full sun. They need a minimum night temperature of 45-50 degrees. The tubers should be planted at the beginning of their growing season, right at the end of their season of rest. This time varies according to kind, but, in general, spring-blooming kinds are started into growth in fall, summer-blooming kinds in spring, and fall-blooming kinds in July or August.

The tubers (bulbs) may be set 6-9 together in a 6-in. flower pan, or slightly fewer in a 5-in. flower pot. They should be covered with soil to a depth of about 1 in.

Watering at first must be sparing, but, as leaves develop and the roots take possession of the soil, may be done more freely; when the plants are in active growth, weekly applications of dilute liquid fertilizer are in order. When the leaves begin to die down naturally after the flowering season is through, watering is gradually reduced and finally stopped altogether. The bulbs are then kept quite dry until the beginning of the next growing season.

During this season of rest the bulbs may be left in the soil or removed and stored in paper bags or other suitable containers in a fairly cool, dry place. Each year the bulbs are repotted in fresh soil at the beginning of the new growing season. At that time, propagation is readily effected by the natural increase of offsets.

These tuberous kinds are also readily raised from seeds sown at the beginning of the growing season of the particular kind. The seeds should be sown in pots or pans of light sandy soil in a cool greenhouse or in the window.

Among the best of these tuberous kinds is O. Bowieana, a South African kind that grows 6-12 in. tall and has large flowers. Bulbs of this Oxalis, planted in spring, produce flowers in late summer; bulbs planted in fall flower late in winter and spring.

Oxalis cernua, called Bermuda Buttercup, is 9-10 in. tall and has bright yellow flowers. It blooms in spring and is a splendid window-garden plant. O. cernua variety flore-pleno is a beautiful double-flowered kind; O. Deppei, 6-10 in., has red or purplish flowers in spring; O. brasiliensis, 3-6 in., has reddish flowers in spring.

O. hirta differs from most tuberous kinds in that it has erect, leafy stems. These grow to a height of 12 in. The plant bears pink flowers in fall and early winter. O. incarnata grows 6-10 in. tall and has purplish or lavender and yellow flowers in spring. O. lasiandra, 12 in. tall, has purple-crimson flowers in summer. O. lobata is a yellow-flowered kind that blooms in fall and is 3-4 in. tall. O. Bowieana (purpurea), a summer bloomer that attains a height of 6-12 in., has pink, purple or purplish-red flowers.

Oxalis variabilis blooms in late fall and early winter and has large flowers of pink, lavender-pink and red coloring. The plants grow 9-12 in. tall. This is the kind often sold under the name "Grand Duchess" Oxalis.

Nontuberous Tender Kinds of Oxalis

Easy to Grow. Among the nontuberous tender kinds are a number suitable for the greenhouse and window garden. Of these, O. rubra, a native of Brazil, is one of the easiest to grow and is one of the commonest. It is often misnamed O. rosea in cultivation.

O. rubra is a very free-blooming and attractive plant suitable for cultivation in a sunny, frost-proof greenhouse and outdoors in mild climates. It is in full beauty in spring and summer. The roots should be potted in January or February. During the season of active growth generous supplies of water are needed. When the leaves have died down, the soil is allowed to become dry.

This kind bears satiny, bright pink flowers over a very long season of bloom. There is a white-flowered variety named O. rubra alba.

Three Shrubby Kinds. Oxalis gigantea is a most interesting plant from northern Chile. It makes an erect shrub up to 6-8 ft. tall, whose woody branches are clothed thickly with short spurs from which come tufts of rather fleshy, trifoliate leaves and numerous bright yellow flowers.

The plant is deciduous, and, when in flower, with the branches wreathed from top to bottom with masses of golden blossom, is extremely handsome. It is best propagated from seeds sown under glass in spring or early summer, and it is a plant for the cool greenhouses. It is rare.

Oxalis Bowieana has large flowers of a beautiful pink color.

More common in the United States is another somewhat shrubby Oxalis, O. Ortgiesii. This native of the Andes of Peru grows to a height of 1½ ft., and has leaves that are rich purple beneath, and small yellow flowers. It needs no season of complete rest and thrives in a rather woodsy soil in a moist atmosphere, with a night minimum temperature of 55 degrees. It needs approximately the same conditions as fibrous-rooted Begonias. It is propagated by cuttings.

O. hedysaroides rubra, a native of Colombia and Brazil, needs similar culture. Sometimes called Firefern, it has slender, erect stems, wine-red foliage and yellow flowers.

A True Shrub. O. dispar is a true shrub, and thrives in a moist atmosphere in a warm, tropical greenhouse. This native of Guiana grows slowly and branches freely. It needs the same conditions as O. Ortgiesii for its successful cultivation. It is propagated by cuttings.

OXEYE. Buphthalmum, which see.

OXEYE DAISY. See Chrysanthemum leucanthemum.

OXLIP. Primula elatior, which see.

OXYCOCCUS. Vaccinium, which see.

OXYDENDRUM ARBOREUM—*Sorrel Tree* (Oxyden'drum). A leaf-losing (deciduous) tree of North America, which, under the most satisfactory conditions, grows 70-80 ft. high. More usually it forms a low tree, often less than 20 ft. high. A common rendering of the name is Oxydendron.

This is a very decorative tree by reason of its dark green leaves, which are 4-6 in. long and 1½-2½ in. wide, and its large terminal clusters of white flowers in summer. In autumn the leaves turn to brilliant shades of red and orange before falling.

Seeds form the only practical means of propagation, and plants should be grown under conditions that suit Rhododendrons—that is, in peaty soil or in limefree loam.

The tree belongs to the Heath family, Ericaceae, and the name is taken from the Greek, *oxys,* sharp or acid, and *dendron,* tree, and alludes to the acid taste of the leaves.

OXYPETALUM CAERULEUM (Oxypet'alum). A tender, somewhat twining subshrub that is a native of Brazil and Uruguay. It belongs in the Milkweed family, the Asclepiada-

The Sorrel Tree, Oxydendrum arboreum, is an extremely handsome native of North America. It belongs in the Heath family and prefers an acid soil.

Although really a perennial, Oxypetalum caeruleum can be grown as an annual, so that it produces its beautiful blue flowers the same year that the seeds are sown.

ceae. Its name is derived from *oxys,* sharp, and *petalon,* petal, and refers to the fact that in some species of the genus the petals are sharp-pointed. This plant is named Tweedia caerulea by some botanists, and by others Amblyopetalum caeruleum.

Oxypetalum caeruleum attains a height of 3 ft. or more and has oblong-lanceolate leaves. Its flowers, which it bears freely, are rotate (wheel-shaped), measure an inch in diameter and are remarkable for the color changes they exhibit. In bud the flowers are pinkish; they open to be pale blue, tinged with lavender and green, change to a purplish hue, and are finally lilac-colored.

Advice on Culture. When seeds are sown early in a greenhouse, Oxypetalum caeruleum may be had in bloom the first year. It may be treated as a flower-garden annual if plants are raised in this way and set in a sunny, well-drained, fertile soil outdoors after the weather is warm and settled. Alternatively, plants may be flowered the first year from seeds sown directly outdoors in early spring.

The plant may also be grown in a large flowerpot in a greenhouse and kept from year to year. Plants grown in this way require a minimum winter temperature of 55-60 degrees and a humid atmosphere. A soil consisting of equal parts of good loam, peat moss and coarse sand, with a sprinkling of bone meal added, is suitable; the pots must be well drained. Repotting

and any necessary pruning back are done in March.

In addition to propagation by seeds, this plant may be increased by means of cuttings inserted in a bed of firmly packed sand or sand and peat moss or vermiculite in spring.

OXYTROPIS (Oxytro'pis). Hardy herbaceous plants which grow wild in North America, Siberia and Europe. They belong to the Pea family, Leguminosae; the name Oxytropis is derived from *oxys,* sharp, and *tropis,* keel, and refers to the sharp end of the keel (lower petal of the flower).

The plants grow 4-12 in. in height and form compact tufts of pinnate (feathery) leaves, which are woolly beneath. The flowers, which are small and pea-shaped, are produced in a spike which carries them well above the foliage. They are white, yellow, cream, pink or purple, and open in June and July.

For a Sunny Rock Garden. Being dwarf and compact in growth, these plants are suitable for growing in the rock garden. A sunny, well-drained position is required and a compost of sandy loam is the most suitable. Planting is done in fall or spring. The plants are set 3-12 in. apart, according to the vigor of the different kinds and the soil is pressed firmly around the roots. As they form strong taproots, they resent disturbance and should only be lifted and replanted when they show signs of poor growth.

Propagation Is Chiefly by Seeds. They are sown in April, where the plants are to grow. The seeds are scattered thinly and covered with a fine layer of soil. They must be kept moist until they have germinated and the seedlings are well established. If more seedlings grow than are required, they should be thinned out.

The plants may be increased by division, but they resent root disturbances and so this method of propagation is not adopted unless seeds are not obtainable.

The Chief Kinds. O. Lambertii, white, blue and purple; O. pyrenaica, purple and lilac; O. pilosa, yellow and O. montana, purple and yellow. The first-named grows 12 in. high, the others reach a height of about 6 in.

OYSTER, VEGETABLE. Salsify, which see.

OZOTHAMNUS. Helichrysum, which see.

P

PACHIRA (Pachir'a). Extremely showy trees, from the warmer parts of South and North America, that may be grown outdoors in the far South. They belong to the Bombax family, Bombacaceae. The name is the Latinized form of a native name.

Pachira aquatica, the Guinea Chestnut, blooms in southern Florida in spring. Its flowers are pink, red or purplish and are very large. P. macrocarpa, found from Mexico to Costa Rica, is a smaller tree with flowers that are pink and yellowish.

These trees may be propagated by seeds and cuttings, and probably by air layering. The seeds of P. aquatica are eaten raw or roasted.

PACHISTIMA (Pachist'ima; Pachisti'ma). Small evergreen shrubs that are natives of North America and belong to the Staff Tree family, Celastraceae. The name is derived from *pachys,* thick, and *stigma,* a part of a flower.

Pachistima Canbyi is a native of rocky woods from West Virginia to southern Ohio and eastern Kentucky. It is known locally as Ratstripper. It is a trailing plant that grows to a height of 1 ft. or less, and forms a neat ground cover. In cultivation it succeeds in sun or shade, but makes a neater, denser growth when it has plenty of sunlight. It needs an acid soil and is easily propagated by cuttings inserted in a cold frame or greenhouse propagating case in late summer, by division in spring, and by seeds. This kind is hardy at least as far north as Massachusetts.

Pachistima Myrsinites, a spreading, stiffish shrub 2-3 ft. tall, occurs as a native from British Columbia to California. Although hardy in southern New York in sheltered places, it does not grow vigorously there. It may be propagated by layers, cuttings and seeds, and it needs a peaty, sandy soil.

PACHYCEREUS (Pachycer'eus). Large-growing Cacti that are natives of Mexico and have thick, ribbed stems furnished with strong spines. They belong to the family Cactaceae and were previously included in the genus Cereus. The name is from *pachys,* thick, and Cereus, and refers to the stems. For cultivation, see Cacti. The chief kinds are P. Columna-Trajani, with massive stems, flowers white; P. Pringlei, a large-growing Cactus of Lower California; and P. pectenaboriginum, Hairbrush Cactus, flowers white and purple.

PACHYPHYTUM (Pachy'phytum; Pachyphy'tum). Tender succulent plants with very thick leaves, covered with a white bloom (fine, waxy meal). All are natives of Mexico. They belong to the Crassula family, Crassulaceae. Previously included in the genera Cotyledon and Echeveria, they require the same kind of treatment as these plants. The name is derived from *pachys,* thick, and *phytos,* plant, and refers to the fleshy stems and leaves.

Noteworthy kinds are: P. bracteosum, 12 in., red; P. Hookeri, 2 ft., red, tipped green or yellow; P. pachyphytoides, 12 in., pink; and P. viride, carmine.

PACHYSANDRA (Pachysan'dra). Evergreen and leaf-losing low-growing subshrubs and herbaceous plants, with soft stems that can hardly be called woody. P. terminalis is frequently planted as a ground cover in shaded and partially shaded

The Japanese Spurge, Pachysandra terminalis, is one of the most satisfactory of evergreen ground covers.

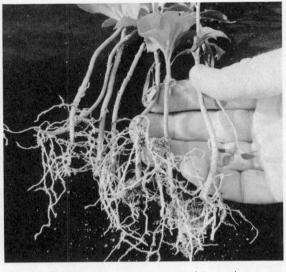

Cuttings of Pachysandra terminalis inserted in sand soon produce healthy roots.

places. The other kinds are less common. A few kinds only are known; they are found wild in China, Japan and in the United States. Pachysandra belongs to the family Buxaceae. The name is derived from the Greek *pachys,* thick, and *andros,* man, and alludes to the thick stamens.

The plants spread by means of a branching rootstock and are increased by division in spring or by cuttings or root cuttings in summer. No particular care is necessary and they may be planted in any ordinary moist garden soil.

P. axillaris, a native of China, grows about 9-10 in. high, with dark green, coarsely toothed leaves and white flowers produced in April. P. procumbens, the Alleghany Spurge, is a North American plant 6-12 in. high with rather large leaves and dull flowers. P. terminalis is a Japanese kind which has creamy white flowers. In the variety variegata the leaves are striped and bordered with silver. P. axillaris and P. terminalis are true evergreens but P. procumbens usually loses all its leaves in winter although some forms of it are evergreen or nearly so.

PACHYSTOMA. See Ancistrochilus.

PACHYVERIA (Pachyver'ia). A group of hybrids between Echeveria and Pachyphytum. They require the same care and culture as Echeveria, which see.

Among the recognized kinds of Pachyveria are the following plants (the names in parentheses indicate the plants from which they are derived): P. clavata (P. bracteosum and E. secunda), P. Clevelandii (P. bracteosum and E. secunda), P. glauca (P. Hookeri and E. species), P. Orpetii (P. bracteosum and E. species), P. Scheideckeri (P. bracteosum and E. secunda), and E. sobrina (P. Hookeri and E. species).

PAEONIA: THE PEONY

Herbaceous and Shrubby Plants of Rare Beauty

Paeonia (Paeo'nia). Popular hardy perennial plants of great beauty, the Peonies are in full bloom in May and June. The herbaceous Peonies are the chief favorites. The Tree Peonies are magnificent, but less well known. The former are natives chiefly of Europe and Asia Minor, the latter of China and Japan. The name Paeonia is said to commemorate the physician of the Greek gods, Paeon. Paeonia belongs to the Buttercup family, Ranunculaceae.

Peonies are hardy in the coldest climates, but do not thrive if their winter dormancy is broken. Therefore, they are not likely to succeed in warm climates. Full sun and well-drained soil are essential. Heavy blooms should be staked to prevent damage from heavy rains.

Comparatively few species or wild types of Peony are grown, but innumerable varieties, having single or double flowers in a wide range of coloring, have been raised, and additions to the number are made annually. Many of the very finest are the result of the work of American breeders. The chief species or wild types from which the May-flowering varieties have been raised by crossbreeding and selection are Paeonia officinalis, the old crimson Peony of southern Europe, and P. albiflora, a Siberian plant which bears white and blush-colored fragrant blooms, and whose offspring are the June-flowering Chinese Peonies.

Soil and Location for Herbaceous Peonies. Herbaceous Peonies thrive in sun or part shade, but they must be planted in deep, rich soil. In poor ground which dries out quickly in summer, they do not flourish; there they grow weakly and flower sparsely. Peonies take some time to become established, and it is necessary to plant them where they can remain undisturbed for years. The sites should be prepared by digging 12-20 in. deep and mixing compost or well-decayed manure in the lower soil. If the ground is light, some heavier loam or clay should be added.

It is a mistake to plant Peonies in a border facing east, for in that position the flower buds are liable to be damaged by the early morning sun, if it happens to shine on them after a frosty night. If, however, the Peonies are in a border facing south, southwest or west, they are unlikely to suffer harm in such circumstances.

How to Succeed with Peonies. As established Peonies are vigorous, leafy plants and take up a

Disbudding Peonies. The side buds of the Peony should be cut (*left*) as they appear. If this is not done, strength will be diverted from the terminal flower (*right*).

good deal of room, it is not wise to use them too prominently in the mixed flower border, where they occupy a disproportionate amount of space after they are through blooming. They may be planted in open spaces among shrubs, in similar places on the edge of woodland, or in other informal parts of the garden where they have room to develop and are not likely to be disturbed. They must not, however, be set in deep shade or in places where the soil becomes impoverished by the roots of neighboring trees or shrubs.

During hot, dry weather in summer, Peonies need a copious watering occasionally; they will not flourish if allowed to become dry at the roots. It is beneficial to mulch the soil around them with decayed manure in spring; this helps to keep the roots moist and feeds them also.

Peonies produce larger blooms if they are disbudded. This operation consists of removing all flower buds except the terminal one from each stem. The buds should be picked or pinched out as early as this can be done without danger of damaging the bud that remains on the stem.

Peonies are quite hardy and require no special winter protection. After frost has killed the foliage it should be cut off slightly below ground level but not deeply enough to injure the buds at the crown (top) of the cluster of roots. Under no circumstances should a mulch of rotted manure, peat moss or other material likely to hold water and exclude air be applied in fall, because it will encourage disease; if a mulch of any kind is used, it should be light and permit the free passage of air through it; salt hay or branches of evergreens laid lightly over the ground are mulches that can be used without ill effect.

The best time to plant Peonies is in September; they may, however, be planted in early spring, provided the ground is in a suitable condition. Set the plants at such a depth that the crowns or tops are covered with about 2 in. of soil; they should be spaced 2½-3 ft. from each other. Planting the roots too deep is a common cause of failure.

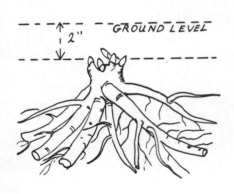

Planting and propagating Peonies: (*Left*) The Peony root should be planted 2 in. below ground level. (*Right*) Peonies are commonly propagated by divisions of the root. Any piece of root with an eye attached will produce a new plant.

When suitably located and cared for, Herbaceous Peonies will bloom satisfactorily each year for a long period, often for 20 years or more; it is not wise to transplant them unless quite necessary so long as they continue to flower well.

Propagation of Herbaceous Peonies. Peonies may be propagated from seed. There are two objections to this method, however. One is the long period (4-8 years) which elapses between the sowing of the seeds and the maturing and blooming of the resultant plants. The second is, that unless it is a wild species, the seed gathered from a Peony plant will not exactly reproduce its parent. If seed is gathered from one of the magnificent double white Chinese Peonies, for instance, the seedlings are liable to be a mixture of white and pink single and double forms, none of them identical with the parent. Hence raising Peonies from seed is of interest chiefly to the specialist and breeder.

For the general gardener the best method of multiplication is by division of the roots. If a Peony root is cut into divisions, every piece of root that has a bud attached to it will grow and produce a new plant of the same variety. This is the standard method of propagating Peony plants.

Each division should, preferably, include 3-5 eyes (buds). September is the most favorable time of the year for dividing herbaceous Peonies.

Tree Peonies. The chief of the Tree Peonies, Peonia suffruticosa (Moutan), is a leaf-losing shrub which reaches a height of 3-5 ft., and bears immense single or double flowers in May and June. It thrives in ordinary loamy garden soil which is well drained; light land can be made suitable by adding old turf, and clayey land by adding old turf, leaf mold and sand. It is necessary to choose a position for these shrubs which is sheltered from the east; they are hardy in the sense that they are unlikely to be damaged by severe frost in winter, but as they start into growth early in spring the fresh shoots are liable to be spoiled by late frosts unless in a sheltered place.

If the shoots become slightly frozen and the sun shines on them early in the morning, they will be injured; if, however, the shrubs are in a position sheltered from the east and open to the south, southwest, or west, the slightly frozen shoots will thaw gradually and no harm will follow.

Tree Peonies are sometimes grown in large flowerpots for the decoration of the conservatory. They should be potted in autumn in loamy (turfy) soil with which some leaf mold and sand have been mixed; they may be left out of doors

A single-flowered Japanese Tree Peony.

Tree Peonies are really low shrubs. They do not die to the ground in winter. They bloom earlier than herbaceous Peonies. This is a double-flowered variety.

until towards the end of the year, or until the approach of severe weather, and then placed under glass. They can be grown in a greenhouse in which a minimum winter temperature of about 45 degrees is maintained.

Kinds of Peonies. Among the wild types or species of herbaceous Peonies there are several attractive flowering plants, some of which should be included in every representative collection.

A young grafted plant of a Tree Peony.

One of the earliest to bloom is Peonia anomala, which bears rose-colored flowers. P. humilis is of comparatively low growth, about 18 in. high, with blooms of rose coloring. Its double form, fimbriata, is very attractive. P. officinalis, a very old garden plant, bears crimson flowers. Its leaves are also attractive when young; they are of reddish-crimson color at first, but they turn green as they age.

The wild type of Tree Peony, Paeonia suffruticosa, has large white flowers blotched with crimson.

Paeonia lutea is a particularly handsome Tree Peony with grayish leaves and yellow flowers which are much smaller than those of the named varieties of Tree Peony.

Other attractive species are: P. Mlokosewitschi, soft primrose-yellow; P. tenuifolia, with finely cut foliage and crimson flowers, and its double form, plena; P. peregrina, red, and its variety Sunshine, salmon-scarlet; and P. Wittmanniana, with pale yellow flowers. All these are in full beauty in May.

Beautiful Varieties. There are innumerable varieties, both single and double, of both herbaceous and Tree Peonies. These are listed and described in the catalogues of dealers in hardy perennial plants and in the catalogues of Peony specialists. They include a wide choice of colors among which are white, pink, red, yellow and many in-between shades and variegations.

Peonies bloom freely in early summer and are especially suitable for planting in sunny borders.

PAINTED DAISY. See Pyrethrum.

PAINTED CUP. Castilleja, which see.

PALISOTA (Paliso'ta). Tropical African, perennial, evergreen, herbaceous plants belonging to the Spiderwort family, the Commelinaceae. The name honors the French botanist and traveler, J. Palisot de Beauvais.

These plants are adaptable for growing in tropical greenhouses and conservatories and are worth trying outdoors in the warmest parts of Florida. They are attractive in foliage and in fruit.

When grown indoors, Palisotas need a rich soil that contains generous amounts of organic material. It should be kept always moist but must be well drained. A minimum temperature of 60 degrees and a moist atmosphere should be maintained. Shade from strong sunshine must be provided. Repotting should be done in late winter or early spring. Plants of this kind normally require this attention every 3-4 years only; in intervening years they may be top-dressed.

Established specimens that have filled their pots with healthy roots benefit greatly from regular applications of dilute liquid fertilizer from spring through fall.

Propagation is readily effected by means of seeds sown in sandy, peaty soil as soon as they are ripe, in a moist atmosphere in a temperature of 70-80 degrees; by cuttings taken in spring or early summer and planted in sandy peat in a close, moist propagating case; and by division at potting time.

Likely to be cultivated is P. Barteri, an almost stemless kind with purplish flowers in fall that are followed by long-lasting bright red fruits in clusters.

Another worthwhile kind is P. Elizabethae, which has erect or more or less sprawling stems. The leaves of P. Elizabethae are rich green with a broad, cream-colored, feathered stripe down their centers. The numerous flowers are crowded into dense spikes; they are dirty white. This plant is very readily propagated by terminal cuttings, as the upper parts of the stems produce roots freely even while still attached to the parent plant.

PALIURUS SPINA-CHRISTI — *Christ's-Thorn* (Paliur'us). A large, leaf-losing (deciduous) shrub or small tree with intensely spiny branches. It is a native of southern Europe and western Asia. Its noteworthy features include its slender shoots, armed at the joints with needle-like spines; its bright green leaves: its dense clusters of small yellow flowers, produced in July and August; and its round, disclike fruits, which are surrounded by a flat wing, the whole fruit being ¾-1 in. across.

This shrub is of chief interest by reason of its legendary associations. It is one of the spiny plants which are said to have been used for plaiting the crown of thorns used for crowning the Saviour before His crucifixion. Although not hardy north of Washington, D. C., it is sometimes grown in greenhouses at botanical gardens because of its interest. The Christ's-Thorn should be planted in well-drained, loamy soil in a sunny position. It is sometimes called Jerusalem Thorn.

Propagation by Seeds and Cuttings. It is best increased by seeds sown in a frame as soon as they are ripe, but it can also be propagated by means of cuttings of half-ripe shoots inserted in a close frame in summer. No regular pruning is necessary, but if a little is required for shaping purposes it may be done in spring.

A Good Hedge Shrub. It is a very good hedge shrub in places where it grows vigorously. When it is used for this purpose, pruning or clipping should be done in summer. Paliurus belongs to the Buckthorn family, Rhamnaceae, and the name is the ancient Greek one for the plant. (Spina-Christi means thorn of Christ.)

PALM. A name given to a large number of tropical evergreen plants belonging in different groups or genera. In the North all must be cultivated under glass, but in the South, especially in southern Florida and southern California, a great many kinds succeed in the open.

Palms may conveniently be divided into two groups, those with palmate (hand-shaped) leaves and those with pinnate (feather-like) leaves. The former are called Fan Palms, the latter Feather Palms. The Palms comprise the botanical family Palmaceae.

A few of the chief kinds in cultivation are Acanthophoenix, Acrocomia, Actinophloeus, Adonidia, Archontophoenix, Areca, Arecastrum, Arenga, Calamus, Caryota, Chamaedorea, Chamaerops, Chrysalidocarpus, Coccothrinax, Cocos, Corypha, Euterpe, Howea, Latania, Licuala, Livistona, Nipa, Phoenix, Ptychosperma, Raphia, Rhapis, Roystonea, Sabal, Thrinax, Trachycarpus, and Washingtonia. For details of cultiva-

Palms growing in the Huntington Botanical Garden, Pasadena, California.

tion and further information regarding these and other kinds, consult articles under their names.

PALMATE. A term used to describe a leaf which has its leaflets, lobes or veins arranged in the manner of a hand with outstretched fingers. The leaflets, lobes or veins originate at and radiate from a common point.

PALM, BETEL. Areca Cathecu; see Areca.

PALM, BRAZILIAN WAX. See Copernicia.

PALM, CARNAUBA. See Copernicia.

PALM, CLUSTER. Actinophloeus, which see.

PALM, COCONUT. See Cocos.

PALM, DATE. See Phoenix.

PALM, DOUM. See Hyphaene.

PALM, EGYPTIAN DOUM. See Hyphaene.

PALMETTO. See Sabal.

PALMETTO, CABBAGE. See Sabal.

PALMETTO, SAW OR SCRUB. Serenoa, which see.

PALM, EVERGLADE. See Paurotis Wrightii.

PALM, FISHTAIL. Caryota, which see.

PALM, KING. Archontophoenix, which see.

PALM, LADY. Rhapis, which see.

PALM, PARLOR. Aspidistra, which see.

PALM, PRINCESS. See Dictyosperma.

PALM, QUEEN. Arecastrum Romanozoffianum, which see.

PALM, RATTAN. Calamus, which see.

PALM, ROYAL. Roystonea, which see.

PALM, SAGO. Cycas revoluta and Metroxylon, which see.

PALM, SEAMBURY. See Coccothrinax.

PALM, SPINDLE. Hyophorbe, which see.

PALM, SUGAR. Arenga, which see.

PALM, TALIPOT. See Corypha.

PALM, WINDMILL. See Trachycarpus.

PAMIANTHE (Pamian'the). A genus of bulbous plants from western tropical America. It belongs to the family Amaryllidaceae, and was named in honor of Major Albert Pam, the first to flower Pamianthe peruviana in Great Britain.

Pamianthe peruviana is the only species in cultivation. It is closely related to Hymenocallis

Pamianthe peruviana is a rare tropical bulbous plant. This is a young specimen. Older plants produce several flowers in a cluster.

and requires cultural treatment similar to the kind given tropical members of that genus. The sheathing leaves are narrow and about 12 in. long, and the large, fragrant, white, long-tubed flowers have, like Narcissus, a conspicuous corona, which is striped and tinted at the throat with green. The flowers are produced in clusters of 2-4 in February–March.

PAMPAS GRASS. See Cortaderia.

PAN. A pan differs from a flower pot in being proportionately wider and less deep than the latter. Pans are generally used in preference to pots

Pans are, essentially, shallow flowerpots. They come in various diameters and depths.

for raising seedlings because of the greater soil surface they provide in proportion to their depth, and because of the greater ease with which seedlings can be removed. Pans are also used in preference to flower pots for the cultivation of some kinds of Orchids, Azaleas, bulbs and alpine plants. The kinds known as Azalea pans, bulb pans and seed pans differ in their proportionate depths, the Azalea pans being the deepest and the seed pans the shallowest.

PANAMIGA. Pilea involucrata, which see.

PANAX—*Ginseng* (Pan'ax). Hardy, perennial, herbaceous plants of low stature that are natives of North America and eastern Asia. They belong in the Aralia or Ginseng family, the Araliaceae. The name is one used by the Greek Theophrastus and is from *pan,* all, and *akos,* cure; the plant was supposed to cure all ills.

These plants are of minor garden value but their roots are highly regarded by the Chinese because of their supposed medicinal virtues. They may be grown in deep, rich, woodsy soil in shade. The soil should be moist but well drained. The plants are raised from seed which is rather slow to germinate. If it is not sown as soon as it is gathered, it should be stratified. This can be done by mixing it with about twice its bulk of peat moss and sand that is just moist, and storing it in a cool, humid place.

Kinds are P. quinquefolium, American Ginseng, which grows to a height of 10-15 in. and is found wild from Quebec to Missouri; P. Schinseng, Asiatic Ginseng, a native of Manchuria and Korea, 9-15 in.; and P. trifolium, Dwarf Ginseng, which grows about 8 in. tall and is found from Nova Scotia to Georgia and

[8—4]
Herbaceous Peony
(Paeonia variety)

[8—4a]
Herbaceous Peony
(Paeonia variety)

[8—4b]
Tree Peony
(Paeonia suffruticosa variety)

[8—4c]
Tree Peony
(Paeonia lutea)

[8—5]
Pansies

[8—5a]
Oriental Poppies
(Papaver orientale)

Wisconsin. In gardens the tropical plants properly named Polyscias are often misnamed Panax.

PANCRATIUM (Pancra'tium). Tender leaf-losing (deciduous) bulbs which bear attractive fragrant flowers. They are natives of tropical Asia, Algeria, Egypt, Arabia, the Mediterranean region and Canary Islands, and belong to the Amaryllis family, Amaryllidaceae.

These plants, which are closely related to Hymenocallis, have large, long-necked, tunicated bulbs (covered with large scales—the coats or tunics) and long, strap-shaped leaves up to 2 ft. in length. The flowers are borne in umbels on the ends of stout scapes (flower stalks). They are white, tubular at the base, 2-3 in. long, and are composed of six long, narrow perianth segments (petals) surrounding a large, cup-shaped corona. Pancratium flowers in summer or winter according to the kind. The name Pancratium is derived from *pan*, all, and *kratys,* potent, and refers to the plant's supposed medicinal properties.

Greenhouse Plants with Fragrant Flowers. When grown in greenhouses, as they must be except in southern Florida and similar mild climates, those from tropical regions need a minimum temperature of 55 degrees, those from the Mediterranean region 45 degrees. The best soil consists of two parts of sandy loam, one part of decayed manure and half a part of sand.

Repotting is done each March, until the plants reach the flowering stage, after which they are repotted once in three or four years. The plants are taken out of the pots and the crocks, as well as any loose soil which can be removed without disturbing the roots, are taken away. They are

Fragrant, white-flowered Pancratium canariense.

then potted in slightly larger pots. These are well drained with crocks, which should be covered with a layer consisting of the rough, fibrous material from the loam. After the plants are re-potted, the soil is not watered until new leaves commence to push up from the bulbs. Then it is thoroughly saturated and is kept moist throughout the summer.

Details of Management. Older plants which have reached the flowering stage are kept growing vigorously for several years by top-dressing annually in spring. A little of the old soil is removed with a pointed stick and replaced with fresh compost. From May to September liquid fertilizer should be applied occasionally.

The atmosphere of the greenhouse must be kept moist by frequently damping the floor and benches, and the foliage should be syringed daily during sunny weather in summer. When the leaves begin to turn yellow, water is gradually withheld and the soil is kept dry during the winter. A light position in the greenhouse is necessary, but they should be shaded from bright sunlight. The leaves must be sponged or sprayed occasionally with insecticide to keep down thrips, red spider mites and mealybugs.

Propagation is principally by offsets or small bulbs which form at the bases of the older ones. They are taken off in spring or summer and half-buried in a seed pan, which is well drained and filled with prepared compost. This consists of equal parts of loam, leaf mold, peat and sand, sifted through a fine sieve. It is essential that the seed pan be well drained with crocks. When a few roots have formed, each plant is potted separately in a 3-in. pot.

When sowing seeds, prepare the flower pans as described for the offsets and sprinkle the seeds thinly on the surface. Cover them with a thin layer of fine soil and moisten by immersing the pan to its rim in water. Then cover it with a pane of glass and set in a propagating case in the hothouse.

When the seedlings have formed a pair of leaves, transplant them, 1½ in. apart, in a deeper pan filled with a similar compost, but in a slightly coarser state. They must be kept moist and growing throughout the winter; they must not be dried off. In the following spring they should be potted separately in 3-in. pots and subsequently into larger ones.

Outdoors in the South. When these plants are cultivated outdoors in the South, the site should be carefully prepared. Unless the soil is well drained, it should be removed to the depth of 2 ft. Six inches of drainage, consisting of broken bricks or stones, is placed in the bottom and covered with pieces of turf. The remainder of the space is then filled with three parts of sandy loam and one part of well-decayed manure or leaf mold or good compost with sand added freely.

When to Plant. The bulbs are planted 3 in. deep in spring. During the summer the soil is kept moist and a mulch of compost or well-decayed manure applied. The bulbs should not be disturbed for several years, or until they show signs of deterioration. Then they should be lifted and divided. New compost is added and the best bulbs are replanted. The smaller ones are planted in a nursery bed if it is desired to increase the stock.

The Chief Kinds. *Tropical:* P. canariense, 18 in., white, autumn; P. zeylanicum, 15 in., white, summer. *From the Mediterranean region:* O. illyricum, 15 in., white, summer; and O. maritimum, 18 in., white, summer.

In the United States, plants grown under the name of Pancratium often belong properly in the genus Hymenocallis.

PANDANUS—*Screw Pine* (Panda'nus). Tropical ornamental foliage plants from Africa, India, Australia and Polynesia. In their native regions some kinds grow 60 ft. in height and have tree-like trunks which are conspicuously ringed with horizontal leaf scars. Stiltlike roots develop at intervals from the trunk and main stems and grow downwards into the soil. These act as props and reduce the danger of the plants' being blown down in storms. The plants belong to the family Pandanaceae. The name Pandanus is derived from *pandang*, a Malayan word meaning conspicuous.

Pandanus leaves, which form tufts at the ends of the branches, are sword-shaped, 2-3 ft. in length and green or green variegated with white or yellowish stripes. The leaves are sessile (without leafstalks), are spirally arranged on the

In warm climates such as that of southern Florida, Pandanus grows to be a sizable tree. In this picture the stilt roots that grow from the stem into the ground are clearly visible.

stems, and are sharp-pointed; their edges and the midveins on their undersides are usually armed with prickles.

These plants produce large clusters of inconspicuous flowers, which are dioecious (male and female on different spikes), and the female flowers are followed by large, conelike fleshy fruits. Pandanus does not flower in a small state but

Young plants of Pandanus are attractive as pot specimens. This is Pandanus Sanderi.

specimens are often grown in pots and tubs for the beauty of their leaves. They are easy to grow and make good house plants.

Greenhouse Plants with Ornamental Leaves. These plants require a winter temperature of 60-70 degrees and a soil consisting of two parts of turfy loam and equal parts of peat moss, leaf mold or humus with a generous sprinkling of crushed charcoal and sand and some bone meal added. Repotting is done February to April. The new pots should be clean and be made ready by placing a layer of crocks in their bottoms, and over this a layer of rough siftings from the compost or rough leaves. Firm potting is essential. The plants are shaded from strong sunlight, and a moist atmosphere is maintained by frequently damping the floor and benches; the leaves, too, must be sprayed.

No water is given until the soil becomes fairly dry, when it is thoroughly saturated. Established plants are watered freely during the summer, but during the winter the soil is moistened only when it becomes moderately dry. The plants require plenty of light at all times of the year, and are shaded in summer from very bright sunlight only.

Propagation is chiefly by suckers or offsets. These are removed in spring or summer and are potted separately in well-drained 3-in. pots filled with sandy soil. The pots are plunged in a propagating case with a bottom heat of 70-75 degrees. When the suckers or shoots are well established, they are repotted in 5-in. pots, and subsequently in larger pots.

Small plants in 5-7-in. pots are useful for decorating the greenhouse and house. Because the leaves of most of these plants are so prickly, it is necessary to keep them clean by spraying them with insecticide, since they are difficult to sponge.

The kind commonly grown is P. Veitchii, with green and white leaves. Other kinds are P. Sanderi, with green and yellow striped leaves; P. Baptistii, with yellow and green leaves; and P. utilis, with blue-green leaves with red spines.

The fibers obtained from various kinds of Pandanus are used for making ropes, baskets, fans, and so forth, and the fruits are used as food by natives.

PANDOREA (Pandor'ea). Chiefly Australasian and tropical Asian twining evergreen vines that belong to the Bignonia family, Bignoniaceae. The name is derived from Pandora, of Greek mythology.

Pandoreas are handsome vines for outdoor cultivation in warm climates where little or no frost is experienced, and for growing in tropical greenhouses. They need rich soil. Plants grown in a greenhouse need exposure to full sun, but benefit from light shade during the hottest months of the summer.

Propagation is easily effected by means of cuttings inserted in a bed of peat moss and sand, sand, or vermiculite in early summer; or plants may be raised from seeds sown in sandy soil in well-drained pots or pans in spring.

Kinds best suited for cultivation are P. jasminioides, Bower Plant, which has white or pale-pink flowers usually with a deeper pink throat (in the variety alba the throat is white and in the variety rosea the whole flower is pink), and P. pandorana, the Wonga Wonga Vine, which has yellowish or pinkish-white flowers that are spotted purple (its variety rosea has pink flowers). Both bloom in summer.

PANICLE. A rather loose flower cluster that is longer than wide and which has the flowers arranged on branching stems. Technically a panicle is a branched, racemose inflorescence. Good examples of panicles are the flower clusters of Lilacs, Catalpas and Oats.

PANIC GRASS. See Panicum.

PANICUM—*Panic Grass* (Pan'icum). A large group of Grasses found wild in most countries, including the United States; they include annual and perennial plants belonging to the Grass family, Gramineae. These plants are not widely cultivated in gardens, as few have any decorative value. The name is an ancient Latin one for a kind of Millet.

Treatment of Hardy Annuals. These are sometimes grown in clumps in the border to impart a light, graceful effect. The seeds are sown in spring in the positions in which the plants are to grow. They are scattered on the surface and raked in, and the seedlings thinned to 6 in. apart. Very little subsequent attention is required, except that they must be watered in dry weather and the soil loosened between the plants with a cultivator to keep down weeds and aerate the soil.

The flower spikes are sometimes dried and used for winter decoration.

The two principal annual kinds are P. capillare, 2 ft., with narrow, grasslike leaves and purplish inflorescences, and P. miliaceum (Millet), 3 ft., with narrow green leaves of soft texture.

Hardy Perennial Grasses. These require a sunny position and ordinary garden soil. They are planted in autumn or spring in clumps in the perennial border or wild garden. They should not be disturbed for several years, or until they show signs of deterioration, when they are lifted, divided, and replanted in fresh soil.

Division, the chief method of propagation, is done as frequently as is necessary to maintain a stock of vigorous plants. Seeds may also be sown in pots of sandy soil in spring. The seeds are lightly covered with soil, and a pane of glass is set over the pot until germination takes place. When large enough to handle, the seedlings are pricked off, 2 in. apart, into a seed pan, and, later on, potted singly in small pots. P. palmifolium (more properly Setaria palmifolia, which see) has broader leaves and is grown in similar fashion. Both P. palmifolium and P. virgatum may be grown without difficulty outdoors in the far South.

The chief hardy perennial kind is P. virgatum, Switch Grass, 3-6 ft. tall, native from Maine to Florida and Arizona, and in the West Indies and Central America. It is sometimes grown as an ornamental. Several Grasses grown in gardens under the name Panicum are placed by botanists in Setaria, which see.

PANSY. The Pansy ranks high in popularity among garden flowers—especially the magnificent large-flowered, richly colored strains of Pansy which modern seedsmen offer. Botanically the Pansy represents a horticultural development of Viola tricolor, a wild species. It belongs in the Violet family, the Violaceae. The word Pansy is from the French *pensée,* which means both thought and Pansy.

Pansies resemble bedding Violas (see Viola) but differ in being of less compact growth and having flowers which are usually larger and dis-

Flowers of rich and varied coloring, representative of a mixed seed strain of modern Pansies.

tinctly marked or blotched to give the appearance of a "face."

Cultivation. Pansies thrive in cool, moist soil, and do best where they are shaded from the hottest sun. It is worth going to some trouble to prepare the soil for them by digging in plenty of old manure or compost, for such treatment results in an abundance of large flowers over a long period, especially if the growths are trimmed back when they become straggly.

Raising Plants. The simplest and best way of raising Pansies is from seeds. To have plants for setting out in the garden in fall or early spring to produce spring blooms, the seeds should be sown about the end of July. A cold frame located in a cool, shaded place outdoors and containing a bed of loose, well-drained soil that contains an abundance of organic matter is a good place to sow the seeds, but they may be sown with good success in drills made directly in the open ground.

As soon as the seedlings are big enough to handle with ease, they should be spaced 6-7 in. apart in outdoor beds or cold frames. Cultivation to keep down weeds must be practiced, and during dry weather the seedlings must be kept watered.

In cold sections the seedlings should remain in the beds or cold frames until spring, and it is wise to protect them with a light covering of salt marsh hay or some similar material. In mild localities they may be set out in the fall in the position where they are to bloom the following

Gaily colored Pansies provide color in this bed in spring. The bordering plant is Veronica incana, a hardy perennial that blooms in summer.

spring. Plants kept in cold frames over winter must be well ventilated on all favorable occasions. This is absolutely necessary if they are to make sturdy, well-rooted plants for setting out in their flowering locations in spring.

Seeds sown in a cool greenhouse in January and then transplanted into flats and kept growing in a temperature of 45-50 degrees will develop into sturdy little plants for setting out in spring. They will bloom later and for a longer season than plants raised from seeds sown the previous summer.

Greenhouse Culture. For winter and early spring flowering in the cool greenhouse (night temperature 45-50 degrees), use seeds of Pansy strains especially recommended by seedsmen for greenhouse culture. Sow these seeds in June or July in a prepared seed bed out of doors or in a frame. The seedlings are transplanted to a lightly shaded nursery bed or frame and kept well supplied with water in dry weather. In September they are planted in their flowering pots or benches in the greenhouse. Such plants will produce blooms throughout the winter and give a lovely show in spring when they attain best growth.

In mild climates winter-flowering strains behave well and flower in winter when planted outdoors.

Cuttings. Specially good varieties of Pansies can be perpetuated by taking cuttings of young unflowered shoots in August–September and rooting them in a cold frame. If, when rooted, they are planted 6 in. apart in a sheltered nursery bed or cold frame, they will provide excellent material for setting in the flower beds in spring. This method of propagation is effective only where summers are not excessively hot; generally it is better to rely upon seed.

Later Treatment. Once the Pansies start blooming, they should be gone over regularly, once a week, for the removal of faded blooms; otherwise, if these are allowed to mature seeds, the plants' display will soon finish. Thorough waterings in dry weather, and occasional soakings with weak liquid fertilizer, will benefit them considerably, as will surface mulches of moist peat or compost. See also Viola.

PANTHER LILY. See Lilium pardalinum.

PAPAVER: THE POPPY

Favorite Annuals, Biennials and Perennials for Garden Decoration and Cut Flowers

Papaver (Papa'ver). Hardy perennial, biennial and annual plants which are of great value in the garden. A collection of different kinds furnishes showy flowers throughout a long season, from early summer until autumn. The Poppies are natives of Europe, eastern Asia and North America, and belong to the family Papaveraceae. The word Papaver is the ancient Latin name for the Poppy.

Poppies flourish in ordinary garden soil, most kinds preferring that which is well drained. They must be grown in a sunny place; they are not successful in the shade. Poppies vary greatly in size, from the tall Oriental Poppy, 2-3 ft. high, to the low-growing Alpine Poppy, which is suitable for the rock garden.

The Oriental Poppy

The Oriental Poppy, Papaver orientale, is a hardy perennial, 2-3 ft. high, with large, deeply cut leaves, which bears immense, cup-shaped flowers of various brilliant colors in early summer.

This is one of the most striking of all the flowering plants which are in full beauty in May and June. In association with Lupines and Bearded Irises, it provides a brilliant display of bloom before many perennial border flowers have opened.

The Oriental Poppy thrives in ordinary, well-cultivated garden soil and may be planted in early autumn or spring. Autumn planting is, however, greatly to be preferred, for, if put in then, the plants are far more likely to bloom the first summer than if planting is delayed until spring.

Dislikes Being Disturbed. The Oriental Poppy has thick, fleshy roots and dislikes being disturbed. It becomes established rather slowly and flowers little, if at all, until the second season after planting. It should, therefore, be placed where it is to remain indefinitely, for the plants increase in size and numbers of flowers annually for many years.

This Poppy looks best in small groups in the perennial border; it should be placed in the middle or towards the back of the border, for the flowers are over in June and afterwards the large leaves are rather untidy.

Taking Root Cuttings. The Oriental Poppy can be increased by means of root cuttings, which should be taken as soon as the leaves have died down. The plant should then be lifted, and the roots cut into pieces 3-4 in. long. These are set in sandy soil in a frame kept close for a few weeks. They may be laid horizontally and covered with an inch or so of soil, or vertically, the tops being covered with ½-1 in. of soil.

The soil must be watered occasionally to keep it moist; water should not, however, be given

An Oriental Poppy in full bloom.

Papaver pilosum is an attractive Poppy with orange-colored blooms.

named varieties, these are some of the most striking: Barr's White, pure white with purplish-black blotches; Cavalier, scarlet; Curtis Giant Flesh Pink, huge flesh-pink flowers; Curtis Giant Flame, immense blazing red flowers; Curtis Salmon Pink, salmon-pink; Enchantress, soft rose; Gold of Ophir, golden orange; Indian Chief, mahogany; May Sadler, salmon-pink with black markings; Perry's White, white with crimson-maroon blotches; Salmon Glow, double flowers of salmon-orange color; Watermelon, deep cerise; Wunderkind, begonia rose-pink.

These named varieties do not breed true from seeds; if an increased stock is required of any of them, it must be obtained by division or root cuttings.

The Iceland Poppy

The Iceland Poppy, Papaver nudicaule, which is a native of Siberia, is an exceptionally fine garden flower for regions where summers are not very hot and humid. The saucer-shaped blooms, in orange, yellow and other colors as well as

until the soil is moderately dry while the cuttings have no roots. If kept in a cold frame during the winter and protected from severe frosts, the cuttings will be well rooted by spring and may be planted out of doors in May where they are to grow. Root cuttings may also be taken in spring and planted in the open ground.

Raising the Oriental Poppy from Seeds. Raising Oriental Poppies from seeds is a perfectly simple matter, though varieties will not, of course, come true to color (most seedlings are likely to have orange-red flowers). Seeds develop profusely on established plants; the pods should be gathered before they open and the seeds saved until spring. Or, of course, seeds can be purchased at that season. The seeds may be sown in sandy soil, in a frame in April, or out of doors in a nursery border in May.

The seeds are very small and, if sowing out of doors is practiced, the soil must be pulverized by forking and raking. The seeds are scattered in very shallow drills and are covered merely by raking the bed over lightly. The seedlings should not be disturbed until autumn, when they will be large enough to be set out in their permanent positions.

Some Brilliantly Colored Varieties. Of the

Flowers of a modern strain of the Iceland Poppy, Papaver nudicaule. They embrace a wide range of brilliant yellow and orange shades and are excellent for cutting.

white, are on long stems and prove invaluable for cutting. They are in full beauty in May and June. The Iceland Poppy is grown as a biennial; that is to say, seeds are sown one year to provide plants that will bloom the year following. After they have flowered, the plants are of little use and a fresh stock is raised annually.

When to Sow Seeds. The seeds are sown out of doors in May or June in a spare border where the soil has been broken down finely with fork and rake; it is necessary to do this because the seeds are very small. They are sown in drills half an inch or so deep and 10 in. apart.

It is wise to sow the seeds thinly because the seedlings should be left undisturbed until autumn, when they are planted out where they are to remain and bloom the following year. If the seedlings are crowded in places, they must be thinned out. They can, if necessary, be transplanted, though it is wiser not to disturb them, for they make better progress and develop into finer plants if not moved before the autumn.

An alternative method is to sow the seeds in small pots in a frame, and grow the seedlings on in these, after thinning them out to one in each pot. Plant them where they are to flower, before they become root-bound.

Iceland Poppies look well in groups towards the front of the perennial border or they may be set out in the rock garden. It is worth while planting some of the seedlings in an out-of-the-way place solely for the purpose of providing flowers for cutting.

Beautiful Varieties of Iceland Poppies. In recent years several grand strains of the Iceland Poppy have been raised. The flowers show a wider range of coloring than the older kinds and the stems are longer. They make showy groups in the garden and, as already suggested, are ideal flowers for cutting for decorative use indoors.

The Annual Poppies

These are beautiful summer flowers, indispensable both for garden decoration and for cutting. The chief types are the Shirley and the Opium Poppies.

These are hardy annuals which are raised from seeds sown out of doors in late August or early

September to provide flowers in May and June, and in early spring to provide flowers in early summer.

Sowing Seeds in Late Summer. The finest possible plants are obtained by sowing the seeds in August–September; they are more vigorous than others raised in spring and yield a profusion of bloom. In gardens where the soil is well drained or light, late-summer sowing is much to be preferred, but on heavy, clayey land the losses among the seedlings during the winter will be severe. If late-summer sowing in this kind of ground is contemplated, the site should be dug and sand and compost added freely to make the soil crumbly.

The seeds should be sown where the plants are to grow; it is unwise to transplant the seedlings. The seedlings must not be thinned out severely before winter because some are certain to disappear before spring. The final thinning out should be deferred until March or April. Each plant will then probably need to be 10-12 in. from its neighbor, to allow room for full development.

Seedlings raised in spring should be thinned out until they are about 6-8 in. apart. Poppy

Shirley Poppies are a particularly fine strain developed by selection from the scarlet Corn Poppy, Papaver Rhoeas.

The large double blooms of the Carnation-flowered strain of the Opium Poppy, Papaver somniferum.

seeds are so small that they are usually sown far too thickly, with the result that the plants are poor, weedy specimens which have a short flowering season. If the seeds are scattered thinly, the seedlings well thinned out, and all faded blooms and seed pods are picked off, annual Poppies will bloom freely for many weeks.

When to Cut Poppy Blooms. If wanted for vases indoors, Poppies should be cut as soon as the buds assume an upright position; they will then open perfectly in water indoors and will last much longer than they would have if left on the plant until the buds were almost ready to burst into blossom.

Shirley Poppies. Seeds of several strains of the Shirley Poppy are sold by seedsmen, including a variety with double flowers which, however, lacks the charm of the single ones, in rose, blush, pink and allied shades.

Opium Poppies. Of the gray-leaved Opium Poppy, there are many varieties with large, double, brilliantly colored flowers—for example, Carnation-flowered, Peony-flowered, White Swan, and Mikado.

Other hardy annual Poppies are Papaver commutàtum, 12 in., and the Tulip Poppy, P. glaucum, 18 in., both having scarlet flowers; and the Peacock Poppy, P. pavoninum, 18 in., scarlet.

Alpine and Other Poppies

The **Alpine Poppy** (Papaver alpinum) is a charming little plant for the rock garden; it grows only about 6 in. high and bears flowers of various shades of color—orange, yellow and salmon as well as white. It thrives in a sunny place in light or well-drained soil, and is increased from seeds sown in spring, preferably where the plants are to grow. It is not long-lived.

Other beautiful Poppies are Papaver pilosum, which bears orange-colored blooms, and P. rupifragum, with flowers of apricot coloring. They are short-lived perennials but easily grown from seeds sown out of doors in summer.

PAPAW. The Papaw, Asimina triloba, a native American fruit, is the only member of the Annonaceae, the Annona family, which is hardy in the northern United States. It is hardy also in parts of Canada. For the Pawpaw, see Carica Papaya.

The fruits of the better types are 4-6 inches long and are shaped like short, fat bananas. They are dull green but turn brown when dead ripe. The flesh is banana-like in texture, sweet, very rich and fragrant and of a delicious flavor. Numerous brown seeds, as large as Lima Beans, are embedded in the flesh. The fruits are borne singly, or in clusters of up to 5 or 6. They ripen from mid-September onward at Geneva, New York.

The tree grows 20-30 ft. in height and produces from the roots suckers which tend to make a dense thicket. The large, long, glossy leaves give the tree an almost tropical appearance. The dull red flowers are interesting, but not beautiful; they appear in late May before the leaves.

The Papaw Is of Easy Culture. It grows naturally in rich soils from Lake Ontario southward nearly to the Gulf of Mexico and will grow on any good, well-drained garden soil.

It is best propagated from seeds which, if not sown outdoors as soon as they are ripe, should be stratified before they are sown. The seedlings grow slowly for 3-4 years and then more rapidly. The suckers have few fibrous roots and, when transplanted, become established with difficulty. The suckers should be removed because the

tree is more attractive with a single stem than when grown as a thicket. See also Asimina.

PAPAYA. See Carica.

PAPER BIRCH. Betula papyrifera, which see.

PAPER BUSH. Edgeworthia papyrifera, which see.

PAPER MULBERRY. See Broussonetia.

PAPHINIA (Paphin'ia). Small but beautiful Orchids which are found wild chiefly in Brazil. All are epiphytal (grow perched on trees) and have evergreen leaves and small, clustered pseudobulbs, from the base of which are produced drooping flower spikes, each with two or three large and attractive flowers. These Orchids have been classified under Lycaste, and they certainly resemble a small Lycaste in growth, but the pendent spikes and the shape of the lip render them of distinct appearance. All flower in summer.

Orchids for the Hothouse. Paphinias are often short-lived under cultivation, but are so beautiful that an effort should be made to grow them. They require a tropical temperature during summer and a moist atmosphere throughout the year. In winter the temperature should never fall below 60 degrees; a temperature of 65 degrees is to be preferred. When growth begins in spring, the plants should be repotted; small pans suit them better than pots. A suitable compost consists of osmunda fiber cut into small pieces or of Fir bark, Redwood bark or Tree Fern fiber.

The flower pans should be suspended near the glass and carefully shaded. Water should never be allowed to remain on the leaves at night. When in full growth, these Orchids must be watered liberally, but in winter the compost is allowed to get moderately dry. Care at all times in watering is essential.

P. cristata has yellowish flowers, thickly lined with purple-chocolate. P. rugosa has slightly smaller, reddish flower.

PAPHIOPEDILUM. A botanical name of a group of Orchids, dealt with in this work under the name of Cypripedium.

PAPOOSEROOT. Caulophyllum thalictroides, which see.

PAPYRUS. Cyperus Papyrus, which see.

PARADISEA LILIASTRUM — *St. Bruno's*

Lily (Paradi'sea). A hardy herbaceous perennial flowering plant from central Europe, which belongs to the Lily family, Liliaceae. From the perennial rootstock rise linear (long, narrow) leaves, 12 in. in length. The flowers, which are funnel-shaped and white, tipped with green, are borne on stems 12 in. high in June. The variety major is a larger and much better plant than the typical kind. The name Paradisea honors Count Giovanni Paradisi, of Modena.

Paradisea requires a partially shaded position and deep, rich soil. The site is prepared by deep digging and incorporating liberal quantities of compost, leaf mold or well-decayed manure. Planting is done in early fall or early spring, when the plants are set 18 in. apart in irregular clumps. In the summer the soil is kept moist by mulching with decayed manure.

Propagation is by division or by seeds. Division is done at planting time, when the plants are lifted carefully to avoid damaging the roots. They are then separated into pieces and replanted in freshly prepared soil.

Seeds are sown in early summer in a well-drained flowerpot or pan. A pane of glass is laid over the pot to prevent the moisture from evaporating, and it is set in a shady frame.

When germination takes place, the glass is removed and the seedlings are exposed to the light. As soon as two or three leaves have formed, the seedlings are transplanted, 2 in. apart, into a flat of soil. They are well watered and shaded until established. When they show signs of becoming overcrowded, they are planted out in a nursery border 6 in. apart, where they remain until large enough to plant in their permanent positions.

PARADISE STOCK. This is a type of rootstock widely employed for budding or grafting the cultivated varieties of Apple on, when quick-fruiting, dwarf-growing trees are required. The stocks are considered by many to have originated from a dwarf form of Malus sylvestris, called paradisiaca.

For many years Paradise stocks were regarded as essentially dwarfing in effect—which was, it seems, their original character. Investigations have shown, however, that the stocks were very mixed, and the name Paradise has covered a wide range of seedling forms of Malus or Crab, some of which were markedly more dwarf in habit of growth than others. (See Apple.)

Special selections of Paradise stocks were made and standardized, so that those now in general use among nurserymen and fruit-tree raisers fall into more or less distinct groups. They are propagated vegetatively, usually by layering, and so remain true to type in all respects.

The term Paradise stock is still popularly applied to dwarfing stocks only, although the types of Paradise stock now in use provide rootstocks suitable for the propagation of each and every kind of Apple tree which may be required in the garden and orchard, from very dwarf bush trees to vigorous, tall trees.

The Chief Paradise Stocks. The Paradise stocks now recommended are as follows:

Very dwarfing: Jaune de Metz Paradise, or Malling No. 9, suitable for cordons, pot trees, espaliers and very dwarf bush trees.

Semidwarfing: Doucin Paradise or Malling No. 2, suitable for quick-fruiting bush trees of medium size, and garden trees.

Semivigorous: Broadleaf English Paradise, or Malling No. 1, suitable for weak varieties when grown as bushes, large permanent bushes and low-headed trees on rich land.

Vigorous: Malling stocks Nos. 12, 13 and 16, suitable for low-headed and high-headed trees of vigorous growth.

PARA RUBBER. The product of Hevea brasiliensis, which see.

PARASOL PINE. Sciadopitys verticillata, which see.

PARASOL TREE. Firmiana simplex, which see.

PARASYRINGA SEMPERVIRENS (Parasyrin'ga). An evergreen shrub of recent introduction from China, belonging to the Olive family, Oleaceae. It grows up to 10 feet tall, has small dark-green leaves and produces clusters of small white flowers in August. It thrives in ordinary well-drained soil and is propagated by layering in autumn, or by cuttings of shoots in sandy soil in a cold frame in August. The name is from *para,* near, and *Syringa,* Lilac.

PARDANTHUS SINENSIS. Belamcanda, which see.

PARIS DAISY. See Marguerite.

PARKINSONIA (Parkinso'nia). Mostly tropical, usually spiny, trees and shrubs, some of which are cultivated for ornament in the warmest parts of North America. They belong to the Pea family, Leguminosae. The name honors the English apothecary and botanical author John Parkinson.

The best-known species is P. aculeata, the Jerusalem Thorn or Ratama, a tree to 30 ft. tall that is a native of tropical America and bears feathery foliage and fragrant yellow flowers in drooping racemes. It makes a good hedge plant when sheared. P. Torreyana is a tree about 25 ft. tall, native to Arizona and Texas.

Seeds afford the simplest and most satisfactory method of propagation. These plants grow well in well-drained soils in sunny locations.

PARLOR PALM. Aspidistra, which see.

PARMENTIERA (Parmentier'a). A small group of trees that belong to the Bignonia family, Bignoniaceae. Natives of Mexico and Central America, they are suitable for planting in southern Florida and similar warm climates. The name honors a French apothecary and writer on plants, A. Parmentier.

The best-known kind is P. cereifera, the Candle Tree, a native of Panama. This kind grows to about 20 ft. tall and has bell-shaped whitish flowers each with a brown calyx. The light yellow fruits, which resemble candles, hang from the branches and are eaten with relish by livestock. Other kinds are P. alata, from Mexico, and P. edulis, the Guajilote, a 30-ft.-tall tree from Mexico and Guatemala that bears greenish-yellow flowers and edible, yellowish-green fruits.

These plants may be propagated by seeds and by cuttings taken in summer.

PARNASSIA—*Grass-of-Parnassus* (Parnass'ia). Dwarf, hardy, perennial flowering plants, which grow in boggy places. They belong to the Saxifrage family, Saxifragaceae, and are found wild in many areas, including North America, India and Europe. Several species are natives of North America, including P. palustris, which also occurs in Europe and Asia. It grows 6 in. in height, and has a thick rootstock which gives rise to a cluster of small, heart-shaped, smooth, green leaves on short stalks. The star-shaped white flowers, veined with green, are produced in early summer, singly on the ends of slender stalks springing direct from the crown. The name Parnassia refers to Mount Parnassus, the abode of grace and beauty.

For the Bog Garden. These plants are grown in a moist position in the bog garden, at the base of a rockery, or near the margin of a stream or pool. If the soil is deficient in humus, liberal quantities of leaf mold or peat should be added.

Planting is done in spring, the plants being set 4 in. apart. After planting, they need not be disturbed except when it is desired to increase them by division. They may then be lifted in spring, separated by pulling them apart, and replanted in their permanent positions.

They are also increased by seeds in early summer, sown in a pan of sandy peat finely sifted, in a moist, shaded position. The seedlings are left in the seed pan until large enough to plant in their permanent positions.

The chief kinds are P. palustris, 12 in., white; P. caroliniana, 6 in., white; P. fimbriata, 6-12 in., white; P. californica, 15 in., white; P. asarifolia, 20 in., white.

PAROCHETUS COMMUNIS — *Shamrock Pea, Blue-flowered Shamrock* (Paro'chetus; Paroche'tus). A tender trailing plant with leaves like those of the Clover, but each of the three leaflets is marked at the base with a brown crescent. Large, blue, pea-shaped flowers are produced in June. This plant is a native of tropical Asia, eastern Africa and the Himalayas, and belongs to the Pea family, Leguminosae. The name Parochetus is derived from *para*, near, and *ochetos*, a brook, and refers to the plant's natural surroundings.

The Blue Shamrock, Parochetus communis.

For a Sunny Rock Garden. This plant is hardy only in warm parts of the country; in cold localities it must be sheltered in a greenhouse or cold frame during the winter.

The plants are set out in spring in a sunny, well-drained position in the rock garden or front of the flower border. Ordinary light garden soil is suitable. If the soil is clayey, it must be dug out to a depth of 12 in. and replaced with light soil or lightened by mixing in sand or ashes.

Once planted, the Parochetus needs little attention, and will eventually cover the soil; if in the rock garden, it will creep between the crevices and hang its trails of attractive flowers and foliage over the face of the rocks.

In cold areas some of the runners or trailing shoots should be detached and placed in 3-in. pots in early autumn. These must be kept in the cold frame or greenhouse in the winter and planted out of doors in spring, to replace plants which have perished during the winter.

If a few plants are repotted in 5-in. pots and taken into a greenhouse with a minimum temperature of 40 degrees, they will continue to bloom and produce flowers in winter. This plant is sometimes grown in hanging baskets in the greenhouse.

Propagation is by detaching pieces of rooted runners in April and replanting them in fresh positions, or they may be pegged down in small pots of sandy soil.

PARODIA (Paro'dia). A genus of small-growing Cacti, family Cactaceae, with rounded or cylindrical stems, the ribs of which are divided into tubercles heavily armed with spines, some of which are hooked. The funnel-shaped flower surmounts the stem. For details of cultivation,

Parodia aureispina flowers freely under cultivation.

see Cacti. The name is in honor of Dr. L. R. Parodi, of Buenos Aires.

Species cultivated include P. aureispina, with white and yellow spines, and golden-yellow flowers; P. chrysacanthion, small yellow flowers; P. microsperma, central spines reddish-brown, flowers orange; P. sanguiniflora, spines white and brown, flowers blood-red; and P. setifera, central spines pink, becoming black, flowers pale yellow. Most of these attractive little Cacti are natives of Argentina.

PARONYCHIA—*Whitlowwort* (Paronych'ia). Dwarf, creeping, perennial rockery plants, which grow wild in southern Europe and the United States and belong to the Knotwort family, Illecebraceae. Paronychia is the old Greek name for the type of inflammation called a whitlow, for which this plant was considered a cure.

Paronychias form dense mats of evergreen leaves which are attractive at all seasons of the year. The slender stems are clothed with opposite leaves, ⅛ in. in length, and minute silvery bracts are formed at their bases. The greenish-white flowers are in tiny clusters along the stems, and they also are surrounded by silvery white bracts.

For the Rock Garden or Flagstone Paths. These plants are very attractive when planted in the rock garden or in the spaces between flagstones forming paths and terraces.

A sunny situation and light, well-drained soil are required. The plants are set out in spring, about 4 in. apart, in the rock garden or in a flagstone path. They are kept moist by watering, after which no further attention is required. Eventually, the clumps grow together, covering the soil and the adjoining rocks with masses of green and silvery leaves.

Propagation is principally by division in early spring. The creeping stems root along their whole length as they run along the soil. Small clusters furnished with roots are therefore always obtainable. These are lifted carefully and replanted in the new position.

Plants may also be raised from seeds sown in sandy soil in spring or summer.

The chief kinds are P. capitata, 9 in.; P. argentea, 6 in.; and P. argyrocoma, 6-8 in. All have white flowers and silvery bracts.

PARROT FLOWER. Heliconia psittacorum, which see.

PARROTIA PERSICA—*Persian Witch Hazel* (Parro'tia). A small, leaf-losing, hardy tree with a widely spreading head, found wild in northern Iran and thence to the Caucasus. It may grow 30-40 ft. high but is usually much dwarfer, for, unless great care is taken in pruning and training the leading shoot in the early days, the tree develops with a short stout trunk from which branches spread to a considerable distance in all directions. The oblong or oval leaves are 5-5½ in. long and nearly 3 in. wide.

Parrotia belongs to the Witch Hazel family, Hamamelidaceae, and the name commemorates a German naturalist and traveler, F. W. Parrot.

Brilliant Autumn-tinted Leaves. The leaves have no special attractions during summer but color brilliantly in autumn with shades of red, orange and bronze. The individual flowers are small, but conspicuous by reason of their many red stamens. They are borne in dense clusters from the leafless shoots in late winter or spring, and, as they appear with great freedom, a well-grown plant is very effective at that period.

Parrotia persica is increased by seeds sown in sandy soil in a frame as soon as they are ripe, and by layers pegged into sandy soil in spring. It requires full sun and well-drained, loamy soil.

Pruning should be given special attention when the tree is young. It is done in summer, and should take the form of shortening the side branches in order to direct additional food material to the leading shoot.

The only other species is P. Jacquemontiana, from the Himalayas, a tree up to 20 ft. tall. It differs from P. persica by having from four to six white bracts, but the most conspicuous part of the flowers, produced in May–June, is the bunch of yellow stamens. The rounded leaves are 2½-3½ in. long and nearly as wide. They remain green longer than the leaves of Parrotia persica, but lack the rich autumnal coloring of that plant. This kind is sometimes called Parrotiopsis Jacquemontiana.

PARROT'S-BILL OR PARROTBEAK. Clianthus, which see.

PARROT'S-FEATHER. Myriophyllum proserpinacoides, which see.

PARROT TULIP. See Tulipa.

PARRYA MENZIESII (Par'rya). An attractive native of the Rocky Mountain region which belongs to the family Cruciferae, the Mustard family. The name commemorates Captain William E. Parry, an Arctic navigator.

Parrya is an excellent subject for a sunny, well-drained position in the rock garden. Of tufted habit, woody at the base, and up to 8 in. tall, it produces its loose racemes of bright purple flowers in May. Its rosettes of leaves are thickly covered with gray hairs. It can be raised from seeds sown in a cold frame or greenhouse in spring, or by cuttings of young shoots inserted in sandy soil in a cold frame in June–July.

PARSLEY. A hardy biennial plant, the leaves of which are used for garnishing and flavoring purposes. The botanical name of Parsley is Petroselinum crispum. The plant is a native of southern Europe and belongs to the Carrot family, the botanical name of which is Umbelliferae.

Moss-curled Parsley is an indispensable herb for use in garnishing and flavoring.

From a short row of Parsley a liberal amount of leaves may be picked.

In many gardens the cultivation of Parsley receives scant attention; it is sown wherever there happens to be room, the seedlings remain crowded together and, as a result, the leaves are small and the plants run to seed early.

Although Parsley cannot be said to be difficult to cultivate, it is an erratic plant. In some gardens it flourishes despite neglect, while in others failures are frequent despite unusual care.

Preparing the Soil. Parsley prefers earth which has been broken into fine particles; whether it be heavy or light, the addition of leaf mold or other organic matter will be found an advantage. On very light ground it is wise to sow Parsley in partial shade.

When to Sow Seeds. Two sowings are sufficient for the average garden. One sowing is made in April, the other in July. Where the climate is

A few plants of Parsley lifted from the garden and planted in pots in fall will provide a supply of fresh leaves all winter in a cool greenhouse or sunroom.

not excessively severe, the later sowing will furnish winter supplies. As one of the most important details in the cultivation of Parsley is to allow the plants plenty of room, it is unwise to sow the seeds thickly. The drills ought to be ½ in. or so deep and 12-14 in. apart; at the final thinning the seedlings should be left 6-8 in. apart.

Seeds Germinate Slowly. Parsley seeds usually take a longer time to germinate than those of

most other vegetables; they may not appear for 5-6 weeks. If the weather is hot and dry after sowing, the soil should be moistened occasionally, and a light top-dressing of leaf mold, compost or peat moss will be beneficial.

To maintain a supply of fresh leaves in winter, except in quite mild climates, some form of protection is necessary. This can be provided by covering the plants with a frame, or a few roots may be set in pots or flats of soil and placed in a frostproof greenhouse or frame or may even be kept in a sunroom window or on a sunny window sill in a cool room.

There are various strains of Parsley with attractively curled leaves, notably Giant Curled and Imperial Curled.

PARSLEY FERN. Cryptogramma crispa acrostichoides, which see.

PARSLEY, HAMBURG. This is a distinct type of Parsley, Petroselinum crispum latifolium, grown solely for its fleshy roots, which are cooked and eaten in the same way as Parsnip. It does

The Parsnip-like roots of Hamburg Parsley make a welcome change in winter root vegetables.

well in ground that was manured for the previous crop. The seed is sown in early spring in drills an inch deep and 12 in. apart; the seedlings are thinned to 9 in. The roots are lifted in October and stored in the same way as Carrots and Beets for use during winter.

PARSNIP

A Root Vegetable for Winter Use

The Parsnip is a root vegetable very easy to cultivate. It is very hardy, and is in season in autumn and throughout the winter months. The botanical name of the Parsnip is Pastinaca sativa. The plant is a biennial, and grows wild in various parts of Europe. It belongs to the family Umbelliferae.

Preparing the Ground. Few vegetables give the grower less trouble than the Parsnip, but large, well-developed roots are obtained only by sowing on land which has been prepared by deep cultivation. On shallow, poorly prepared or stony ground, the roots of Parsnip will be small and unshapely.

The amateur gardener who wishes to have good-sized and shapely roots must have the ground plowed, rototilled or spaded deeply, thus allowing the roots to penetrate easily. If the soil is hard or lumpy the roots will certainly be poor. It is important that fresh manure should not be used when preparing the site for Parsnips; badly shaped roots will result. Very old, well-rotted manure may be incorporated with the soil, and so may good compost.

The bed in which Parsnips are to be grown should be turned over deeply in the fall. In spring, when it is fairly dry, it should be forked and leveled to bring it into a fit condition for sowing. A week or two before sowing, a scattering of bone meal—2 oz. for each square yard of ground—is beneficial. Superphosphate may be substituted for this.

Deep, Rich Soil Necessary. Parsnips, like other root crops that require deep, rich soil free from fresh manure, are best grown on a plot planted the previous year with vegetables for which the land was dug and manured. For example, Parsnips might well be sown where Onions, Beans or Peas were grown.

When to Sow Seeds. Since the Parsnip needs as long a season of growth as possible, the seeds must be sown as soon as the conditions of soil and weather will allow. It is, however, useless to sow when the weather is wintry or the ground sodden. It is wiser to defer sowing for a week or two than to set the seeds in lumpy or sodden ground.

How to Sow. There are two ways of sowing the seeds. One way is to scatter them thinly along the full length of the row: the other is to

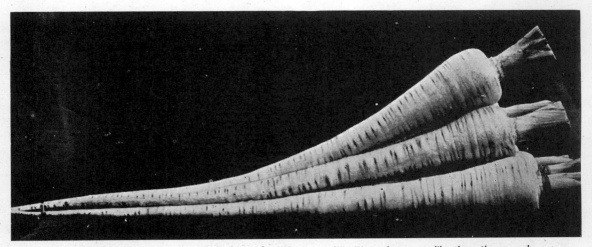

Roots of the Student Parsnip, of prize-winning exhibition quality. To produce roots like these the ground must be deeply cultivated and fertile but not freshly manured.

[8—6]
Geranium
(Pelargonium)

[8—6a]
Geranium
(Pelargonium) Mrs. Burdette Coutts

[8—6b]
Geranium
(Pelargonium) Mrs. Parker

[8—6c]
Ivy-leaved Geranium
(Pelargonium peltatum variety)

[8—7]
Picking Parsley

[8—7c]
Lombardy Poplar
(Populus nigra italica)

[8—7b]
Virginia Creeper
(Parthenocissus quinquefolia)

[8—7a]
Boston Ivy
(Parthenocissus tricuspidata)

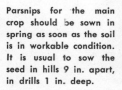
Parsnips for the main crop should be sown in spring as soon as the soil is in workable condition. It is usual to sow the seed in hills 9 in. apart, in drills 1 in. deep.

set groups (hills) of three or four seeds at 6-9-in. intervals. The latter method is recommended as it is less wasteful of seeds, and time in thinning. If this plan is followed the seedlings must be reduced until only one is left in each group. The drills should be 15 in. apart and 1 in. deep, and when hill sowing is practiced it is a good plan to sprinkle a few radish seeds between the clusters. These will germinate quickly and mark the rows for hoeing.

Sowing Parsnips for Exhibition. The way to ensure first-rate Parsnips for exhibition at flower and vegetable shows, if the soil is poor, shallow or stony, is to make holes 3 ft. deep and about 12 in. apart, with a crowbar. The holes should be 4-5 in. wide across the top and tapering almost to a point at the base. Good garden soil, which has been sifted and mixed with some sand and thoroughly decayed manure, is used to fill the holes to within an inch or two of their tops. It is important that the soil be made firm by packing it down with a long wooden rammer—the handle of a disused broom makes a suitable tool for this purpose. After the holes are filled and the soil is firmed, four or five seeds

are sown near the center of the top of each hole and are covered with about ½ in. of soil.

Thinning the Seedlings. When the seedlings are well up, they must be thinned out. The superfluous seedlings are removed gradually until only one sturdy plant, as near the center of the hole as possible, remains. First-rate Parsnips can be grown by this method. In hot weather the soil in the holes is more liable to dry out than the surrounding soil. If the roots suffer from lack of moisture, their development will be checked seriously. Therefore it is necessary to water the plants freely in dry periods.

Later Management. During the summer the only attention required, after the final thinning has been done, is to cultivate frequently between the rows to keep down weeds and to encourage the free growth of the Parsnips.

As Parsnips are perfectly hardy, the roots may be left in the ground to be dug as they are required. If this plan is followed where winters are severe, the ground should be covered heavily in fall with leaves, hay or straw to prevent heaving by frost.

In really cold climates it is usually wisest to lift and store the crop as soon as the leaves have died down in autumn. In lifting Parsnip

Preparing holes for the production of exhibition Parsnips. These are filled with fine, stone-free compost.

roots, care must be taken to insert the garden fork well away from them, and to dig deeply so that the fork will be thrust beneath the base of the roots; otherwise they will be pierced and their keeping properties will be impaired. Parsnips keep best when stored between layers of sand, soil or ashes in a cool cellar.

If the crop is left in the ground, to be dug as required for use, it is necessary, if severe frost threatens, to lift sufficient roots and to store them to provide a supply for a few weeks.

Favorite Varieties. There are several varieties of Parsnip. The best are the Student, Hollow Crown, All-American and Guernsey.

PARSNIP, COW. See Heracleum.

PARTHENOCISSUS—*Boston Ivy, Virginia Creeper* (Parthenocis'sus). Botanists have divided what was the genus Vitis into several genera, and Parthenocissus is the name of the group which have twining tendrils, or tendrils which end with discs or sucker-like tips. It includes such well-known plants as the Virginia Creeper, P. quinquefolia and its varieties; P. Henryana, and the popular Boston Ivy, P. tricuspidata, which was previously called Ampelopsis tricuspidata and Vitis inconstans. The name Parthenocissus is derived from the Greek *parthenos,* virgin, and *kissos,* Ivy.

The self-clinging P. tricuspidata (Boston Ivy) is a most colorful member of the genus. It

The Boston Ivy, Parthenocissus tricuspidata, is one of the most popular of self-clinging vines. Its foliage colors handsomely in the fall.

forms long, slender stems and ascends very high walls by means of its sucker-like tendrils. The leaves are very variable in shape and size. They may be small, with sawlike margins, or several inches across and divided into large lobes, or they may be definitely three-parted. They are often brightly colored when they appear in spring, and turn to vivid shades of red before they fall in autumn. The berries are very small and bluish-black.

A very small-leaved variety called Lowii is charming and colors well in autumn. The variety purpurea is distinguished by its purplish leaves. In variety Veitchii the leaves are smaller and are purplish when young but become green later. Where these plants are grown, great care should be taken to keep them out of gutters and from growing between the tiles or shingles of roofs.

The Virginia Creeper. P. quinquefolia is a vigorous plant with large, long-stalked leaves which are usually divided into five leaflets. It is a native of eastern North America and is the climber usually referred to as the Virginia Creeper and sometimes as Woodbine. It is more useful for planting against the trunks of trees or for climbing over large bushes than for growing against a wall. The variety Engelmannii is of neater growth, with smaller leaflets. The foliage of these vines colors brilliantly in fall.

Other Attractive Kinds. P. Henryana is a very vigorous species from central China, with five-parted leaves which are deep velvety green, marked with white and pink along the midrib and veins. The leaves turn bright red in autumn. It is very attractive and is capable of reaching the top of a high wall.

P. himalayana is a vigorous climber from the Himalayas and China, with sucker-tipped tendrils. It colors rich red in autumn, but is not as hardy as the others and is adapted only for planting in the far South.

PARTRIDGEBERRY. See Mitchella repens.

PARTRIDGE-BREASTED ALOE. Aloe variegata, which see.

PASQUEFLOWER. Anemone Pulsatilla, which see.

PASSIFLORA — *Passion Flower* (Passiflor'a). Mostly tender climbing plants with attractive

The beautiful climbing Passion
Flower, Passiflora caerulea.

flowers. They are found wild in South America, North America and Australia, and belong to the family Passifloraceae. These plants have slender stems, usually 20-30 ft. in length, which are covered with small, dark green, vinelike leaves. They climb by means of the tendrils which are formed in the axils of the leaves. The flowers, produced singly in the axils of the leaves, are 3-5 in. in diameter, and crimson, red, purple, blue or white.

From the peculiar arrangement of the various parts of the blooms, this plant has been given the name of Passion Flower. The flower consists of an outer ring consisting of ten petals, which were thought to represent the ten apostles, who witnessed the crucifixion or passion of Christ. Within these there is a ring of filaments, suggesting the crown of thorns, while the five stamens represent the wounds, and the three stigmas the nails. The name Passiflora is derived from *passio,* passion, and *flora,* a flower.

Treatment in Greenhouses. The treatment of

Passiflora racemosa is an attractive vine for growing in a large greenhouse. It bears red flowers.

all these plants is similar except for the temperature required. The tropical kinds need a minimum winter temperature of 55 degrees and the subtropical kinds one of 45 degrees.

The best potting compost consists of two parts of fibrous loam and equal parts of peat and leaf mold with a liberal amount of sand added. The plants are grown in large pots or tubs, or planted in a prepared bed or border in the greenhouse.

Repotting of plants that are in small pots is done in February or March. They are taken out of their pots and the crocks and loose soil are removed from the roots. The new pots, two sizes larger, are filled to one quarter their depth with crocks, which are covered with rough siftings from the compost or rough leaves. Sufficient compost is then added, so that when the plant is set in position the uppermost roots are an inch below the rim of the pot. The remainder of the compost is filled in and made firm.

After potting, the plants are set in a shady part of the greenhouse. The atmosphere is kept moist by damping the floor and benches as well as spraying the foliage two or three times a day. They are watered sparingly until well rooted, but during summer the soil must be kept moist by watering freely; throughout the winter very little water is required.

Planting and Potting. Well-rooted plants in 5-7-in. pots are set in their permanent positions in large pots or tubs, or are planted in a bed of soil in the greenhouse. Pots or tubs, 18-24 in. in diameter, are necessary, and these are prepared in the manner described above.

The best results are obtained by planting in a bed of soil in February or March. For a single plant, half a cubic yard of soil should be removed; a layer of broken bricks, 9 in. in depth, is placed in the bottom of the hole, and covered with pieces of fibrous turf, to prevent the compost from washing into the drainage and blocking it up. The remainder of the space is then filled with the prepared compost. The roots are spread out to their fullest extent and the compost made firm around them; otherwise the growth will be soft and sappy.

Plants in pots or tubs can be kept growing vigorously for many years by top-dressing them each spring with fresh compost. If they are in a bed of soil this attention is only necessary occasionally.

Pruning is done as soon as the plants have finished flowering. It consists of thinning out weak shoots and regulating the growths so that they fill the allotted space, without overcrowding. The main branches are secured to wires or a trellis fixed to the greenhouse wall or roof, and the short lateral shoots are allowed to hang down freely in order to display their attractive blossoms.

Cultivation Outdoors. Passion Flowers can be grown outdoors in the deep South, and one, P. incarnata, at least as far north as Virginia. They require a sunny position and well-drained loamy soil. Very heavy soil should be excavated and replaced with loam or good garden soil; light, sandy soil is made suitable by incorporating a liberal dressing of well-decayed manure or compost. Planting is done in spring. Pruning is the same as for the indoor kinds. The soil must be kept moist in dry weather and liquid fertilizer applied occasionally to plants which are not making satisfactory growth.

Propagating Passion Flowers. Propagation is by cuttings, seeds and layering. Seeds are sown in spring or summer in well-drained pots filled with sandy soil sifted through a 1/2-in. sieve. Before the seeds are sown, the pots of soil should be watered, then set aside to drain; the seeds are scattered thinly on the soil surface and are covered with 1/4 in. of fine soil. A pane of glass is laid over the seed pot, which is kept in a temperature of 60-70 degrees if the seeds are of tropical kinds, 50-60 degrees if the kinds are Passion Flowers that require cool greenhouse culture. When the seedlings show above the soil, the pane of glass is removed from the seed pot.

When the seedlings are big enough, they are potted separately in 3-in. pots, and later into larger pots. A sandy, peaty soil is recommended for this first potting.

When to Take Cuttings. Cuttings are taken in early summer. Shoots about 3 in. in length are taken; the lower leaves are then removed from these and the basal cut is made just below a node (joint). The cuttings are inserted under a bell jar or in a propagating case in a greenhouse and are shaded from direct sunshine. As soon as they have produced roots 1-2 in. long, they are planted individually in 2½-in. or 3-in. pots in a sandy, peaty soil mixture.

Layering can be done at any time during the summer. A shoot which can conveniently be bent down to touch the soil is prepared by making an inch-long cut in a lengthwise direction through a node (joint) and extending nearly to the center of the stem. The cut should be made in a place where the stem is quite firm—which will usually be 1 ft. or more from the tip of the shoot. The cut part of the stem is pegged down on to sandy soil and is covered with the same kind of soil. The soil is kept moist until roots 1-2 in. long have formed. The rooted shoot is then severed from the parent plant and is potted in sandy, peaty soil in a pot just big enough to hold the roots without crowding.

The Chief Kinds. *For the tropical greenhouse:* P. alata, pink and purple; P. edulis, the Purple Granadilla, purple and white, edible fruits; P. quadrangularis, the Giant Granadilla, red, violet and white, grown extensively in certain tropical countries for its fruits; P. racemosa, purple, white and red; P. coccinea, scarlet and purple, fruit edible; P. laurifolia, Yellow Granadilla, white, red and violet, fruit edible; P. tetraden, scarlet; P. vitifolia, orange-scarlet to blood red. P. alato-caerulea is a handsome hybrid with white, pink, purple and blue flowers. P. coriacea, P. maculifolia, and P. trifasciata are interesting kinds grown for the beauty of their variegated foliage.

For the cool greenhouse: p. atropurpurea, purple, violet and white; P. caerulea, white and purple; P. caerulea grandiflora, with larger flowers; P. incarnata, native from Virginia to Florida and Texas, white and purple.

P. caerulea has several varieties, of which Constance Elliott, white, is one of the best.

PASSION FLOWER. Passiflora, which see.

PATHS: ORNAMENTAL AND USEFUL

How to Make and Maintain Garden Paths

Paths are a most important feature of the garden and, according to the way they are laid and the materials they are made of, may add to or detract from its appearance.

The chief materials used in the construction of garden paths are stone chips, gravel, flagstones, brick, asphalt, cement and cinders. Gravel or stone chips (finely crushed stone) are commonly used but in small gardens, paved paths are often preferred. The initial cost of a paved path is greater than that of one of gravel or chips, and in a large garden may be prohibitive. The disadvantage of gravel paths is that the surface must be renewed from time to time if it is to remain presentable and, unless carefully tended, it is less pleasant to walk on during wet weather than a paved path.

Making a Gravel or Stone-Chip Path

To make a gravel or stone-chip path that will be really satisfactory and permanent, it is necessary to provide a proper foundation. The site must be excavated to a depth of not less than 12 in., and drainage is provided by placing a layer of broken brick or stone to a depth of 6 in. in the bottom of the excavated site. On top of this is placed a layer of smaller stones or clinkers, and

Garden paths surfaced with stone chips are attractive. It is important that they have a good foundation.

this is followed by coarse gravel and finally a surfacing of fine gravel or stone chips.

Each layer must be made firm by rolling and tamping before the next layer of material is put on. When the path is finished, it should be higher in the middle than at the sides, so that the water will drain away quickly. Unless the layers of material are rolled thoroughly as they are put on, the path will become uneven in places, and, as a result, rain water will collect in the hollows, spoil the appearance of the path, and prove a nuisance. Rolling and perfect drainage are the chief details of importance in making a gravel path or one of crushed stone.

Draining the Path. If a gravel or stone-chip path is made on heavy clay soil, it is usually necessary to lay agricultural tile drain pipes to ensure a satisfactory surface from which superfluous water will drain away quickly in wet weather. The best method is to lay a main drain down the center of the path, with a slight fall to a dry well or free outlet.

In the course of time the gravel and stone-chip paths lose their bright, clean appearance, and become dull and soiled. They can be improved if the surface, to a depth of 2-3 in., is forked or raked in spring to expose the cleaner gravel or stone chips beneath, then swept and finally

This path, surfaced with bluestone chips, requires frequent raking over to keep it looking well.

rolled. Frequent raking of the surface from spring through fall is necessary to keep a stone-chip path looking well.

The Use of Weed Killers. Weeds and moss may spoil the appearance of these paths if they are not destroyed. Hand weeding is an out-of-date practice so far as the care of garden paths is concerned; the weeds can be destroyed so much more easily and conveniently by using a weed killer. Both poisonous and nonpoisonous weed killers are sold, and if they are applied in spring, according to the directions supplied by the manufacturer, they will keep the paths clean for the whole year, except perhaps in very rainy seasons, when a second application may be necessary.

Many owners of gardens now use one of the special bitumen products sold for the purpose of surfacing paths. It provides a smooth, hard-wearing, clean surface which is weedless and saves a good deal of labor in maintenance.

Paths Made of Bricks

Paths made of bricks are very attractive and strongly to be recommended in gardens of moderate size, or in special parts of a large garden, as, for example, alongside the perennial border, or in a formal garden or Rose garden. They always look well, they blend pleasingly with plants and flowers and afford a dry footing at all times of the year and in all weathers if laid correctly.

It is necessary to choose hard bricks for this purpose; soft bricks are useless, for during frosty weather they are damaged—pieces are broken off, and the path soon becomes uneven. Dark red bricks are most pleasing, but ordinary light-colored stock bricks may be used; they will tone down after a few months' exposure to the weather and lose their harsh coloring.

It is necessary that a brick path be laid carefully to ensure a perfectly level surface. This can be done by anyone who will take the necessary trouble.

How to Lay a Brick Path. The first essential is to provide a suitable foundation on which the bricks can be embedded firmly. The site should be excavated to a depth of about 8 in.; the bottom is raked over to remove all stones, and made firm by rolling. Finely sifted ashes or sand are placed in to a depth of 5-6 in. or even more, according to the level at which it is desired to have the top of the path.

In laying a straight brick path it is necessary to work with the help of a garden line to ensure perfectly straight edges. If the edges are uneven, the appearance of the path will be spoiled. Each brick must be embedded firmly in the ashes, sand or sifted soil and, to ensure a perfectly level surface, it is advisable to use a straightedge and level. If the bricks are laid unevenly the path

An attractive curved brick path flanked by low hedges.

Firmly tamped cinders form the foundation of this brick path. The bricks are embedded evenly in a layer of sand spread over the cinders.

will be unpleasant to walk on and, in some degree, dangerous.

When all the bricks are laid, sifted soil, sand or ashes should be scattered over the path and brushed in the spaces between the bricks. It should not be used for a week or two, to allow the bricks to settle down firmly and evenly. After a few weeks it is usually necessary to examine the path to make sure that the bricks have settled at a uniform level. Any that are higher than the neighboring ones should be lifted and reset.

Cementing the Spaces Between the Bricks. The disadvantage of a brick path finished off with sifted soil, ashes or sand in the joints is that the latter provide a home for weeds. These can, however, be destroyed by one or two applications annually of a weed killer. This should be put on while the weeds are small and before they have flowered. The most satisfactory way of finishing off a brick path is to place cement in the spaces between the bricks, but this is not practicable in regions of heavy winter frosts unless the bricks

Brick paths were favorites in colonial times. This example is at Williamsburg, Virginia.

Many interesting patterns can be achieved by using bricks to form paths.

Flagstone paths are practical and give distinction to the garden.

are laid on a solid concrete foundation. If this is not done, the cement between the joints will crack as a result of movement due to heaving by frost. Cement between joints gives a neat appearance to the path and prevents the growth of weeds.

If a brick path is laid alongside a flower border, the path should be edged with bricks raised slightly above the path level to prevent soil from falling on it.

Many designs can be worked out for brick paths. The bricks may be laid in herringbone fashion, with an edging of bricks laid at right angles to those in the center of the path, and in numerous other ways.

Flagstone Paths

Flagstone paths have many advantages: they provide a dry footing throughout the year, they add to the charm of trees and flowering plants, and their first cost is almost the last.

Rectangular pieces of flagstone form an ideal path, and if the path is a wide one they are to be preferred to random (irregular) paving (see below). If the path is a long one, its appearance is improved if the stones are bordered by wide strips of grass.

If a paved path surrounds the house, running alongside the borders at the foot of the house

walls, large rectangular pieces of stone are more suitable than random paving: because of their larger and more even surface they are pleasanter to walk on. The large stones are especially useful for making a wide paved area or terrace on which to set garden seats and tables.

How to Lay Flagstone Paths. Stone paving must be set very firmly, embedded in finely sifted ashes, soil or sand, in the way recommended for

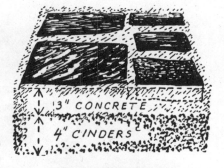

3" CONCRETE
4" CINDERS

SAND
3" OR 4" CINDERS

Flagstone path: cross section of path set (above) in concrete, and (below) in sand.

laying brick paths. If there are stones or lumpy soil beneath them, the flagstones will lie unevenly, and will move when trodden on. The depth of the sifted material should be not less than 4-5 in. to provide a satisfactory foundation. If the stones are set on, and bound with, cement, this ensures a firm, weedfree path that will last a lifetime.

If the cost of natural flagstone is prohibitive, precast concrete slabs may be used, or the slabs can be made where they are to lie. See Cement: Its Use in the Garden.

Random paving is a favorite form of path in small gardens and, if restricted to those positions for which it is suitable, it is attractive and to be recommended. It looks well in a small garden of formal design, in a rock garden, or around a garden seat, sundial, or birdbath, and provides a pleasant walk beneath a pergola. It is not recommended for main paths that will be walked on frequently, unless the stones are set in concrete.

In setting random paving, the sides of the path must be laid first, pieces of stone with one straight side being chosen for the purpose. The inner spaces are then filled in.

The stones will remain firm if they are embedded in finely sifted soil or ashes, or they may be set in concrete after the base of the site has been made thoroughly firm by rolling. As the spaces between the stones are so numerous, and become filled with grass and weeds, it is usual to cement them, places being left here and there, if desired, in which creeping plants can be grown.

Other Kinds of Paths

Concrete Paths. Paths made of concrete are an advantage; they are very durable and easily kept clean, especially if there is a raised edging of concrete separating them from the borders of soil. Concrete tinted gray or brown is usually preferred to ordinary uncolored concrete.

Asphalt paths are of unattractive appearance, and should not be laid in prominent and picturesque parts of the garden. They are, however, very serviceable and long-lasting. They are useful in service areas and at the back of the house.

Cinder Paths. Coal cinders make excellent paths in unobtrusive parts of the garden. If laid on a foundation of clinkers, stones, pieces of flowerpot, or other waste material which provides drainage, they will remain dry and, if kept firm by rolling, will prove entirely satisfactory. Unless adequate drainage is provided, they remain moist and weeds soon take possession of them.

A path of random flagstone bordered by a row of neatly set bricks forms an attractive entranceway to this house.

A charming path made by laying random flagstones level with a grass lawn.

This charming path at Williamsburg, Virginia, is surfaced with tiles.

An excavation about 9 in. in depth should be made; this must be filled to half its depth with drainage material made firm by tamping and rolling before the ashes are filled in. The cinders should be sifted before use, the coarser pieces being placed on the top of the drainage and the finer material used for surfacing.

It is a perfectly simple matter to keep a cinder path in good condition. If it becomes weedy or mossy, it is necessary merely to fork over the surface to the depth of a few inches, remove the weeds or moss, and make the cinders firm again by rolling.

Tanbark Paths. Spent tanbark is a splendid surfacing for paths in woodlands and other shaded areas. It should be spread to a depth of 2-4 in. over a foundation of cinders or crushed stone. Tanbark paths are soft to walk upon, easily maintained and their warm brown color complements both the greens of foliage and the bright colors of flowers.

Tile Paths. Paths of tile are not so common now as in the past. They were popular in colonial times. The tiles are laid in the same way as bricks.

Unsatisfactory garden paths are generally due to faulty drainage caused by an insufficient depth of foundation and to failure to use weed killers. Since the introduction of weed killers which are harmless to animals and birds, those who object to the use of poisonous weed killers can keep garden paths clean by one or two applications annually. The nonpoisonous type of weed killer is caustic and will kill any vegetation with which it comes in contact, so care in using it is necessary to prevent damage to grass and edging plants.

PATIENCE PLANT. See Impatiens.

PATRINIA — *Eastern Valerian* (Patrin'ia). Hardy perennial flowering plants with graceful foliage. They are found wild in Japan and Siberia, and belong to the Valerian family, Valerianaceae. They grow from 9 in. to 2 ft. in height, have finely divided, feathery leaves and produce large, spreading clusters of small yellow or white flowers in early summer. They are not very popular and are chiefly to be found in botanical collections. The name Patrinia commemorates Patrin, a French botanist.

Cultivation. Seeds are sown out of doors in early summer, in drills ½ in. deep. The seedlings, when large enough to handle, are transplanted 6 in. apart in a nursery border, and are set in their permanent positions in fall or spring. They are planted 9-12 in. apart. Light, well-drained soil and a sunny position are required. New plants can also be obtained by dividing the clumps in October or March.

The chief kinds are P. triloba, 15 in., yellow, and P. scabiosaefolia, 18 in., yellow.

PAULLINIA (Paulli'nia). Tropical evergreen climbing plants which are grown for their ornamental foliage. They are natives of South America and belong to the family Sapindaceae. P. thalictrifolia, the principal kind, grows 20 ft. high and has twining stems clothed with finely divided leaves resembling those of Thalictrum. The leaves are bronze-pink when young and change to green as they mature. The small pinkish flowers are inconspicuous. The name Paullinia commemorates Simon Paulli, a professor of botany at Copenhagen during the 17th century.

Foliage Plants for the Greenhouse. Paullinias require a minimum winter temperature of 55 degrees and a soil compost of equal parts of loam and leaf mold or peat moss with sand added freely.

The plants are grown in large pots or in a bed of soil in the greenhouse and the shoots are trained to wires or a trellis fixed to the roof. They should be set in their permanent locations in March.

Well-rooted plants in 5-in. pots are the most suitable for planting. The pots to which they are permanently transplanted should be at least 12 in. in diameter and filled to one fifth of their capacity with crocks, these being covered with a layer of rough leaves. Sufficient soil is added to bring the top of the ball of roots 2 in. below the rim of the pot. The plant is then knocked out of its old pot, and the crocks and loose soil are removed from the roots before the plant is set in the large pot. Next, soil is filled in and made firm, a 1-in. space being left at the top for watering.

To prepare a bed for planting, the soil is taken out to a depth of 18-30 in., and a 6-in. layer of broken bricks is placed in the bottom. These are covered with pieces of leaves or turf to prevent the soil from washing into the drainage, and the remainder of the hole is filled with good soil.

After a few days a hole is taken out sufficiently wide to allow the roots to spread out to their fullest extent, and deep enough for the ball of soil to be covered to a depth of 1 in.

After planting or potting, the soil is well watered and the plants are shaded from sunlight. When they are established, the soil is kept moist throughout the summer, and the plants are exposed to full light to develop a bronze-pink tint in the leaves.

Summer and Winter Care. A moist atmosphere must be maintained by frequently damping the floor and benches, and the foliage should be sprayed twice a day in summer. Less atmospheric moisture is required in winter, and in this season the soil is only watered when it becomes almost dry.

Instead of training the shoots to wires fixed to the greenhouse roof, you may grow the plants in pots and train the shoots to a tripod of stakes fixed in the pot. If the shoots are regularly pinched, a compact pyramid of greenery will be formed.

Pruning consists of cutting back extra-long shoots in February.

Propagation Is by Cuttings. Shoots 2 in. in length are taken off in spring. The leaves from the lower half of the shoot are removed and a cut is made just below the bottom joint. The shoots are then inserted in a propagating case with a bottom heat of 65-70 degrees. Each morning the top of the case should be raised to change the air, and the surplus moisture must be wiped from the underside of the glass.

When roots have formed, the plants are potted separately in 3-in. pots and later on in 5-in. pots, from which they are planted out or set in the large permanent pots.

PAULOWNIA (Paulow'nia). Leaf-losing (deciduous) trees that are beautiful both in leaf and flower. They are natives of China. P. tomentosa (also called P. imperialis) is hardy about as far north as New York City, and has established itself in some parts of the eastern United States where it has "escaped" from gardens. One other kind of recent introduction, P. Fargesii, may be a hardier tree, and it flowers in a younger stage. P. Fortunei is a less hardy kind that is grown in California and the South.

Handsome Trees with Violet-colored Flowers. The chief characteristics of the Paulownias are

Paulownia tomentosa, forms a handsome specimen. In spring it bears panicles of lilac-blue flowers.

their large handsome leaves and violet or deep lilac flowers, which are borne in panicles from the points of branches in May. Unfortunately, the flower buds are produced at the end of the growing season, and thus remain fully exposed to the weather throughout winter and spring; as a result, when winters are severe the inflorescences may be killed even though the trees survive. Paulownia belongs to the Snapdragon family, Scropulariaceae, and the name was given in honor of Anna Paulownia, Princess of the Netherlands.

Raising Seedlings. Propagation is best carried out by means of seeds. They may be sown as soon as ripe in sandy soil in a shaded cold frame or greenhouse. Seedlings appear in a few weeks. When large enough to handle, they should be potted singly or dibbled into a bed of light soil in a cold frame. The young plants are kept in a cold frame for the first winter and planted in a nursery the following spring.

Growth is very rapid, and soft shoots, 6-8 ft. high, may be formed the first season; they have enormous leaves, sometimes 2 ft. or more across.

Planting and Pruning. Paulownias should be planted in well-drained loamy soil in a sunny position. While the trees are young, pruning is necessary in order to train them into tree form, for cutting back the soft ends of the shoots tends to produce a bushy habit. Dead ends of shoots should be removed in spring. New shoots that are not required for the future tree should be cut off when an inch or two long, and any other pruning required for shaping purposes should be carried out during summer.

The Chief Kinds. P. tomentosa (imperialis) forms a round-headed tree, 40-50 ft. high; the leaves are almost as broad as long, with lobed margins 2 ft. across on vigorous young plants, and about 6-9 in. long and wide on adult trees; they are soft and velvety in texture. The inflorescences may be 9-12 in. long and broad, made up of a large number of violet or bluish purple flowers, shaped like those of the Foxglove, individual flowers being 1½-2 in. long. Each fruit contains a large number of seeds. This kind makes a very good lawn tree.

P. Fargesii was introduced from Szechuan, China, in about 1896. It grows rapidly into a tall tree and bears handsome heads of sweetly

scented violet or deep lilac flowers freely in May. P. Duclouxii is a closely allied kind that has been described, but does not appear to be in cultivation.

PAUROTIS—*Saw Palmetto* (Pauro'tis). Attractive Palms with fan-shaped leaves that are native to Florida, the West Indies and, reportedly, Central America. They belong to the Palm family, Palmaceae. The name is derived from *pauros,* small, and *otis,* ear.

Paurotis Wrightii is variously known as the Everglade Palm, the Silver Saw Palm and the Saw Cabbage Palm. It grows to a height of 30-40 ft. and has nearly round leaves that measure 2-3 ft. or sometimes more across. The leaves are green above and silvery beneath.

This Palm requires the same culture as Sabal, which see. It has also been known as Seranoa arborescens and Acoelorraphe arborescens.

PAVIA. A name at one time used for the North American kinds of Aesculus or Horse Chestnut. See Aesculus.

PAVONIA (Pavo'nia). Tropical and subtropical evergreen flowering shrubs which belong to the Mallow family, Malvaceae. The chief kind in cultivation is P. multiflora. This grows 2 feet in height, has simple (undivided) leaves which are ovate-lanceolate, serrate (toothed at the edge) and from 6-10 in. long. The flowers, which are produced in autumn, are 1½ in. long, tubular and purplish-red, in small clusters on the ends of the branches. The name Pavonia commemorates

Pavonia multiflora, an evergreen shrub for the warm greenhouse.

Don José Pavon, a Spanish traveler and botanical author.

For a Warm Greenhouse. These plants, when cultivated indoors, require a minimum winter temperature of 55 degrees and a soil compost of two parts of turfy loam and one part of peat moss, with sand added freely. Repotting is done in March. The plants are first pruned into shape by shortening the longest branches; they are then taken out of their pots, and after all loose soil and crocks have been removed from their roots, are set in slightly larger pots.

After potting, they are watered sparingly until established. During the remainder of the summer the soil is kept moist, but throughout the winter the compost is only moistened when it becomes quite dry.

Propagation Is by Cuttings. Shoots 2 in. in length are removed from the plants in April. These shoots are prepared by cutting off the lower leaves from each and making a cut below the bottom joint. The shoots are then inserted in a greenhouse propagating bench containing sharp sand or vermiculite, or a mixture of sand and peat moss.

The rooting medium is kept moderately moist and the atmosphere inside the case close until roots are formed. When this occurs the young plants are potted separately in 3-in. pots. After they are established in the small pots, the tips of the shoots are removed and the resulting side branches are similarly treated to make bushy plants. Repotting into 6-in. pots is necessary.

Outdoors in the South. In the far South some kinds can be grown outdoors successfully. At least two, P. hastata and P. spinifex, have naturalized themselves in some places, and produce seedlings spontaneously. They thrive without trouble in a variety of soils.

The Chief Kinds. The kinds chiefly grown in greenhouses, and most useful for that purpose, are P. multiflora and its derivatives, among which must be numbered the varieties called by gardeners P. intermedia, P. intermedia Kermesina and P. intermedia rosea. These P. intermedia varieties of gardens are apparently quite distinct from the true P. intermedia of botanists.

Pavonia multiflora, a native of Brazil, has purplish-red flowers and, as seen in gardens, does not usually exceed 2 ft. in height; it is a native of Brazil. P. intermedia (of gardens) is similar but has white flowers. The flowers of P. intermedia Kermesina (of gardens) are carmine, and those of P. intermedia rosea (of gardens), rose-pink. P. hastata, of South America, attains a height of about 6 ft. and bears its pale red flowers, each with a dark spot at its base, singly rather than in clusters. P. praemorsa is a South African shrub with solitary yellow flowers, each with a dark center. P. spinifex, from tropical America, has solitary yellow flowers. It forms a shrub about 20 ft. tall.

PAWPAW. Carica Papaya, which see. See also Papaw.

PEA: MOST WELCOME OF EARLY SUMMER VEGETABLES

How to Grow Peas to Produce Delicious Crops

The garden Pea, which provides pods of edible seeds for use chiefly in the early summer months, is one of the most delicious of vegetables. The numerous varieties now in cultivation are descended from an annual plant whose botanical name is Pisum sativum; it belongs to the family Leguminosae. This Pea is said to be a native of parts of Europe and western Asia.

Because the Pea is very intolerant of hot weather and can be grown only when the days, and more particularly the nights, are compara-tively cool, the chief sowing time in most parts of North America is spring. It is generally true that the earlier the seeds can be sown, once danger of severe frost has passed, the better. Light frosts do not harm Pea seeds in the ground or even young plants showing above ground. In parts of the South, Peas sown in fall give good results because the months that follow sowing are cool enough to be favorable to the growth of Peas, yet not so cold as to prevent their growth or the maturing of crops.

Pea Little Marvel, a heavy-cropping dwarf early variety.

Peas can be grown well only in deep and fairly rich soil that does not dry out in hot weather; they are not a success on poor or sandy, light land.

The ideal way to prepare the ground for the cultivation of Peas, especially if crops of the best quality are desired, is as follows:

Dig a trench 2 ft. deep in the garden in the autumn. Add manure or rich compost to the lower soil and leave the rest of the excavated

Well-cropped Pea vines in a home garden give promise of an abundant harvest.

soil at the sides of the trench so that it will be exposed to the weather during the winter months. In very early spring the soil will be crumbly, and easily broken into fine particles with the garden fork. The soil should then be filled into the trench and trodden moderately firm while it is fairly dry. Unless the soil contains plenty of lime, a scattering of this substance should be put on the surface and forked in lightly.

What we have just described is an ideal way of preparing the soil, because Peas are a deep-rooting crop and thrive best in deeply prepared soil. Fortunately, on most soils, good crops can be obtained with less effort than taking out a 2-ft.-deep trench in the way described. The ground should, however, be plowed or spaded to a depth of 9-10 in. and be well enriched with manure or compost and an application of fertilizer.

Any good complete vegetable garden fertilizer, such as a 5-10-5, may be substituted for the fertilizer mixture mentioned above. (See Fertilizers.)

In the vegetable-garden rotation of crops, Peas should occupy a section of the garden that has been deeply dug and manured in preparation for sowing and planting; this section, the following year, without any further manuring, may be devoted to root crops such as Beets, Carrots, Parsnips and Turnips—all vegetables that thrive best on ground that has not been recently manured but has been enriched by manure incorporated in preparation for a previous crop.

In cultivating Peas on light (sandy) land, a location shaded slightly from the midday sun should be selected. Rotted manure or compost should be added at 10-12 in. beneath the surface and decayed organic material of any type mixed in liberal amounts with the soil above. As soon as the Peas are 6 in. or so high, the soil alongside the rows should be mulched with decayed manure, compost or other suitable material.

Sowing the Seeds. As the seeds of Peas germinate freely, it is wasteful to scatter the seeds thickly. A good plan is to make a 6-in.-wide, shallow, 3-4-in.-deep drill or furrow on the prepared site, and to scatter the seeds over the bottom, the seeds being set about 2 in. from each other. They should be covered with an inch or so

Peas should be sown as early in spring as possible. Sowing in broad shallow drills is a good method for the home garden.

After the Pea seeds are scattered evenly along the drill, about 1 in. of soil is raked over them.

of soil. An alternative method is to make two drills or furrows 6-8 in. apart and 3-4 in. deep, and sow in these. The space between the two drills gives a place into which to insert the peasticks or other supports for the double row of seedlings.

Distance Between the Rows. The rows, whether single and 6 in. or so broad, or consisting each of two furrows, should be set at a distance from each other equal to the height of the plants when they are full grown. Thus, if the Peas will eventually reach a height of 4 ft., the rows should be 4 ft. apart, and so on. To make the most of the ground between the rows, it is usual to sow Spinach or Lettuce there. Before sowing the seeds of Peas, many gardeners stir them in a dish

containing a mixture of red lead and kerosene to prevent damage by mice.

Staking Peas. A detail of importance is to provide the seedlings, when they are only 2 or 3 in. high, with small twiggy sticks or other suitable supports. If this is neglected, the seedlings will fall over for lack of support, and if that happens they never do really well afterwards. Before the Peas reach the tops of the twiggy sticks, tall brushwood, of a height suited to the particular variety, should be put in; or a fence of chicken wire may be substituted for this tall brushwood.

Amateurs almost always insert the peasticks so that they meet at the top, but a better way is to set them so that they slope slightly outwards at the top.

During early growth the soil between the rows should be hoed frequently to keep down weeds. If dry weather sets in, the Peas must be watered thoroughly at regular intervals. If a mulch of compost or other moisture-retaining material that will keep the roots cool is placed alongside the rows, it will prove of great benefit.

Peas should be picked while they are young and tender, but not before the seeds in the pots are sufficiently large to make picking them worth while. If they are picked when too young, the total weight of crop gathered is greatly reduced.

Varieties. Garden Peas are of two main types,

A row of Peas staked with brushwood.

Chicken wire, stretched to form a fence, will give support to the Peas which are sown in two rows, one on each side of the bottom of the .fence.

the smooth-seeded and the wrinkled-seeded. The former are hardier, may be sown a week or so before the wrinkled-seeded varieties, and are especially useful in cold sections. Their seeds are less liable to rot in the soil under unfavorable conditions than are those of wrinkled-seeded

kinds. The quality of the Peas, however, is markedly inferior to that of wrinkled-seeded Peas.

Wrinkled-seeded Peas are the choicest, and a wide selection of varieties of these are offered in seed dealers' catalogues, from which the gardener may make a selection to suit his needs. The varieties vary in height from about 2 ft. to 6 ft. or higher. They also vary in the length of time they take from sowing to maturity. Some gardeners choose one or two varieties and make two or three sowings spaced ten days to two weeks apart to ensure harvesting a crop over as long a period as possible. However, it is usually a better plan to select varieties that need different lengths of time to mature, and sow all of them as early as practicable. This gives the plants an opportunity to send their roots deeply into the earth before hot weather comes, and also ensures successional harvesting.

Edible-podded Peas or Sugar Peas are something of a novelty, and are well worth growing. Their culture is exactly the same as for other kinds. With these varieties both the pods and the seeds they contain are cooked and eaten.

PEA, BUTTERFLY. See Clitoria.

PEA, DARLING RIVER. See Swainsona.

PEACH: A MOST DELICIOUS FRUIT
How to Grow Crops of Fine Quality

The Peach, Prunus Persica, is probably a native of China, although it was once thought to be of Persian origin (hence the name Persica). From China, where it has long been cultivated, it spread westward to Persia and southern Europe, and reached England in the Anglo-Saxon period. Spanish colonists brought the Peach to St. Augustine, Florida, in the sixteenth century, and it spread northward rapidly. Commercial planting in the United States began early in the nineteenth century, and from 1850 onward many varieties were selected and propagated. Peach breeding at the Agricultural Experiment Stations began in about 1920, and from this work many new and valuable varieties have been introduced.

Peaches are grown commercially in more than

half of the states and in Ontario and British Columbia in Canada. Areas of heavy production are central California, the Great Lakes region (particularly southwestern Michigan), western New York and northern Ohio, Georgia, the Carolinas, New Jersey, Maryland, Pennsylvania, and Ontario in Canada. Many other states, except those in northern New England, the Great Plains, and Rocky Mountain regions, have extensive Peach plantings.

The Peach is the least hardy of our temperate-region fruit trees. The site of a planting must be chosen with great care if serious losses from low-temperature injury to the fruit buds and wood are to be avoided. A temperature of —15 degrees F. is critical for the blossom buds on dormant trees in midwinter. A few of the hardiest

Peaches, well cared for, give good crops in localities favorable to their cultivation.

varieties will produce some fruit after experiencing temperatures a few degrees lower. On the other hand, trees that are low in vigor or that in early winter or spring have experienced sudden severe cold following a mild spell, may be injured by temperatures considerably higher than —15 degrees.

Injury to Peach wood may be expected when temperatures reach —18 to —20 degrees F.

The Peach tree should, therefore, be planted where experience has shown that these critical temperatures occur very infrequently. For garden plantings, one may take chances that the commercial grower would not take, as Peach trees grow fast, bear early and are easily replaced when killed by the cold. The loss of an ocsional crop in the home orchard is not a serious matter.

Good air drainage is very important, as temperatures vary greatly at different levels on a slope, and the differences may be great enough on still nights in winter, or when the trees are blooming in the spring, to cause serious injury to trees or blossoms near the base of a slope, while those at higher levels remain unharmed.

The proximity of large bodies of water also prevents sudden severe drops in temperature and tends to delay blossoming until the danger of frost is past.

The best sites for Peach trees are, therefore, on sloping land or near large bodies of water.

Peaches prefer lighter soils than the other tree fruits but will do well on soils ranging from coarse sands to well-drained clay loams if these are deep and well drained. Deep, fertile, well-drained sandy loam soils that permit root penetration to a depth of 3-5 ft. are best if available. Poorly drained soils with a hard subsoil near the surface prevent deep root penetration, and the trees are unproductive and short-lived. Heavily eroded soils are also undesirable.

Peaches should not be planted after other Peach trees have been removed without an interval of several years, as experience has shown that poor growth may be expected if this is done. Other crops, preferably of a soil-building nature, should be grown for several years before the land is returned to Peaches.

Propagation. Peaches are propagated by budding selected varieties on seedling Peach rootstocks. Formerly the seed came from wild seedling trees in the Carolinas, Kentucky and Tennessee, but now seedlings of Lovell, a California drying Peach, are often used because they are available in large quantities.

The seeds are stratified over winter in moist sand or peat at a temperature of 35-40 degrees, and then planted in rows in the nursery in the spring. In late July, or August, in the North, the trees are budded by the shield, or T-bud, method (see Budding). The following spring the bud starts to grow, and the top of the seedling stock is cut off just above the base of the new shoot. In the South the seedlings are budded in June, the bud soon starts to grow, and the seedling top is cut off so that by fall a one-year-old tree, or June bud, as it is called, is ready for planting.

Plum and Apricot rootstocks are sometimes used for Peaches, but they are less satisfactory than Peach rootstocks. Where nematodes are present, the Shalil and Bokhara strains of Peaches are used as rootstocks because of their resistance to these root pests.

Planting. One-year-old Peach trees are commonly used for planting, but June buds, which are smaller, are satisfactory where the growing season is long. The largest size June bud or the medium-sized (4-6 ft.) one-year tree should be used.

Newly planted Peach trees intercropped with Beans.

Peaches should be planted in the spring in New England and the north central states, in late fall farther south, and in late fall or early winter in the Southeast and Southwest. Spring planting should be done as early as possible while the trees are fully dormant.

The trees are commonly spaced 20 by 20 ft., but vigorous varieties on fertile soils will need 25 by 25 ft. or more. In a small home orchard a spacing of 15 by 20 ft. may be used and the trees kept small by pruning.

On slopes steep enough to suffer erosion, the orchard should be planted on the contour; otherwise the soil may easily be damaged by erosion. Contour orchards should be planned well in advance of planting.

Soil preparation and planting the tree are the same as for the Apple, which see.

Pruning. Peach trees are pruned to develop a strong framework to support heavy crops, to avoid weak, narrow-angled crotches that are subject to winter injury, and to shape the tree for convenience in orchard operations. Pruning is also a form of thinning, as it improves the size and quality of the fruit by removing weak and crowded wood. It stimulates vigorous shoot

growth on mature trees, which is essential, as the Peach bears its fruit on one-year-old wood.

The tree, as received from the nursery, is usually 3-7 ft. tall and has some branches. An open-center tree with 3 scaffold or framework branches is best, and these branches should be selected for retaining when the first pruning is done. At planting time the tree is often cut back to a height of 20-24 in., but 36 in. is better—it will give a better spacing of the scaffold or main limbs. The laterals on the young nursery tree are often too weak to be developed as scaffold branches, and they should be cut back to stubs to encourage the growth of strong shoots. When these shoots are a few inches long, three of them that spread at wide angles and are well spaced should be selected and the rest removed. Very vigorous trees, with strong branches, may have the scaffold branches selected at planting time.

The second spring, all weak or crowded laterals that may have grown since planting are removed, and the main branches are headed (pruned) back lightly. The third spring the scaffold branches are again headed back lightly and weak laterals are thinned from the main branches. Pruning during the first 4 years, before the tree is in full bearing, should be as light as possible, just a light thinning with no general heading back of one-year growths.

A Peach tree full of flower buds in the home garden.

An espaliered Peach tree on a fence in a New Jersey garden.

As the trees come into full bearing, more severe pruning is necessary to maintain good growth and renew vigorous fruiting wood throughout the tree. Terminal shoot growth in vigorous trees should be from 12-15 in. each year. Over 20 in. is too vigorous, and poor-colored fruit and winter injury may result.

Young bearing trees on fertile soils and in good vigor are pruned chiefly by thinning out the weak wood. Older, heavy-bearing trees that are slowing down in growth are headed back to well-placed branches on 2- and 3-year-old wood and the weak growth is thinned. This should be done uniformly throughout the tree rather than in just the top.

The Peach should be pruned in late winter in the northern states, as severe cold may cause serious winterkilling of trees pruned earlier. In the South, pruning may be done any time that the trees are dormant.

Thinning out of the young fruits is very essential, as Peaches usually bear several times as much fruit as the tree can properly mature. Peaches should be thinned to leave one fruit to 30 to 50 leaves. Hand thinning is usually done just after the June drop (when the tree naturally drops some of its small fruits), and the earlier it is done the greater the benefit in terms of size of fruit and future crop. The vigorous wood in the top of the tree produces the largest and best-colored fruits, so more fruits should be left there than on the weaker wood that occupies the inside of the tree.

Chemical thinning of the blossoms with dinitro materials and hormones is practiced by large growers, but, as recommendations are changing frequently, the Agricultural Experiment Stations should be consulted for the latest

To insure good size and quality, Peach fruits should be thinned gradually to average one for each 30-50 leaves.

recommendations. Blossom thinning, when it can be done properly, is better than hand thinning of the young fruits.

Soil Management. In controlling weeds and grass in Peach orchards, one should compromise between clean cultivation (the common practice in the past) and the maintenance of a sod which is kept mowed, as is done in Apple orchards. Clean cultivation, which means eliminating all grass, weeds and other ground-cover plants by the frequent use of the cultivator, is too harmful to the soil, and the sod provides too much competition for the roots of the trees. The best practice is what is known as trashy cultivation. Under this system the development of heavy sod is discouraged by using a disc harrow, but the sod is not turned under. As much should be left on the surface as is needed to prevent erosion and to act as a light mulch.

Rye Grass is excellent for growing in the Peach orchard, and if 5 to 10 per cent of the plants are left when discing, it will reseed and provide good cover again by fall.

Nitrogen is usually the chief nutrient needed in the Peach orchard; the other elements are not often in short supply. Young trees making 18 in. of growth each season in the top of the tree, and bearing trees making 12 in. of growth, are making optimum growth. Bearing trees making over 16 in. of growth should not receive nitrogen. If growth is less than 8 in., the amount of nitrogen should be increased.

The basic amount for 1-3-year-old trees is one-half pound of nitrate of soda per tree. Three-to-five-year-old trees should get ½-2 pounds, while trees over 5 years of age should receive 2-4 pounds.

Mulching as described for the Apple is also satisfactory for Peaches but the expense, mice and the possibility of fire should be considered.

Harvesting. A ripe Peach is a very delicious fruit, but unfortunately many that reach the market are picked too green and never realize their full quality. The quality of the fruit increases only while it is on the tree, where the leaves can manufacture the sugars and flavoring substances that make Peaches good to eat.

Peaches increase rapidly in size, and thus the crop is much greater as the fruit approaches the tree-ripe condition. One hundred bushels of Peaches on August 15, if not picked until tree-ripe a few days later, will make 124 bushels of much finer peaches.

Peaches should not be picked until the ground color of the fruit changes from green to yellow with the yellow-fleshed varieties and from green to white with the white-fleshed varieties. Two or three pickings are desirable with most varieties.

Varieties

There are many good varieties of Peaches, but a comparatively few provide the bulk of the commercial crop. Many more are adaptable for growing in home gardens. Generally, a succession of varieties is desirable to spread the harvesting and marketing over a period of several weeks to avoid labor difficulties and to avoid glutting the markets.

Peaches are yellow-fleshed and white-fleshed, clingstone and freestone. The yellow-fleshed freestone varieties are preferred on most markets, but the others may be grown for unusual earliness, quality or hardiness. Peach varieties vary in hardiness of blossom buds and wood, but the range from the tenderest to the hardiest is not enough to extend Peach growing into colder regions than where they are now being grown. In border-line regions the hardiest varieties may produce crops in years when the less hardy varieties fail because of low temperatures.

The hardiest varieties are Greensboro, Oriole, Rochester, Veteran, Carman, Erly-Red-Fre, and Champion. Fairly hardy are Redhaven, Halehaven, Ambergem, Jerseyland, Golden Jubilee and Prairie Dawn.

Tender varieties are Elberta, J. H. Hale and many others, but these are not tender enough to prevent their culture on good sites in the important commercial Peach-growing areas.

The canning Peaches in California are yellow-fleshed clingstone varieties without red color around the pit. Important varieties are Phillips Cling, Walton, Hauss, Johnson, Paloro, Peak, Libbee, Gaume, Sims and Halford No. 2. Newer ones are Stanford and Ellis.

Varieties grown in California for drying are

Lovell, Muir and Elberta. Small-pitted freestone peaches with firm, sweet, clear yellow flesh with no red at the pit are preferred.

Varieties for growing outside of California for canning are as follows:

Very Good	Good
Dixigem	Jerseyland
Redhaven	Golden Jubilee
Vedette	Sunhigh
June Elberta	Southland
Ambergem	Goldeneast
Valiant	Halehaven
	Veteran
	Early Elberta

Varieties Suitable for Freezing. Those with nonbrowning flesh are Redhaven, Triogem, Fairhaven and Redkin. Other good freezing varieties are Vedette, Sunhigh, Halehaven, Veteran.

Variety Descriptions. These are yellow-fleshed freestone varieties unless otherwise noted.

Very early:

Mayflower: White, cling, poor.

Mikado: Cling, fair, needs cross-pollination.

Dixired: Cling, fair to good, attractive, promising.

Erly-Red-Fre: Partly cling until ripe, fair.

Early:

Dixigem: Good.

Redhaven: Good, promising new variety.

Raritan Rose: Good, fine early white variety.

Golden Jubilee: Good, soft, widely grown standard variety.

Triogem: Good, firm, attractive.

Midseason:

Fairhaven: Good, promising, new.

Sunhigh: Good, firm, attractive.

Southland: Good, firm, good shipping variety in South.

Goldeneast: Good, large, firm.

July Elberta: Good, one of best varieties.

Halehaven: Good, fairly firm, widely planted, one of best varieties, needs thinning.

Valiant: Good, firm, attractive.

Veteran: Good, needs thinning.

Belle: Standard, white, good.

Sullivan Elberta: Fair, widely planted in the Southeast.

Champion: White, high quality.

Early Elberta: Good, standard variety.

Elberta: Fair, long the leading variety because of size and shipping quality. Slowly being replaced by hardier, more attractive and better-quality varieties.

J. H. Hale: Good. Very large, attractive, unproductive. Needs cross-pollination.

Late:

White Hale: Good, white, large.

Afterglow: Good, large.

Rio Oso Gem: Good, large. Weak tree.

Salberta: Fair, large, lacks color.

Laterose: Good, white, new, promising.

Goodcheer: Good, firm, new, promising.

PEACH-LEAVED BELLFLOWER. Campanula persicifolia, which see.

PEACOCK FLOWER. Delonix regia, which see.

PEACOCK FLOWER FENCE. Adenanthera pavonina, which see.

PEA, EVERLASTING. Lathyrus latifolius, which see.

PEA, GLORY. Clianthus Dampieri, which see.

PEA, LORD ANSON'S. Lathyrus magellanicus, which see.

PEANUT. The Peanut, botanically Arachis hypogaea and a member of the Pea family, Leguminosae, is a tender annual and a native of Brazil. In the South it is much cultivated for its seeds (Peanuts), which are of considerable commercial value, but it is of minor importance as a garden crop. Because it is very susceptible to frost, it is not generally grown outdoors north of Virginia. However, where seasons are shorter and cooler, it is sometimes cultivated as a garden novelty, and is also grown in greenhouse collections that are maintained for educational purposes, as in botanical gardens.

The Peanut, Goober or Groundnut, as it is variously called, is of more or less trailing habit, usually not growing more than 18-20 in. high. It bears two kinds of flowers: male or staminate ones, which are bright yellow and quite decorative, and inconspicuous female or pistillate ones. The female flowers, after fertilization with pollen from the staminate blooms, develop small pods which bury themselves in the soil and there complete their growth, to become the familiar mature Peanuts. These are not nuts botanically, but are pods containing seeds, and correspond to

Peas and Beans in their form and structure.

Peanuts are sown outdoors in fertile soil about the time that Corn is planted. A rather sandy earth, that has been limed if it is at all acid, suits them best. The rows are spaced about 30 in. apart. Throughout the summer clean cultivation is practiced to keep down weeds.

After frost has blackened the tops, the Peanut plants are dug up or pulled up and are permitted to dry for a time before the pods are picked off and stored or used.

PEA, PERENNIAL. Several kinds of perennial Peas are useful hardy climbing plants. They are described under Lathyrus.

PEAR: CHOICE FRUIT FOR GARDEN AND ORCHARD
The Best Kinds to Grow and How to Care for Them

The Pear has long been associated with man as a cultivated fruit. The European Pear, Pyrus communis, originated in southeastern Europe and the Caucasian region, from whence it spread westward through Europe. The earliest settlers brought it to America.

Pears are grown throughout the Temperate Zone where winter temperatures are not too severe and soil and moisture supply are favorable. The commercial industry is located in California, Oregon, and Washington, and in the fruit regions near the Great Lakes. New York near Lake Ontario, and the Hudson Valley, western Michigan, Illinois, Pennsylvania, Ohio, and Ontario in Canada are eastern Pear-producing areas.

Pears are less hardy than Apples but hardier than Peaches. Temperatures lower than —20 to —25 degrees F. are likely to injure fully dormant Pear trees. The moderating effect of large bodies of water and a uniform moisture supply are important factors in determining the location of the

commercial Pear industry. The high temperatures and high humidity of the southern states favor the rapid development of Pear blight and limit Pear culture in these states to the low-quality, blight-resistant Sand Pear hybrids, Kieffer, Le Conte, Pineapple and others.

Site and Soil. Good air circulation is essential, as Pears bloom earlier than Apples, and the flowers may be frosted on low land surrounded by higher ground from which the cold air drains on still, cool nights. A sloping site is preferable except where a nearby large body of water affords protection from frost.

Pears are considered to prefer the heavier soil types. Clay loams with porous subsoils which permit the deep root penetration required by the Pear tree are best. Medium loams and sandy loams are satisfactory if they are in good physical condition and well drained. Pear trees do not thrive on soils that are waterlogged during the growing season. In the home garden a wider

Seckel Pears are of small size but excellent flavor.

Beurre Bosc Pear is a most excellent late variety for home planting.

range of soils is adaptable than is true for commercial planting. Very fertile moist soils that stimulate unusually vigorous growth should be avoided, as Pear fire blight disease is more troublesome on trees making overvigorous growth.

Pollination. Pears, for all practical purposes, are self-sterile, and provision should be made for cross-pollination by planting more than one variety in the Pear orchard. Bartlett and Seckel do not pollinate each other, and a planting of these two varieties should contain a third variety for pollination.

Propagation. Pears in the past have generally been propagated by budding on rootstocks of Pyrus communis, known as the French Pear among nurserymen. The seeds were obtained

from Perry Pears in France. The French Pear seedlings were susceptible to blight disease, and in about 1900 Pyrus pyrifolia seedlings were used as rootstocks because of their blight resistance. Unfortunately, however, the fruit borne on trees having these rootstocks developed a black area of hard grit-cell tissue called black end. This happened when other Oriental Pear species were used as rootstocks, and the Oriental Pears were abandoned as rootstocks.

The best practice now is to bud or graft the blight-resistant Old Home variety on P. communis roots, grow the resulting tree 3 or 4 years in the orchard, and top-work (top-graft) it to the desired variety, leaving long scaffold branches of the blight-resistant intermediate stock. The

A young Pear tree bearing a heavy crop of fruit.

These dwarf trees are trained in espalier shapes against a support. Grown in this way, they require a minimum of space. The trees may be sprayed more easily, the fruit may be picked with less difficulty, and the trees come into bearing earlier.

roots and framework of the tree are thus protected against Pear blight disease.

Dwarf Pear trees are produced by using the Quince as the rootstock. The Angers Quince (Malling A) is considered the best Quince rootstock for Pears. Some Pear varieties do not grow well on Quince roots; hence an intermediate stock is used (another variety of Pear grafted on the Quince stock), and on this the Pear variety that does not grow well on Quince is grafted. Varieties not compatible with the Quince are Beurré Bosc, Sheldon and Winter Nelis. The Pears used as the intermediate stocks for these varieties are Beurré Hardy and Pitmaston Duchess. Some nurseries also use intermediate stocks for Bartlett and Seckel on Quince roots.

Soil Preparation and Planting. The soil is prepared for planting the same as for Apple, and the planting operation is the same as for Apple, which see.

The trees may be set in the spring or, in mild climates, in the fall. Standard trees are set about 20 ft. apart each way, but the more vigorous varieties, such as Kieffer, Beurré d'Anjou and Flemish Beauty, may need 25 ft. Trees on Quince roots are planted 12-15 ft. apart, and care should be taken that the point of union of the scion and stock is a few inches above the ground

level, or the scion may soon develop its own roots and become a full-sized tree.

Care and Fertilizing. The soil may be managed as for the Apple except that, because vigorous or overvigorous growth may be very susceptible to fire blight, great care must be taken not to stimulate it. The injury to the trees from fire blight may cause far greater loss to the grower than the crop reduction which may occur from trees that are kept somewhat below average in vigor.

The object in managing the soil should be to stimulate only as much growth as the trees can make without becoming too susceptible to blight and yet be sufficiently vigorous to set enough fruit buds for profitable crops. One should err, if necessary, on the side of too little growth.

In humid regions, as in the East, or in the West where ample irrigation water is available, the orchard may be maintained in a permanent

These fine specimens of espaliered Pear trees decorate the Long Island, New York garden of the landscape architect, Umberto Innocenti.

Pear Clapp Favorite, bearing a
heavy crop of fruit.

sod. Enough nitrogen is used to promote moderately vigorous growth. A heavy sod may need discouraging in the spring by partial cultivation and then be allowed to re-establish in late summer. If clean cultivation is practiced, a cover crop should be sown in midsummer to occupy the ground until the following spring.

Phosphorus and potassium are not likely to be needed on most soils, except possibly for the sod or cover crop.

Pruning. Pear trees are pruned much like Apple trees, except that overpruning and the resulting vigorous growth may result in succulent tissues which are very susceptible to blight injury, as already mentioned. Pruning, therefore, should be as light as is consistent with developing a structurally sound tree and maintaining the fruiting wood in good vigor.

The modified leader type of tree is preferred for the Pear. A one-year tree is headed (cut back) at 3½-4 ft. at planting time. At the end of the first season's growth, 4 to 6 scaffold or framework branches are selected. These are spaced about 6 in. apart and are selected to point in different directions. The other branches are removed. If insufficient growth is made the first year, additional scaffold (main framework) branches may be selected for retention a year later.

For the next few years, until the tree is in bearing, pruning should be light and corrective in nature to produce a well-shaped tree that can support heavy crops without breakage. Bad crotches (those likely to break apart because of their weight as the trees become older) should be prevented from developing by cutting back one member of the pair of young branches that diverge to form the crotch. Light thinning of the shoots to prevent crowding may be needed, but moderation should be the rule to reduce the possibility of injury from blight.

The shoots of bearing trees should be thinned out lightly and regularly. Heavy pruning should never be practiced with blight-susceptible Pears. Frequently, the removal of blight-infected twigs will be all the pruning that is necessary. The tree, however, should be kept from getting too dense, and some weak (thin) branches should be pruned out from the centers of the trees. Water sprouts (long, erect-growing shoots that spring from old branches) should be removed, as their succulent growth invites infection by the fire blight organism, and the disease, by moving rapidly downward, may invade a large limb, thus making necessary a heavy cut to remove the infected wood.

Harvesting. Pears must be harvested greener than the other fruits, as they ripen better off than on the tree. Fruits ripened on the tree turn brown at the core. The Bartlett Pear is ready when the green color between the lenticels, or dots, becomes paler than the lenticels, giving the fruit a speckled appearance.

Pears mostly have more tender skins than Apples, and more careful handling is necessary.

Pears do not keep well at room temperatures and have a much shorter life in cold storage than Apples.

Varieties. The Pear varieties of the world are very numerous and have mostly originated as the result of definite attempts to improve them through breeding.

During the eighteenth and nineteenth centuries a great interest in Pears stimulated the raising of thousands of seedlings in Belgium and France. Van Mons, a Belgian, at one time had 80,000 Pear seedlings in his plantings. From this work many of our best Pear varieties came. Now the Agricultural Experiment Stations in the United States are producing new Pear varieties for American conditions, but the European varieties are still the basis of the commercial Pear industry and are likely to remain so for many years.

Bartlett (William's Bon Chrétien of Europe): This is the leading Pear variety of the world and first choice for commercial as well as home-garden planting. Tree bears early and regularly. Fruit yellow, large, excellent for dessert and canning; midseason.

Beurré Bosc: Large, attractive, excellent qual-

An espalier-trained dwarf Pear tree in full bloom.

ity, late. Tree productive and slow in coming into bearing. A good variety for market and home use.

Beurré d'Anjou: The standard winter Pear—large, good, late, keeping most of the winter. Tree slow in coming into bearing, but productive.

Clairgeau: A very attractive, large, late-keeping Pear of only fair quality. Tree productive.

Clapp Favorite: Large, attractive, good quality, midseason. Tree susceptible to blight.

Comice: The best-flavored of all Pears, but grown only in Oregon and the Santa Clara Valley of California. It bruises easily, and the tree is not productive enough for commercial planting but is a splendid variety for home gardens.

Dana Hovey: A small, late-ripening, very high-quality Pear suitable for home use, but the tree is not productive enough for commercial planting.

Ewart: Large, greenish-yellow, good quality. Tree productive. A promising new Pear well worthy of trial. A late variety.

Flemish Beauty: This is a high-quality Pear that is very susceptible to scab disease. The trees are hardier than those of most varieties. A midseason variety.

Giffard: Very early, but of low quality.

Gorham: Large, good, midseason. Tree moderately productive.

Seckel: Small, attractive, highest quality, midseason. Tree slow in coming into bearing, blight-resistant, one of the best for home use and for pickling.

Sheldon: Medium sized; reddish brown, high-quality, late. Tree not very productive. Excellent for home use.

Tyson: Small, sweet, good, early. Tree vigorous, hardy, blight-resistant. A good variety for home use.

Winter Nelis: Medium sized, greenish-yellow, russeted, very good. Tree regular in bearing, small and of poor growth habit. A widely distributed winter Pear on the West Coast but little grown in the East.

Several unusually hardy Pears recommended for culture in Minnesota are Bantam, Mendel, Parker, Patten and Tait No. 2.

The European Pear has been hybridized with

the Sand Pear from China, and a number of varieties have been introduced. They are coarse-fleshed, contain many grit cells, and are much inferior in flavor to the European Pears. They are, however, sufficiently resistant to blight to be grown in the warmer parts of the eastern United States where blight prevents the culture of the European Pears. Kieffer, the best-known variety of this group, is heavy yielding and is extensively grown, especially for canning.

Others of the same type are Garber, Le Conte, Pineapple and Douglas. New and promising is Waite, a very blight-resistant variety. Orient and several recently introduced varieties from the Tennessee Agricultural Experiment Station belong in this group and should be tried in areas where Pear blight disease is severe.

PEAR, AVOCADO. See Persea.

PEARLBUSH. Exochorda, which see.

PEARLY EVERLASTING. See Anaphalis.

PEARLFRUIT. Margyricarpus setosus, which see.

PEARLWORT. See Sagina.

PEA, ROSARY. Abrus precatorius, which see.

PEAR, PRICKLY. Opuntia, which see.

PEA, SHAMROCK. Parochetus communis, which see.

PEA SHRUB. Caragana, which see.

PEASTICKS. This is a name that gardeners give to pieces of twiggy brushwood that are sometimes used for supporting Peas, Sweet Peas and occasionally other kinds of plants. Each piece is sharpened at its lower end so that it can more readily be thrust into the ground. Peasticks vary in length from about 2-7 feet.

PEA, SWEET. See Sweet Pea.

PEAT: IT ENRICHES THE SOIL
The Different Kinds and How to Use Them

Peat of various kinds is purchased each year in huge quantities by amateur gardeners and landscape men for incorporating with the soil to improve its quality.

Wherever new homes are built and lawns are to be made, wherever the planting of trees, shrubs and evergreens is to be undertaken, peat products may be employed. They may also be considered for use wherever new flower borders are to be prepared or old ones refurbished, vegetable gardens improved, rock gardens and wild gardens conditioned, or wherever seeds are to be sown in pots or flats or cold frames, and wherever mulching is to be practiced. Whether or not a peat product is actually used may depend upon comparative costs and other circumstances.

Leaf mold and other decayed vegetation play an important role in enriching the soil. Under natural, uncultivated conditions, they are returned to the earth by the plants that spring from it. Under garden conditions, however, they are mostly removed in the form of crops, or in the various tidying-up and hygienic processes that go with gardening. Peat is a good replacement for these valuable materials, and in its various forms (these will be discussed shortly) affords an easy and effective means of adding to the soil the bulky organic matter it needs.

Needs of Garden Soil

Most garden soils require periodic additions of organic matter (humus or humus-forming materials) to maintain them in reasonably fertile condition. Ordinary fertilizers do not supply organic matter in sufficient amounts to bring about significant improvement in the physical condition of the soil.

Fertilizers add plant nutrients (nitrogen, phosphorus, potassium and other elements necessary for plant growth) and because of this are valuable and needed aids to good gardening. By themselves, however, they are rarely enough.

To improve garden soils and to maintain them in a high state of fertility, it is important to add to them periodically both plant nutrients and bulk organic matter. Organic matter is particularly important in improving soil structure—in maintaining a desirable physical condition.

Peat moss may be purchased in bales of convenient sizes.

It is true that all bulk organic matter contains some nutrient elements, which, as the material decays, are gradually made available to the plants. Likewise, all fertilizers of organic origin (but not those of synthetic or mineral origin) add some humus to the soil.

But organic fertilizers, such as dried blood, tankage, and cottonseed meal, are used primarily for their nutrient content; the small amount of humus they add is of little importance. On the other hand, many bulky organic materials such as compost, leaf mold, commercial humus, peat moss and green cover crops are valued chiefly for the very considerable amounts of humus or humus-forming material they provide.

In a simpler horticultural age the gardener and farmer supplied their soils with both bulk organic material *and* liberal amounts of nutrients by the generous use of animal manure mixed with straw or other bedding materials. This was sometimes supplemented with bone meal or superphosphate, to make up for the phosphorus deficiency of most animal manures.

Most mid-twentieth-century gardeners cannot obtain manure in amounts sufficient to maintain the humus content of their soils at desired levels, and many, even if they could, would prefer to use other forms of bulk organic matter. There are several of these fairly commonly available; among the most popular and easily procurable

are the various kinds of peat. Because peats (including peat moss) vary greatly, it is essential to know something about their characteristics to be able to purchase them advantageously. Unfortunately these materials are not well standardized.

What Peat Is

The term "peat" is correctly applied to vegetable matter (plant remains) that has accumulated and partially decayed under water or in locations waterlogged most of the time. The character of a particular peat depends upon the kinds of plants of which it is composed, the rate and state of their decomposition, and the chemical contents of the water in which the decay took place.

Peats are related to "mucks" so closely that it is not practicable to draw a fine line of distinction between the two. There are intermediate soils that one expert might term muck, another peat. In general, muck contains much more mineral material than peat, and the plant remains in it have decayed so far that they can no longer be recognized; they have become formless humus.

In true peats the structure of the stems, leaves,

Sedge and reed peat, which is often sold under the name humus, may be bought in bulk, in bags and by the bushel.

etc., of the plants of which the material has been formed can be clearly discerned, at least by an experienced person with a good magnifying glass. Peat is more spongy or more fluffy than muck and weighs much less. Mucks are rich soils and can be worked to give most excellent crops, but unless muck can be obtained locally at comparatively small expense it should not be considered as a substitute for peat; even if obtainable at advantageous prices, it cannot be employed in all capacities as a peat substitute, as will be shown later.

Kinds of Peat

Peat moss, moss peat or Sphagnum peat is formed chiefly from the decay of Sphagnum mosses, although it frequently contains small quantities of the remains of other Sphagnum bog plants such as Ferns, Sundews and terrestrial Orchids. Characteristically it is strongly acid (pH 3.5 to 5.0) in its reaction. It is loose, spongy and normally varies from yellowish-brown to rich dark brown.

Its nitrogen content is low (about 1 per cent) and other nutrients it contains are negligible. Peat moss will absorb between six and fifteen times its own dry weight of water.

Sedge and Reed peat, often sold commercially as humus or peat humus, is formed chiefly by the partial decay of Sedges, Reeds, Cat-tails, certain Grasses and other shallow-water and swamp plants. It is ordinarily much less acid than peat moss, its pH value ranging between 4.4 and 6.5 When of good quality, it is light, powdery when dry, and usually dark brown to black. Its nitrogen content is decidedly higher than that of peat moss, being 2 to $3\frac{1}{2}$ per cent. Other nutrients are negligible. Sedge and Reed peat will absorb between three and six times its own dry weight of water.

In addition to being sold in a raw state, Sedge and Reed peat is offered as cultivated peat. To produce cultivated peat, the bogs are drained and sown down with cover crops. The green cover crops are then disced under and allowed to decay. When this has occurred, the surface layer is scraped off, piled in heaps to drain and then is screened and packaged.

This cultivating process is akin to composting, and the product is claimed to encourage plant growth better than unprepared peats.

Other Peats. The two types of peat described above are those that most commonly enter commerce. Another peat is Hypnum peat, derived from the partial decay of Hypnum and mosses other than Sphagnum, together with Sedges and some other plants. It is light and spongy, brownish or drab and usually slightly acid, neutral or even alkaline. Hypnum peat is low in nitrogen and absorbs water to about the same extent as Sphagnum peat.

Forest peat or peat mold consists of the partially decayed roots, trunks, branches, bark, leaves, etc., of various trees and shrubs. It is brown and fluffy but less fibrous than peat moss and usually contains an abundance of small particles of wood. Its nitrogen content is 1 to $2\frac{1}{2}$ per cent and it absorbs between four and eight times its own dry weight of water.

Sources of Peat. Peat deposits occur in many parts of North America, and a considerable amount of domestic peat is marketed. This includes Sphagnum peat moss, which is found chiefly north of a line stretching from south-central Maine through north-central New York to north-central Minnesota and British Columbia, and Sedge and Reed peat, which predominates south of that line. Some Hypnum peat is marketed from northern states. The domestic supplies that come to market are supplemented by peat moss imported from northern Europe, chiefly Germany and Holland.

Buying Peat

Peat is marketed in bulk and in bales, cartons and bags. Bulk peat is often nearly saturated with water, but packaged and baled samples normally contain little moisture, and most frequently its percentage is not stated. Wet bulk peat is commonly sold by the cubic yard rather than weight. If of good quality, a cubic yard is likely to contain about 450 pounds of organic matter. Dried and shredded peat is much lighter, weighing usually about 8 pounds per bushel when loose. Bales of peat vary considerably in size and this the buyer must take into account

[8—8]

Perennial Border

[8—9]
Centaurea macrocephala

[8—9a]
Bee Balm
(Monarda fistulosa alba)

[8—9b]
Regal Lily
(Lilium regale)

[8—9c]
Coreopsis verticillata

when comparing prices. Their compressed volume may be from five to sometimes more than eight bushels (considerably more, of course, when the peat is opened and loosened up).

A typical bale of peat moss of a large size measures about 36 by 23 by 23 inches and weighs about 175 pounds. Such bales are sold as containing 22 bushels (measured before compression) or about one cubic yard of loosened, fluffed-up material. Smaller bales, weighing about 100 pounds and containing about 12 bushels, or slightly more than half a cubic yard of loosened material, are commonly sold.

Measurements and the contents of bales as expressed in bushels of peat moss vary considerably. As the United States Department of Agriculture points out in one of its circulars, "The consumer's interest would be better served if the quantity of peat in a bale could be standardized, and the standardization put on the basis of weight rather than volume."

And there lies the crux of the whole situation. The purchaser of peat for horticultural use is primarily interested in the actual weight of organic matter he gets for his money (he should not pay for water content).

In addition to learning the actual weight of organic matter it contains, the gardener is interested in knowing how acid peat is—in other words, its pH value.

Acidity and alkalinity are measured according to a scale in which pH 7 represents a neutral condition, neither acid nor alkaline. As the figure following the pH symbol increases above 7, so does the degree of alkalinity it represents; as it decreases, it indicates increasing acidity. A soil having a reaction of pH 6 is considered slightly acid, one rating pH 5 is considered acid, and one rating pH 4 very acid.

Some Points to Remember. In the United States, because of the Federal Trade Commission's regulations, you are sure to get a fairly good product if you buy peat or peat moss under brand names or from reputable dealers.

Remember, however, that the value of these products, as measured by the actual weight of organic matter contained in a given quantity, may vary considerably within the Federal Trade Commission's specifications. Under those regu-

lations a content of 75 per cent peat is sufficient to warrant the use of the term "peat" to describe a product, and a content of 75 per cent peat derived from mosses makes it permissible to describe a product as peat moss or moss peat. Yet a really tiptop peat moss contains 95-99 per cent organic matter and a first-rate Sedge and Reed peat 85-95 per cent organic matter.

When comparing prices, remember that sizes of bales and other containers vary; and if you buy by weight, remember that moisture content of moist and wet peats varies.

Beware of irresponsible local "landscapers" and peddlers who sell black mucks as "humus" and "peat" to unsuspecting customers to spread on their lawns and for other garden purposes. Such sellers are most active in spring.

Muck, because it cakes over and partially seals the soil surface against the free entry of air, is not suitable for use as a lawn dressing or mulch.

Because it lacks sponginess and the water-holding and soil-loosening capacities of peat, muck is much less useful as a soil amendment. Its organic content is usually not more than 40-50 per cent.

If it can be procured cheaply enough, muck may be mixed with very sandy and gravelly soils with considerable advantage, but it cannot be regarded as a satisfactory substitute for peats having organic contents of 75 per cent or higher.

Because peats are used primarily as sources of organic matter, the economics of employing them should be balanced against the costs of other materials that provide this—for example, compost, leaf mold and decayed manure (here the fertilizer or plant nutrient values must be taken into consideration also).

Peat for Particular Uses

While the actual amount of organic matter you get for your money should be the first consideration when you buy peat, and its acidity a close runner-up for your interest and attention, other factors may rightly influence your judgment as to which particular peat product to favor.

On light, sandy or gravelly soils that are not

retentive of water and that dry out excessively in summer, peat moss, because of its much greater water-holding capacity, is to be preferred to other peats, provided its price per unit of actual organic matter does not differ greatly from that of other types.

On very heavy, clayey soils that tend to hold water rather than permit it to drain away quickly, Sedge and Reed peat is usually to be preferred to peat moss if it can be obtained at approximately the same price for the same amount of actual organic matter.

For propagating purposes, peat moss, alone or mixed with sand, is the most useful product to make up beds in which cuttings are to be inserted to form roots. For mixing with soils in which seeds are to be started, either peat moss or Sedge and Reed peat is satisfactory. If the plants to be raised are kinds known to prefer acid soil, be sure an acid peat is used.

For mixing with soils in which pot plants are to be grown, peat moss is considered most satisfactory for acid-soil plants such as Azaleas and Camellias; Sedge and Reed peats are recommended for other types of plants.

For mulching (spreading as a surface layer on the ground over the roots), all types of peat are valuable but the more acid (low pH) types are the ones to use for acid-soil plants such as Rhododendrons, Azaleas, Mountain Laurel and Blueberries.

Peat for horticultural use should be finely shredded. Coarser grades are much used as litter in stables and chicken houses. Through this use, such materials are fortified by the addition of animal excrement and urine; used in gardens afterwards, they supply both plant nutrients and considerable organic matter.

Such peats are extremely valuable and are worth more (because of their *fertilizer* value) than plain peats. They may be available in local markets in bulk and are also dehydrated, ground, screened, packaged and sold over wider areas.

PEAT-LOVING PLANTS. Chief among plants that thrive best in acid, peaty soils are Arbutus, Azalea, Camellia, Daboecia, Enkianthus, Epigaea repens, Erica, Ferns, Gaultheria, Gentiana sino-ornata and others, Haberlea, Kalmia, Leucothoë, some of the Lilies, Magnolia, Pernettya, Pieris (Andromeda), Polygala Chamaebuxus, hardy Primulas, Ramondia, Rhododendron, Ledum, Shortia, hardy Cypripediums, Vaccinium and Zenobia.

PEAT, ORCHID. See Osmunda fiber.

PEA TREE. Caragana, which see.

PECAN. The Pecan (Carya Pecan) is a type of Hickory that grows naturally from Indiana to Mexico. It is much valued for its edible nuts, for which the trees are cultivated extensively in parts of the South. Wild Pecan trees usually bear nuts of inferior quality; therefore, growers depend upon trees that are propagated by budding. In most cases, named varieties of superior quality are budded on to young seedling stocks, but sometimes old wild trees or trees of poor quality are top-worked (top-grafted) with scions of named varieties.

When Pecans are to be grown under orchard conditions, it is usual to plant them 60-70 ft. apart. These trees thrive best on deep, rich, well-drained soils. Because many varieties of Pecan are self-sterile or partly so, it is important to include in any planting more than one variety, and to be sure that the flowers of the various kinds mature at the same time.

When transplanting young Pecan trees, great care should be exercised not to damage the strong, deep taproots and to make sure that the hole in which each is placed is deep enough to take the taproot without breaking or bending it, and that good soil is packed around it. Clean but shallow cultivation of the surface soil is beneficial.

Varieties of Pecans are numerous and not all that have been named are superior; some are of value under special local conditions only. Before planting Pecans, the gardener should consult his State Agricultural Experiment Station for recommendations of varieties likely to be most satisfactory under his conditions. It should be remembered that Pecan trees are hardy and will flourish and form attractive specimens considerably north of regions where they will mature satisfactory crops of nuts.

PEDATE. A botanical term used in describing a leaf which bears some resemblance to a bird's foot—a compound leaf of which the segments are deeply divided.

PEDICULARIS—*Lousewort, Wood Betony* (Pedicular'is). A considerable group of herbaceous perennial plants that are of no great horticultural importance, although they may sometimes be included in wild-garden plantings. Because they are semiparasitic on the roots of other plants, they are not always easy to establish in cultivation. Pedicularis takes its name from *pediculus,* a louse, because it was supposed that sheep grazing where these plants grew became infested with lice. It belongs in the Figwort family, Scrophulariaceae.

These plants may be increased by seeds and division. Kinds include P. canadensis, a woodland plant of eastern North America, with yellowish flowers that are often tinted red, and yellow-flowered P. lanceolata, which is found in wet ground in eastern North America.

PEDILANTHUS (Pedilanth'us). Only one kind is in common cultivation, Pedilanthus tith-

Pedilanthus tithymaloides variety variegatus has nice stems and green, white and pink variegated foliage.

ymaloides, a shrub which grows wild in tropical America and the West Indies. It belongs to the Spurge family, Euphorbiaceae, will reach a height of 5-6 feet, and bears purple or reddish flowers. The name is derived from *pedilon,* a shoe, and *anthos,* a flower, and alludes to the shape of the latter. It is called Redbird Cactus, Jewbush and Slipperflower.

This shrub, when grown in the greenhouse or window garden, needs a minimum winter temperature of 60 degrees; during the summer months a warm, rather dry atmosphere suits it best, as the shoots are fleshy or succulent. The soil must be kept moist in summer, but in winter it should be watered only when fairly dry. The most suitable potting compost consists of loam with which sand and crushed brick or small pieces of flowerpot have been mixed freely. The pots must be well drained.

Propagation is by cuttings in the summer months. The cuttings must be treated like those of other succulent plants—laid on the greenhouse bench for a day so that they may harden somewhat before they are inserted. They should be set in pots of very sandy soil, but not covered with a bell jar. Very little water is needed until the cuttings are rooted.

Pedilanthus tithymaloides has varieties with variegated foliage. It and related kinds are planted outdoors in the warmest parts of the United States. Of kinds other than P. tithymaloides, the most likely to be found in gardens are P. aphyllus, a native of Mexico, P. smallii, a native of Brazil and P. macrocarpus which has its home in western Mexico.

PEDIOCACTUS—*Snowball Cactus* (Pediocact'us). A species of Cactus, family Cactaceae, that occurs natively from Kansas to Washington and New Mexico. It forms a globular specimen which, when young, is covered with white wool, from which fact its common name derives. Its flowers are pinkish. The name Pediocactus (*pedios* means plain) refers to the Great Plains, which are the common habitat of this plant in nature. For culture, see Cacti.

PEDUNCLE. A botanical term used to describe the stalk of a single flower, as in the Tulip, or of a cluster or group of flowers, as in the Geranium.

PELARGONIUM: THE GERANIUM

Favorite Greenhouse, Garden and Window Plants

Pelargonium (Pelargo'nium). Tender, shrubby and herbaceous flowering plants. The shrubby kinds are found wild in South Africa and the herbaceous kinds in Asia Minor and Syria. They belong to the Geranium family, Geraniaceae. The name is derived from *pelargos,* a stork, from the shape of the fruit, which somewhat resembles the beak of a stork.

Pelargoniums are divided into several groups, of which the Zonal Pelargonium, popularly known as Geranium, is of chief importance.

Zonal Pelargoniums or Geraniums

These plants are woody at the base, but the young shoots are soft and succulent. The leaves are evergreen, long-stalked, roundish, from 1-4 in. in diameter, wavy-edged and unequally lobed at the base. The whole plant is covered with very fine hairs. A horseshoe-shaped zone of dark coloring, found on the leaves of many varieties, has given rise to the name of Zonal Pelargonium.

Zonal Pelargoniums blooming freely in an amateur's greenhouse.

In addition to those Zonal Pelargoniums which have plain green leaves or green leaves marked with the characteristic horseshoe-shaped zone there are many varieties which have variegated foliage. Those in which the variation consists of a single color, such as creamy-white, in addition to green are called bicolors. In tricolor and quadricolor varieties the green leaves are beautifully

A single-flowered Zonal Pelargonium (Geranium).

marked with two or three other colors such as yellow, orange, bronze, pink, copper red, creamy-white and dark purple.

A few varieties are distinguished by the fact that their petals are clearly spotted with pin-point dots of red or pink. These are called Birds-egg Geraniums. Rosebud Geraniums are varieties that have flowers which superficially resemble double Roses. In addition to the usual varieties of Geraniums which, under favorable conditions, attain heights of 3-4 ft. or more, there is a group of varieties called Dwarf Geraniums which normally do not exceed 8-9 in. in height and a group of still lower varieties, which are called Miniature Geraniums.

The normally five-petaled, rotate flowers of Pelargoniums are in dense clusters on the ends of stout, upright stalks, which spring from the axils of the leaves all the way up the stems. There are single-, semidouble- and double-flowered varieties in a wide range of colors including crimson, red,

Ivy-leaved Pelargoniums have distinctly lobed leaves and more or less trailing stems. They are useful for growing in baskets and pots.

Variegated Zonal Pelargonium (Geranium) variety Skies of Italy.

scarlet, rose-pink, salmon-pink, purple and white.

For summer bedding, Zonal Pelargoniums are unequaled in many areas, where they produce masses of color from the time they are planted out until frost puts an end to the display in the autumn. They are suitable for window and porch boxes.

These plants are grand subjects also for a greenhouse, as with careful management they can be had in flower all the year round. As window plants they are popular favorites, for they withstand exceptionally well the dry atmosphere of a dwelling room where the temperature is not excessively high.

Treatment in Winter. During the winter, except in such mild climates as that of California, they must be kept in a room or greenhouse where the temperature can be maintained above freezing point. A minimum temperature of 40 degrees is sufficient and night temperatures of more than 50-55 are detrimental. Moderate watering is required from October to March, sufficient only being given to prevent the leaves from wilting.

A basket planted with Ivy-leaved Pelargoniums in bloom in a greenhouse.

Zonal Pelargonium Black Vesuvius is a dwarf variety with dark-colored foliage and red flowers.

A Geranium to be repotted is watered a few hours previously, then is taken out of its pot and the old crocks are removed.

Pruning and Repotting in Spring. When growth becomes active in March or April the branches are pruned back, this ensures bushy plants; if pruning is neglected, they develop into leggy specimens with leaves and flowers at the ends of the shoots only. When side shoots begin to push forth, the plants are taken out of their

A clean pot somewhat larger than the root ball is then prepared by crocking it to provide drainage and the plant is set in it and centered.

pots and, after the crocks and all loose soil have been removed from the roots, are repotted in pots two sizes larger. The compost should be made firm with a potting stick to assist the plants to make firm, short-jointed shoots.

The best potting compost consists of two parts of fibrous loam, one part of leaf mold or peat moss, a little lime and a liberal sprinkling of sand. After potting, no water is given until the soil becomes nearly dry; then it is thoroughly soaked. This method of watering is continued until the plants are well rooted, when they are kept moist throughout the summer; a feeding with fertilizer or liquid manure is applied once a week until they are well rooted. The water supply is gradually lessened as autumn approaches, and through-

New soil is filled in around the old ball and is made firm with the fingers or with a potting stick. Room is left at the top for watering.

out the winter the soil is moistened only when it becomes moderately dry.

Excessive shade and too much nitrogen in the soil encourage lush growth and few flowers.

Zonal Geraniums for Winter Flowering. By giving them special treatment, you can make these plants bloom throughout the winter. Cuttings are inserted from March to May. When well rooted, they are potted in 3-in. pots and subsequently into 5-7 in. pots, according to the vigor of the plants. The tip of the main shoot is pinched out and the subsequent side branches are similarly treated. They are then allowed to

Zonal Pelargoniums (Geraniums) are easy to train as standards.

develop unchecked, except that all flower buds are removed until the end of September. From June to September, when the plants are well rooted in their final pots, they are placed out of doors, buried to the rims of their pots in a bed of ashes or sand in a sunny position, to ripen the shoots.

The soil is kept moist and weak liquid fertilizer given once a week. About the end of September they are taken into a sunny window or greenhouse with a minimum temperature of 50 degrees, where the flowers are produced continually throughout the winter. Daytime temperatures should not exceed 55-60 degrees.

In the spring the plants are pruned and potted as already recommended, and the side shoots are taken off as cuttings.

Propagation. Dwarf bushy plants set out from 4-in. or 5-in. pots are most effective for producing a continuous display of flowers in beds, window boxes and porch boxes during summer. Plants may be obtained by inserting cuttings in late summer or in winter; the summer ones make the best plants. These may be obtained by taking the cuttings from the plants in August or

September while they are still in the flower bed, or, if a sufficient number cannot be obtained without spoiling the floral display, the tops of all the shoots are utilized after the plants are taken from the flower beds.

The old plants are lifted from the flower beds before frost, all shoots being cut back to about three or four buds. The long roots are also shortened and the plants are packed closely together in deep flats with moist soil covering their roots. They are then placed in a light, well-ventilated position in the greenhouse and watered very sparingly throughout the winter. In the following spring they are either potted separately in 5-in. pots to form large specimens for bedding out or for greenhouse decoration, or the shoots are taken off and inserted as cuttings.

The tops of the shoots which are trimmed off in August–September provide the main supply of plants for summer bedding in the following year. A cut is made below the third or fourth joint, and only two leaves are left at the apex. All flower buds are also removed as well as the stipules (small leaflike appendages at the base of the leafstalks). The prepared cuttings are then laid on a shelf or bench in a dry atmosphere for a few hours to allow a corky skin to form over the cut ends. This preparation is desirable to prevent the shoots from rotting.

The cuttings are inserted in a firmly packed bed of sand in a greenhouse or under a bell jar in a window. The sand is kept moderately moist but not saturated. Sufficient ventilation is given to prevent the atmosphere from being humid and close. When the cuttings have formed roots 2 in. long, they are potted separately in 3-in. pots. When well rooted, they are gradually hardened off and planted out of doors in May or June. To obtain bushy plants, the tips of the main shoots are pinched out.

Standard Pelargoniums. Zonal Pelargoniums are sometimes grown as standards (in "tree" form) which are used as "dot" plants in the summer flower beds or as terrace or greenhouse decorations. These are obtained by inserting cuttings in August–September. The rooted cuttings are potted separately in 3-in. pots, and, when well rooted in these, are moved to 5-in. and finally to 7-in. pots.

The main stem is not pinched, but allowed to grow straight up and the side shoots are rubbed out while they are quite small. When the main stem is 3-4 ft. tall, the tip is pinched out and three side branches are allowed to develop at the apex. These are also stopped when 6 in. in length, and a head of branches is thus formed.

Ivy-leaved Pelargoniums or Geraniums

The plants in this group are quite distinct in habit from the Zonal Pelargoniums. They have slender trailing stems, and leaves shaped like those of the Ivy, and bear trusses of crimson, scarlet, salmon-pink, pale pink and white, single or double flowers. Owing to their trailing habit of growth they are useful for many purposes— for furnishing hanging baskets, as pot plants trained to stakes, or for summer bedding.

Geraniums in Hanging Baskets. To prepare the hanging baskets, line them with moss and fill them with potting compost. Well-rooted plants of Ivy-leaved Geraniums are removed from the pots and are planted 6 in. apart, in the top of the baskets in April. They are well watered, and are kept in the greenhouse until the end of May or early June, when they are hung

Martha Washington Pelargoniums (Geraniums) have large pansy-like blooms.

out of doors in suitable and attractive positions.

As pot plants for the greenhouse, the Ivy-leaved Pelargoniums are potted in 6-in. pots or larger ones, and the shoots are tied to a single central stake or to a tripod of sticks fixed in the pot. Sometimes the pots are placed on a shelf or the edge of the benches, and the shoots are allowed to droop over the sides. They are nice window-garden plants.

For Summer Bedding. The plants are planted out in late May or early June, and the shoots, as they develop, are pegged down in the soil. By this method the ground is thickly carpeted by their foliage, and the flowers are shown to better advantage. In some cases they are planted as "dot" plants, and the shoots are then tied to a central stake. The propagation, soil requirements and general treatment are the same as for the Zonal Pelargoniums.

Show or Regal Pelargoniums (Martha Washington or Lady Washington Geraniums)

The plants in this group have woody stems, but the young shoots are soft and sappy, and not as stout as those of the Zonal Pelargoniums. The leaves are palmate, toothed at the margins, and wrinkled. The flowers are large and richly colored with conspicuous blotches in many varieties. The plants in this group are used for early summer decoration of the greenhouse only, or they may be grown in a sunny window.

When to Take Cuttings. The stems of the old plants are cut back to three or four buds in July, and they are syringed occasionally to cause them to break into growth. When the side shoots are 2 in. in length, they are taken off and inserted in pots of sandy soil. They are placed in a cold frame, where they are shaded, and the atmosphere is kept moist until roots are formed.

When rooted, each cutting is potted in a 4-in. pot, and placed on a shelf near the glass in a greenhouse with a winter temperature of 45-50 degrees at night. The soil is not watered until it becomes fairly dry, and throughout the early part of winter the same method of watering is adopted.

In January the plants are repotted in 5-in. pots. The points of the main shoots are pinched out when the plants are established and, as the pots become filled with healthy roots and the days lengthen, increased supplies of water are given. Weekly applications of dilute liquid fertilizer from March until the flowers open are very beneficial.

After flowering, these Pelargoniums are placed in a sunny spot out of doors to ripen the growth. From then until they are pruned, only enough water is given to prevent them from absolutely drying up. They are pruned in July as already described and either repotted in larger pots, or the side shoots are taken off and utilized as cuttings.

Scented-leaved Pelargoniums or Geraniums

In this class are included varieties and species with leaves of varied and often very attractive forms, which are strongly scented and aromatic

Pelargonium echinatum is a beautiful species with rosy magenta flowers that are blotched with deep crimson.

Pelargonium denticulatum.

when crushed. The treatment of these is the same as advised for the Zonal Pelargoniums when grown as pot plants. They are excellent window plants and may be planted in the outdoor garden in summer.

A Herbaceous Pelargonium

P. Endlicherianum is a herbaceous perennial which grows about 2 ft. in height, has rather fleshy stems clothed with hairy, heart-shaped leaves, and bears umbels of rose-colored flowers in summer. It should be planted in well-drained sandy soil. It is hardy only in moderately mild climates. Propagation is by division or by seeds.

The seeds are sown in a well-drained pan of sandy soil which is moistened and covered with a pane of glass. It is then set in a cold frame until the seeds have germinated. The glass is removed and, when the seedlings are large enough to handle, they are pricked out into a seed box, watered and shaded from sunlight until established. They are hardened off and planted out, 6 in. apart, in a sunny bed, and finally transplanted to their permanent positions in spring.

Pelargonium ardens.

Succulent Species of Pelargonium

In addition to the many improved varieties of Pelargoniums or Geraniums which have originated in cultivation and which are the kinds chiefly grown a number of species (unimproved kinds as they are found in the wild in their native habitats) are cultivated. Some of these are included under the Scented-leaved group mentioned above; the herbaceous P. Endlicherianum is another. Yet others are distinctly succulent types of curious appearance. Usually these have thick stems and at some period of the year, normally in winter, they drop all their leaves and should then be kept quite dry and not given water until signs of renewed growth become evident.

These succulent Geraniums thrive in well-drained pots in very porous soil. The addition of some broken limestone to the soil compost is beneficial. They revel in full sun and should be watered freely during their active growing season. They may be propagated by cuttings and by seeds. A window in a cool room or a cool, airy greenhouse provide the best growing conditions for these plants.

Growing Pelargoniums from Seed

Both the Zonal and Show Pelargoniums can easily be grown from seeds. The seeds are sown in pots of sandy soil in spring or summer, and placed in a warm greenhouse to germinate. The seedlings are pricked off, 1 in. apart, into a seed pan, and before they become overcrowded they are potted separately in 3-in. pots and subsequently in larger sizes.

When the seedlings bloom, the best kinds should be noted, and increased by inserting cuttings, as they do not come true from seeds. Seeds often germinate very irregularly; one should not be in too much haste to discard the seed pots or pans from which a few seedlings have been taken; it is quite likely that more may show up upon inspection.

Growing Geraniums Outdoors

In California and similar climates that are frost-free or nearly so, Geraniums can be grown outdoors throughout the year. They thrive in a variety of soils and in full sun, or in places where they receive part-day shade. They should be trimmed into shape in the fall and periodically through the growing season. During the growing season they should be watered periodically to ensure free growth and the retention of their leaves.

Frost is the greatest enemy; the Martha Washington types are in danger at temperatures of 28 degrees or lower, the Zonal and Ivy-leaved varieties when the temperature goes below 25 degrees. Plants that have their tops injured by frost may recover if their tops are cut back to sound wood. A covering of 6 in. of coarse sand mounded around the base of each plant in fall will often prevent total killing, even though the tops are injured.

Some Good Varieties

Zonals. The numerous varieties in cultivation have originated from crossbreeding between P. zonale and P. inquinans. The most popular Zonal Pelargoniums for summer bedding, and for window-box and pot cultivation, are:

Alphonse Ricard, scarlet, double; California Beauty, pink with white centers to flowers, double; Enchantress Fiat, delicate pink, double; Fiat Queen, salmon-pink, semidouble; Fiat Supreme, salmon, semidouble; Madonna, white, double; Mme. Buchner, white, double; Maxine Kovaleski, orange-red; New Phlox, white with red eye; Olympic Red, scarlet, double; Pink Phenomenal, rose-pink, double; Poinsettia, bright red, many narrow petals of varying lengths; Radio Red, bright red, double; Red Fiat, bright scarlet, double; Snowflake, white.

Ornamental-leaved Zonals. Leaves green variegated with white or cream: Beckwith Pride, Flower of Spring, Hills of Snow, Mary Ann, Mme. Languth, Mme. Salleroi, Silver Leaf S. A. Nutt. *Leaves green variegated with yellow:* Crystal Palace Gem. *Leaves yellow variegated with bronze:* Alpha, Bismark, Bronze Beauty, Graves Jubilee, Jubilee, Pink Maréchal MacMahon, Red Marechal MacMahon. *Leaves green with a narrow, black-purple band:* Distinction. *Leaves*

Pelargonium zonale Hills of Snow, a handsome kind with variegated leaves.

yellow: Cloth of Gold, Dwarf Gold Leaf, Gold Leaf, Golden MacMahon, Verona. *Tricolors and quadricolors:* Achievement (black-purple, red and yellow), Happy Thought (green, yellow and bronze), Miss Burdett Coutts (green, cream, bronze and pink), Mrs. Cox (green, red, purple and cream), Mrs. Pollock (green, red, yellow and orange), Pink Happy Thought (green, yellow and bronze), Skies of Italy (green, cream, purple and orange).

Dwarf and Miniature Zonals. Black Vesuvius, foliage black-green, flowers orange-scarlet; Carlton Pet, leaves green, flowers white and pink; Dopey, foliage green, flowers pink; Imp, dark foliage, flowers bright salmon-pink; Madame

Zonal Pelargonium variety Distinction.

Fournier, leaves black-green, flowers scarlet; Kleiner Liebling (Little Darling), leaves bright green, flowers rose pink; Madame Fournier, leaves black-green, flowers scarlet; Milky Way, leaves dark green, flowers white or tinged pink; Pigmy, leaves green, flowers double, scarlet; Pixie, foliage olive-green, flowers salmon pink; Sirus, foliage dark, flower pink with white center. Venus, dark foliage, flowers double, pale pink.

Birds-egg Geraniums. Baudelaire, flowers pink with white centers, dotted crimson; Curiosa, flowers double, mauve-pink, dotted carmine; J. J.

Zonal Pelargonium variety Happy Thought.

Knight, flowers pale pink, dotted deep pink; Skylark, flowers white or tinged pink, dotted carmine.

Rosebud Geraniums. Apple Blossom Rosebud, flowers double, white edged pink; Crimson Rosebud, flowers double, magenta-crimson; Pink Rosebud, flowers double, pink; Salmon Rosebud, flowers double, salmon-pink; Scarlet Rosebud, flowers double, scarlet.

Ivy-leaved Geraniums. Alliance, lilac-white with rose markings, double; Charles Turner, rose-pink, double; Comtesse de Grey, soft pink marked with violet, semidouble; Diener's Lavender, deep lavender marked with cerise, double; Galilee, salmon-pink to rose, double; Intensity, bright red, semidouble; Jeanne d' Arc, pale lavender with red stripes; Mme. Margot, lilac-white with violet marks, leaves cream-edged often

Scented-leaf Pelargonium Lady Plymouth.

Pelargonium dasycaule.

flushed with pink; Sunset, salmon-pink, leaves mottled yellow and edged with cream.

Show and Regal Pelargoniums. Autumn Glow, tangerine-orange with white eye; Chicago Market, orchid, deeper towards center, upper petals marked red; Diener's Giant, bright, deep pink, red spots on upper petals; Duchess of Kent, white, upper petals feathered purple; Easter Greeting, cerise-pink, with almost black markings, early blooming; Empress of Russia, black and rose, petals with narrow white margins; Lavender Queen, lavender with darker markings; Marie Rober, magenta to almost black; Mrs. Layal, purple, rose and white; Rhapsody, salmon-pink, upper petals maroon; Royal Velvet, orchid or orchid-pink, bases of petals darker; Springtime, pink with white flower centers and petal margins; Winter Cheer, clear salmon-pink.

Scented-leaf Pelargonium variety Dr. Livingston.

Scented-leaved Pelargoniums. P. Camphor Rose, camphor-scented, otherwise similar to P. graveolens; P. capitatum, rose-scented, flowers rose-purple; P. citrosum (often called P. citriodorum in gardens), lemon-scented, flowers pale pink feathered with dark red; P. Clorinda, mildly pungent, large rose-red and cerise flowers; P. crispum, lemon-scented, crisped leaves, flowers lavender with purple markings; P. crispum variety minor, similar to P. crispum but with smaller leaves, lemon-scented; P. denticulatum but has more finely divided leaves; P. Dr. Livingston (sometimes called Skeleton Rose), rose-scented, finely cut foliage, flowers lavender with two purple spots; P. Fair Ellen, pungent-scented, similar to P. quercifolium but more bushy and flowers larger; P. fragrans, nutmeg-scented, small white-tinged-red flowers; P. graveolens, the Rose Geranium, rose-scented, lavender pink purple-veined flowers; P. graveolens minor has smaller leaves and darker colored flowers than P. graveolens but otherwise is similar; P. Gray Lady Plymouth, rose-scented, leaves grayish edged with creamy-white, flowers lavender with darker veinings; P. Lady Plymouth, rose-scented, leaves grayish blotched with creamy-white, flowers lavender with darker veining; P. limoneum, lemon-scented, flowers lavender marked with red; P. limonium variety Lady Mary, lemon-scented, flowers magenta with carmine spots; P. odoratissimum, apple-scented, small white flowers marked with pin points of red; P. Old Scarlet Unique, pungent-scented, leaves grayish, flowers large, scarlet with nearly black markings; P. Prince of Orange,

orange-scented, flowers lavender feathered with dark red; Prince Rupert, leaves larger than those of P. crispum, lemon-scented; P. Rober's Lemon Rose, lemon-rose-scented, leaves less finely divided than those of P. graveolens, otherwise similar; P. quercifolium, the Oak-leaved Geranium, pungent-scented; flowers pink with darker markings; P. radens (often called P. radula), pungent-scented, flowers small, pink with magenta markings; P. Rollison's Unique, mint-scented, flowers magenta-crimson; P. scabrum, pungent-scented, flowers deep pink with darker markings.

Pelargonium glaucifolium.

Succulent Pelargoniums. P. echinatum, stems covered with conspicuous spines, foliage gray-green, flowers magenta-purple or magenta-purple and white; P. gibbosum, stems much swollen at the nodes, flowers greenish-yellow; P. glaucifolium, leaves divided, flowers very dark maroon-red; P. tetragonum, semi-climbing, stems very distinctly quadrangular, leaves fleshy, flowers pink and white; P. dasycaule, leaves deeply divided, flowers whitish with red spot in center.

PELECYPHORA—*Hatchet Cactus* (Pelecy'-phora). A small genus belonging to the Cactus family, Cactaceae. It somewhat resembles Mammillaria, to which it is closely related. The best-known kind is P. aselliformis from Mexico. It grows about 4 in. in height, and has stout, peg-top-like, fleshy stems, covered with tubercules.

These tubercles, instead of being nipple-like, as in the Mammillaria, are wedge-shaped or hatchet-shaped, hence the common name. At the tip of each tubercule is a small crevice surrounded by overlapping scalelike tissue. The large, many-petaled flowers are formed at the apex of the stems in early summer. They are purple or yellow. The name Pelecyphora is from the Greek *pelekus,* hatchet, and *phoros,* bearing, and refers to the shape of the tubercles.

The flowers are borne at the top of the stem and are deep purple, with paler sepals.

Cultivation. These plants require a minimum winter temperature of 50 degrees, and a soil consisting of equal parts of loam, sand and crushed bricks. Repotting is done in March or April, but it is not necessary every year. Plants which are growing satisfactorily should not be disturbed. When repotting becomes necessary, the plants are taken out of their pots and the crocks and all loose soil removed from the roots with a pointed stick. The new pots are filled to one third their capacity with crocks which are covered with a layer of leaves or of the coarse fiber sifted from the loam. After the plants are set in position, the soil is made firm.

After potting, the soil is not watered until it becomes quite dry; this system of watering is continued until the plants are well rooted, when the soil is kept moist throughout the summer. During the winter very little water is required, sufficient only to prevent the stems from shriveling. In midwinter several weeks may elapse between waterings. No shade is required, and the greenhouse must be freely ventilated.

When to Sow Seeds. Propagation is by seeds or cuttings. The seeds are sown in pots of sandy soil in spring or summer (see Cacti).

Cuttings are not produced freely, but when they become available they are taken off in spring or summer. A cut is made at the base of each one, and they are laid on a shelf to allow a corky skin to form over the cut surface. They are then inserted in well-drained pots of sand or sandy soil as advised for the seedlings. They are set on a sunny shelf, and not watered until the soil becomes fairly dry.

The chief kinds are P. aselliformis, deep purple petals, pale purple sepals, and P. concolor, purple.

PELEXIA (Pelex' ia). Tropical American terrestrial Orchids, family Orchidaceae. The name, derived from *pelex,* refers to the shape of the dorsal sepal. A loose, moist, humus-rich soil, a night temperature of 55-60 degrees and shade from strong sun suits these Orchids. P. maculata is cultivated.

PELICAN FLOWER. Aristolochia grandiflora, which see.

PELLAEA—*Cliff Brake* (Pell'aea). Tender and hardy evergreen and deciduous (leaf-losing) Ferns of New Zealand, South Africa, Australia and the Americas, which belong to the family Polypodiaceae. They vary from a few inches to 2 or 3 ft. in height and have scaly rhizomes (underground rootstocks). The spikes (leaf-stalks) are wiry, smooth and shining and vary in color from light brown to black.

The fronds are either pinnate (once divided), bipinnate (twice divided), or tripinnate (three times divided), and the pinnae (leaflets) are either round, oval, ovate, oblong or hastate (spear-shaped). The spores are formed in a continuous band around the pinnae. The name Pellaea is derived from *pellos,* dusky, and refers

Pellaea falcata which is native from India to New Zealand.

Pellaea rotundifolia, a native of New Zealand, is an unusual-looking Fern that is cultivated in greenhouses and terrariums.

to the leafstalks of some kinds, which are dark-colored.

For Outdoors. P. atropurpurea, a native of eastern North America, is an interesting kind for the Fern garden and wild garden. It thrives best in a well-drained position on limestone rocks. Several other species occur in the West and require similar growing conditions.

Ferns for the Amateur's Greenhouse. The majority of these Ferns require a minimum winter temperature of 45 degrees F. The best compost consists of equal parts of peat, leaf mold and loam, with some crushed limestone and sand added freely. A little powdered charcoal should be added to the compost. Repotting is done in March or as soon as new fronds begin to develop. The plants are taken out of their pots and the roots examined; if they are not sufficiently well rooted, they are put back in the same pots and are not disturbed until the following year.

Hints on Repotting. Plants which have filled the pots with roots need repotting in slightly larger pots. The new pots are well drained with crocks which are covered with the rough siftings from the compost. All the old crocks and loose soil are removed from the roots with a pointed stick. The plant is then set in the new pot and the soil made moderately firm by pressing with the fingers. After potting, the plants are set in a shaded position in the greenhouse and the atmosphere is kept moist by damping the floor and benches two or three times a day.

No water is given until the soil approaches dryness; it is then saturated. These Ferns will prove disappointing if they are overwatered before the soil has become filled with roots, though then, as with most other kinds, the soil must always be kept moist during the summer. Throughout the winter less watering is required but the soil must not be allowed to remain in a dry condition for long.

These Ferns are raised by sowing spores as soon as they are ripe. See Ferns.

Propagation by Division. Another method of propagation is by division. The plants are removed from their pots in March or April, and all the soil is washed away from the roots. The rhizomes are then cut through so as to separate them into small pieces, each containing a few fronds. The divided portions are set in pots just large enough to hold them, and treated as advised for older plants.

Popular kinds include P. atropurpurea, 1 ft.; P. viridis, 1 ft.; P. rotundifolia, 12 in.; P. cordata, 6-9 in.; P. falcata, 3-6 in.; P. mucronata, 10 in. These measurements refer to the length of the fronds.

PELLIONIA (Pellio'nia). Tender ornamental foliage plants from Cochin China, which belong to the Nettle family, Urticaceae. They have creeping, fleshy stems, clothed with oval leaves 1-2 in. in length. The leaves are olive-green, with violet and greenish-white markings. The small clusters of greenish flowers are insignificant. These plants may be grown in hanging baskets or in pots to form an edging to the greenhouse benches and in terrariums. They may also be planted under the benches to form a carpet of ornamental greenery.

They require a minimum winter temperature of 55 degrees and a soil compost of equal parts of loam and leaf mold or peat with sand added, freely.

Ornamental-leaved Plants for Hanging Baskets. When these plants are grown in hanging baskets, the latter are first lined with moss and then filled with the prepared compost. Rooted cuttings are inserted, 4 in. apart, in the top and sides of the basket. The basket is hung in a shaded position in the greenhouse and the plants are syringed with water daily to help them to become established quickly.

The soil is well moistened when the plants are

Pellionia Daveauana is a low-creeping plant suitable for terrariums and greenhouses.

inserted, but no more water is given until it becomes moderately dry. This method of watering is continued until the plants are well rooted, when the soil is kept moist throughout the summer. As autumn approaches, the water supply is lessened, and during winter the soil is only moistened when it becomes fairly dry.

Cultivation in Pots. Small plants, well rooted in 3-in. pots, are repotted singly in 5-in. pots in April, or several are set in a seed pan. When well established, the plants are set along the edge of the greenhouse benches, where the pendent shoots of attractive leaves are effectively displayed. The general treatment is the same as advised for basket plants. They are not repotted in large pots each year, as plants in small pots are most effective.

Planting Under Greenhouse Benches. A bed of prepared soil is made up under the greenhouse benches and the plants are inserted about 6 in. apart. As they develop, the plants are allowed to ramble, so that their shoots intermingle and form a dense carpet of foliage.

When they show signs of deterioration, they are taken up, the soil is renewed and fresh plants are inserted.

The chief kinds are P. Daveauana, leaves olive-green with violet and greenish-white markings, and P. pulchra, leaves dark green, purplish underneath.

PELTANDRA VIRGINICA—*Arrow Arum* (Peltan'dra). A hardy herbaceous plant with ornamental leaves. It is a native of North America and belongs to the Arum family, Araceae. This rather uncommon plant has thick, cordlike roots and produces large, dark green, glossy, arum-like leaves. It grows 12 in. in height, and has green, arum-like flowers, 6 in. in length. Peltandra, which is grown principally for its attractive foliage, is used for ornamenting the margins of bog gardens, or other damp places. The name is derived from *pelta,* round, and refers to the shape of the anthers.

For the Bog Garden. The roots are planted in spring in boggy or muddy soil on the margins of ponds, or in the bog garden. They may also be planted in shallow water. For this purpose the roots are set in a flowerpot or wicker basket and lowered into the water. After planting, they require very little attention, except to remove those which are outgrowing their allotted space.

Propagation is by division in spring. The clumps are lifted, divided into smaller portions, each containing a few shoots, and are replanted in the positions in which they are to grow.

PELTARIA ALLIACEA (Pelta'ria). A hardy herbaceous flowering plant, from eastern Europe, which belongs to the Mustard family, Cruciferae. It grows about 12 in. in height, has smooth, slender stems, clothed with oval leaves, heart-shaped at the base and sessile (stalkless). The stems are terminated by corymbs (widespreading clusters) of small, white, four-petaled flowers in summer. The whole of the plant smells like Garlic. The name Peltaria is derived from *pelta,* a small shield, and refers to the roundish seed pods.

This plant requires a sunny position and thrives in ordinary garden soil. The roots are planted in autumn or spring, 6 in. apart, in irregular clumps. Very little attention is required, but when they show signs of deterioration they should be lifted, divided, and replanted in fresh soil. This is the principal system of propagation. Seeds, when obtainable, are sown out of doors in April, in the position in which the plants are to grow, the seedlings being afterwards thinned out to 6 in. apart.

PELTATE. A botanical term used in describing a leaf in which the leafstalk is connected to the center of the leaf, as in Tropaeolum (Nasturtium). See Leaf.

PELTIPHYLLUM—*Umbrella Plant* (Peltiphyl'lum). A genus of the family Saxifragaceae

The pink flowers of the native Californian, Peltiphyllum peltatum, are borne in clusters at the tops of stout stems before the leaves appear in spring.

consisting of a single species, Peltiphyllum peltatum, a native of California and previously named Saxifraga peltata. The name is from *pelta,* a shield, and *phyllon,* leaf, and alludes to the shape of the leaves.

This handsome herbaceous perennial is a grand subject for planting on the margins of pools and streams. The root is a thick, fleshy rhizome which creeps over the ground, rooting as it spreads. The flowers, produced in April, are white or rose-pink, in large heads carried on stout, erect stems 2-3 ft. tall. As the flowers fade the leaves appear, peltate in shape (as in the garden Nasturtium), 6 in. or more across and carried on stalks 2 ft. or more tall. It is a noble plant for wet positions. Increase is by division in autumn. It is reasonably hardy and may be grown outdoors, where winters are not excessively severe, in the East.

PENIOCEREUS (Peniocer'eus). Cacti with large, bulbous roots of great size and slender stems. They belong to the Cactus family, Cactaceae. The name is derived from *penios,* a thread, and Cereus. It refers to the slender character of the stems.

The best-known kind is P. Greggii from western Texas to Arizona and Mexico. It has stems

[8–10]

A garden of Petunias

[8—11]
*Passion Flower
(Passiflora caerulea)*

[8—11a]
Sweet or Bell Peppers

[8—11b]
Petunias

[8—11c]
Double-flowered Petunias

to 10 ft. long. Its flowers, which open at night, are white, tinged red on the outsides. For the culture of this plant, see Cacti.

PENNISETUM (Pennise'tum). Tender and hardy Grasses, found wild in Argentina, Abyssinia, and South Africa, and belonging to the family Gramineae. They vary in height from 12 in. to 10 ft., have linear, grasslike leaves and bear large plumes of flowers with bristle-like awns in summer. The name Pennisetum is derived from *penna*, a feather, and *seta*, a bristle, and refers to the feathery bristles (awns).

An Ornamental Grass. P. villosum (longistylum), which grows 1-2 ft. in height, is best treated as an annual in the North, although in mild climates it is perennial. The site is prepared by deep digging and, if the soil is poor, manure or compost and bone meal are added. A sunny, well-drained location is best. When the soil is crumbly in spring, the surface is raked down to a fine condition and the seeds are scattered thinly on the surface and raked in. When the seedlings are 2 in. high, they are thinned out to 6 in. apart.

For Mild Places Only. P. latifolium is a more vigorous plant growing up to 10 ft. in height, but it is hardy only in mild climates. A sunny location and light, well-drained soil are needed. Planting is done in April and the soil is kept moist by watering and mulching in dry weather. During severe winter weather the plants should be protected or lifted, placed in large pots or tubs with soil around the roots, and stored in a frostproof greenhouse.

This kind is also propagated by sowing seeds out of doors in April. The seedlings are transplanted 4 in. apart in a nursery bed when they are a few inches high, and, when large enough, are planted in their permanent quarters. New plants are also obtained by division in April.

P. Ruppelii, Fountain Grass, is a most attractive perennial species with arching, graceful flower spikes in summer. Where not reliably winter-hardy, it can be grown as an annual as advised above for P. villosum.

The plumes of these grasses are useful for winter decoration. They are cut when fully expanded, tied in bundles, and suspended upside down in a cool, airy position to dry.

PENNSYLVANIA, GARDENING IN. See Regional Gardening.

PENNYROYAL. Mentha Pulegium, which see.

PENNYWORT. Umbilicus pendulinus, which see.

PENSTEMON — *Beardtongue* (Penste'mon). Hardy and more or less tender perennial plants which are found wild chiefly in North America. They belong to the Figwort family, Scrophulariaceae. The name, from *pente*, five, and *stemon*, stamen, means five stamens.

Some of the Penstemons are admirable summer-flowering plants for the herbaceous border, others are suitable for the rock garden, and, in climates where they succeed, as they do on parts of the West Coast, the florists' varieties are grand summer bedding plants. They grow 9 in. to 2 ft. in height and bear tube-shaped flowers of various colors during the summer months.

Some of the wild types or species are beautiful rock-garden plants, and a few may be planted in the herbaceous border. The bedding or florists' types, which are more common in Europe than in America, are descended chiefly from the species or wild types named P. Hartwegii, which species bears red flowers, and P. Cobaea, which has purple flowers. Both are North American plants.

Planting and Suitable Soil. Although the

Spikes of large-flowered bedding Penstemons.

Penstemon hirsutus, a native of eastern North America, has pale lavender flowers.

bedding Penstemons are perennials, they may be grown as annuals and raised from seeds or cuttings every year. They thrive in ordinary well-cultivated garden soil in a sunny or slightly shady place. They are planted out of doors in spring—the large-flowered varieties about 10 in., the smaller ones 6-8 in., apart. The former generally need to be supported by sticks.

When to Take Cuttings. Penstemons of the bedding varieties are increased by cuttings, which are inserted in a cold frame in September. The cuttings are made from nonflowering side shoots on the old plants; they should be 3 or 4 in. long, the lower leaves being removed and the base of the cutting made by cutting beneath a joint. The soil should be watered after the cuttings are put in and the frame must be kept close for several weeks.

As soon as the cuttings are rooted, the frame must be ventilated, a little at first, the ventilation being increased gradually. During the winter months the plants must be protected in severe weather by covering the frame, but on mild days air should be admitted freely. The plants need little water at that season and the soil should be moistened only when it is fairly dry.

Management in Winter. As soon as the cuttings are well rooted, they should be potted separately in 3-in. pots, in which they will pass the winter. A compost of loam, two thirds, and leaf mold, one third, with a free scattering of sand is used.

In the spring, as the weather becomes warmer, the Penstemons are hardened off gradually and are then planted out of doors in the flower beds or borders.

Named varieties of bedding Penstemon can be increased only by taking cuttings in the way described. The method of raising Penstemons annually from seeds has, however, much in its favor, for the grower is saved the trouble of tending the plants during the winter months. If a good strain of seeds is used, the flowers compare favorably with those of named varieties.

Raising Bedding Penstemons from Seeds. The seeds are sown in pots or flats in February and placed in a greenhouse having a temperature of about 60 degrees. The seed receptacles are covered with glass and paper, and the soil must be kept just moist. When the seedlings are an inch or so high, they are placed separately in 3-in. pots filled with sandy, loamy soil containing a little leaf mold or peat moss. When well rooted, they must be gradually hardened off so that they shall be ready to be planted out of doors in April or May.

Treatment of Old Plants. In gardens in comparatively mild climates bedding Penstemons live through the winter, and start into fresh growth in spring. At New York City they will do this in mild winters but they are more usually killed if left outdoors. Second-year specimens develop into much larger plants than those raised annually from seeds or cuttings.

If, in winter, the stems die back to some extent, they should be cut down to where fresh young shoots have started to grow.

Some of the Best Varieties of Penstemon. But few named varieties of bedding Penstemons are grown in North America. Some of the best of the European large-flowered varieties are Barbara Hope, red and white; Captain Penwell, bright red; Chester Scarlet, scarlet; George Holmes, scarlet; Glamis White, white; Hon. Alan Gibbs, bright red; Princess Elizabeth, cherry red and

Penstemon barbatus, with spikes of cerise-scarlet flowers, is a border plant.

white; Pink Beauty, soft pink; and William Kelway, red and white.

Of the smaller-flowered Penstemons, best are Newbury Gem, of which there are varieties of white, cerise and red coloring; Southgate Gem, rich red and white; and Mydellton Gem, carmine-rose.

Other Penstemons. Among the wild types or species of Penstemon there are several very beautiful flowering plants which can be grown in well-drained, sandy, loamy soil in a sunny place towards the front of the flower border, or in the rock garden. One of the loveliest of these is P. heterophyllus, 18 in., which bears blue flowers tinged with purple.

Others are P. azureus, 3 ft., blue; P. Davidsonii, 6 in., ruby, a gem for the rock garden; P.

The beautiful herbaceous, blue-flowered Penstemon heterophyllus.

confertus, 12 in., pale yellow; P. Cobaea, 18 in., purple; P. glaber, 12 in., purple-blue; P. Hartwegii, 2 ft., red; P. isophyllus, 3 ft. or more, scarlet-crimson; P. laevigatus, 2 ft., white or blush; P. Menziesii, 1 ft., violet-blue, a grand rock-garden plant; P. Newberryi, 1½ ft., red; P. Scouleri, 1 ft., lavender-blue; P. Bridgesii, 18 in., scarlet, shrubby; P. Roezlii, 12 in., crimson; P. rupicola, rose-red; and P. unilateralis, 2 ft., blue.

As these plants are not usually long-lived, in most gardens it is advisable to raise fresh stocks every year or two by inserting cuttings in September or by sowing seeds in late summer or spring in a greenhouse, cold frame or outdoors.

Penstemon barbatus (often listed as Chelone barbata) is a handsome border plant which reaches a height of about 3 ft., and in July and August bears narrow, tube-shaped blooms of cerise-scarlet P. hirsutus, lavender-violet flowers, and P. Digitalis, white or pinkish flowers, are eastern American natives that are well suited for naturalistic plantings and for flower borders. P. Digitalis needs moist soil.

PENTAPTERYGIUM (Pentapteryg'ium). Attractive epiphytic shrubs from the eastern Himalayas, suitable for cultivation in a greenhouse with a minimum winter temperature of 50 degrees, and outdoors in California and similar climates. They belong to the family Ericaceae.

These plants thrive in a peaty compost in well-drained pots or suspended baskets, and are propagated by cuttings of young shoots in peat moss and sand in a close propagating case.

Pentapterygium is closely related to Agapetes and thrives under similar conditions. The name is from pente, five, and pterygion, a small wing, and refers to the winged calyx.

Kinds Worth Growing. P. flavum, 1-3 ft., with pendulous, yellow, red-margined flowers; P. rugosum, 1-3 ft., white, with purple or deep red markings and tipped with green; P. serpens, 2-3 ft., of drooping habit, with red flowers drooping from the axils of the leaves.

PENTAS (Pen'tas). Tender, evergreen flowering shrubs, from tropical Africa, which closely resemble Bouvardia. They belong to the family Rubiaceae. The principal kind, P. lanceolata, grows about 18 in. in height, has branching, woody stems, clothed with large, ovate to lanceo-

late-oblong pointed leaves, and bears terminal clusters of white or pink flowers in winter. It may be grown permanently outdoors in the far South. The name Pentas is derived from pente, five, and refers to the floral organs.

Summer and Winter Management. When grown indoors, these shrubs require a minimum winter temperature of 55 degrees, and a soil compost of equal parts of peat, leaf mold and loam, with a scattering of sand. Repotting is done in March. The shoots are first shortened slightly to make the plants shapely. These are then sprayed lightly with water several times a day to assist new shoots to form. When the shoots are ¼ in. in length the plants are taken out of their pots. The loose soil and the crocks are removed from the roots, and the plants are repotted in well-drained pots two sizes larger.

After potting, the plants are set in a shaded part of the greenhouse and frequently syringed to assist them while rooting into the new soil. The atmosphere is kept moist by frequently damping the floor and benches. When established, the plants are exposed to full light, but shaded from the fiercest rays of the sun.

Water is applied very sparingly to the soil until the plants are well rooted, but for the remainder of the summer the compost is kept moist. During the winter less moisture is required, but the compost is not allowed to become dry until the flowers have faded. The water supply is then gradually lessened and the soil is kept on the dry side until it is time for repotting.

As Summer Bedding Plants. In the North, Pentas make good summer bedding plants. They bloom continuously all summer and until the coming of frost. When used for this purpose, good plants in 4-in. or 5-in. pots should be planted in sun, or where light shade for part of the day is received. The soil should be deep and rich, and the planting should not be done until the weather is quite settled and warm.

Propagation Is by Cuttings. Side shoots or the tips of shoots, 2 or 3 in. long, are taken in early spring or in August-September. The cuttings are inserted in a propagating case having a bottom heat of 65-70 degrees.

The frame is kept close except for a few minutes each morning, when the top is lifted and the moisture is wiped from the underside of the glass. Condensed moisture must be removed, otherwise it may drip on the cuttings and set up decay.

When roots have formed, the cuttings are ventilated more freely, and after a few days are hardened off sufficiently. They are then potted separately in 3-in. pots and, when well rooted in these, they are transferred to 5-in. pots.

To make bushy plants, the tips of the main shoots are pinched out and the resulting side shoots are similarly treated. The remainder of the treatment is as advised for the older plants.

The chief kind is P. lanceolata (carnea), pink. There are three varieties of this: alba, white; kermesina, carmine-rose and violet; and Quartiniana, pink.

PEONY. See Paeonia.

PEPEROMIA (Pepero′mia). Tropical ornamental-leaved plants which are chiefly natives of tropical America and belong to the Pepper family, Piperaceae. The name Peperomia means pepper-like.

There are many kinds of Peperomia, and they are useful as house plants and for greenhouse decoration. Dwarf and compact, they rarely exceed 12 in. in height, and they vary considerably in appearance. Some have threadlike, trailing stems and others thick, succulent, upright stems.

The leaves are entire (undivided), smooth

Peperomia hederifolia.

and fleshy, and may be ovate, peltate (leafstalks at or near the center of the leaf blade), cordate (heart-shaped) or lanceolate (lance-shaped); they vary from 1-4 in. in length. They are green or striped, marbled or margined with pale green, red or gray, and the petioles of some kinds are red.

The flowers, which are inconspicuous, are very minute and produced in the form of a cordlike spike. P. resedeflora, which has white, fragrant flowers, is the only kind grown for its blossoms.

Summer and Winter Management. These plants may be grown in pots, shallow pans or in hanging baskets. They require a minimum winter temperature of 55 degrees and a soil compost

Peperomia Sandersii variety argyreia.

Peperomia obtusifolia.

Peperomia capreata.

of equal parts of peat moss, loam and sand.

Repotting is done in March. The new pots should be well drained. The plants are removed from the old pots, the crocks and as much as possible of the old soil being removed without damaging the roots. The plants should then be set in the new pots, which should be slightly larger, and just big enough to hold the roots comfortably without cramping them.

No water is given until the soil becomes

A young Peperomia propagated from a leaf cutting.

nearly dry, and then it is thoroughly saturated. This method of watering is followed throughout the year, but the intervals between the waterings are longer in winter.

Suitable for Hanging Baskets. P. rotundifolia, P. brevipes and others of trailing growth are suitable for growing in hanging baskets. The baskets are first lined with sphagnum moss and then filled with the prepared soil. Small plants, or rooted cuttings, are planted at the top of the baskets, 3 in. or so apart. The baskets are hung in a shaded corner of the greenhouse and watered in the manner recommended for pot plants.

Propagation is by cuttings, leaf cuttings or division. The plants are divided at potting time, when they are removed from the pots and separated into smaller pieces, each of which should have a few roots attached. They are potted separately in small pots.

When to Take Cuttings. Cuttings are taken in spring or summer. The shoots are removed, the lower leaves cut off, and a cut made below the bottom node (joint). The prepared cuttings are laid on the potting bench for an hour or two to allow a corky skin to form over the cut end. They are then inserted in a propagating case with a bottom heat of 70-75 degrees, but the top is not entirely closed as the plants, being of a semisucculent nature, do not transpire (give off water) very rapidly. When sufficient roots are formed, the plants are either potted separately in 3-in. pots or planted in hanging baskets.

The Chief Kinds. P. acuminata, narrow grass-green leaves; P. clusiaefolia, thick green leaves with narrow red edges; P. crassifolia, leaves round, fleshy, dill green; P. griseo-argentea, leaves metallic-gray with olive veins, rounded, glossy; P. incana, thick, gray-green leaves; P. rotundifolia, small roundish leaves; P. obtusifolia variegata, leaves green, well variegated with white and creamy yellow; P. rubella, tiny olive-green leaves that are red beneath; P. Sandersii, leafstalks red, leaves green; P. Sandersii variety argyreia is similar, with silvery blotches between the veins; P. velutina, silky green with light veins; P. maculosa, gray-green with silver-green veins; P. glabella variegata, green, pale green and creamy yellow; and P. capreata (Emerald Ripples), leaves bright green with dark veins.

Sweet Peppers or Bell Peppers.

PEPPER. The Peppers of the vegetable garden, including those from which red pepper, cayenne pepper, paprika and tabasco are made, are all considered to be varieties of one very variable species, Capsicum frutescens, a native of the tropics. This is quite different from, and is not closely related botanically to, Piper nigrum, the plant from which the condiments, black and white pepper, are prepared.

Capsicum frutescens belongs in the Nightshade family, the Solanaceae, and thus is closely related to the Tomato and Potato. In tropical countries it is perennial and becomes a shrub as high as 8 ft., but as commonly grown in gardens it is treated as an annual and new plants are raised from seeds each year. This is true of the kinds that are grown as ornamental pot plants as well as of those cultivated in the vegetable garden.

Varieties of garden Peppers are numerous. They can be divided into two groups, the sweet Peppers or mild-flavored varieties, which are used for stuffing and for salads and garnishing, and the hot Peppers, which are used in sauces and flavoring. The latter are seldom grown in the North but in the South, especially among people of Spanish descent, they are popular. The Spanish word "Chili" describes Peppers of all kinds, but in English the name is usually applied only to the pungent varieties used for flavoring. The hot Peppers include C. frutescens abbreviatum (Short Pepper), C. frutescens conoides (Cone Pepper), C. frutescens fasciculatum (Red Cluster Pepper), and C. frutescens longum (Long Pepper). The last named includes Chili, Cayenne and Long Yellow. Varieties of hot Pepper offered commercially include Hungarian Wax, Large Cherry, Long Red Cayenne, Maule's Red Hot, Red Chili and Tabasco. All have red or orange-scarlet fruits when ripe.

The Sweet Pepper or Bell Pepper, C. frutescens grossum, is a popular vegetable. The fruit, when ripe, is red or yellow, but is used as a vegetable in the green state. It is ready for picking 58-70 days from the time of sowing, according to the variety and the weather conditions. Early-fruiting varieties such as Merrimack Wonder, Patrick Henry, Harris' Early Giant, Ruby King and Ozark Giant are best for the home gardener who can give only limited space to their culture. They continue to bear throughout summer, provided the fruits are picked regularly as soon as they are large enough. Gather the fruits by snapping off the brittle stems or cut them off with a sharp knife; any fruits that have not been picked and are hanging on the plants when frost threatens in early fall should be cut off at that time and be stored in a cool but frost-free cellar or similar place. Under such conditions they will keep for three months or longer.

Cultural Requirements. Peppers require about the same cultural care as Tomatoes but they stand even less cold. They are distinctly a warm-weather crop. The soil in which they thrive best is one that does not dry out too rapidly and is well supplied with organic matter. Caution should be exercised in applying fertilizers containing much nitrogen because an excess of this is likely to cause the plants to make gross foliage growth and not set many fruits. The plants should be grown in a sunny location.

Raising Plants from Seeds. The seeds should be sown in light, well-drained soil in a warm (60 degree minimum), sunny greenhouse some 6-8 weeks before the resulting plants are to be planted in the garden. When calculating the correct time to sow the seeds, remember that the plants must not be put out in the garden until the weather is really warm and settled—about 2 weeks later than it is safe to set out Tomatoes. The seeds take 16-20 days to germinate. Transplant the seedlings into flats as soon as they are big enough to handle easily, spacing them 2-3 in. apart, or plant them individually in small pots. In either case, use well-drained soil. The plants must never be allowed to suffer from drought or from low temperatures. Keep them growing steadily and harden them gradually before planting them in the garden.

Planting and Aftercare. A sunny position in the garden suits Peppers. They should be spaced 18 in. apart in the rows with 2 ft. allowed between the rows. Cultivate the surface soil frequently to kill weeds, but avoid deep cultivation that is likely to harm the roots. If the soil is at all retentive of moisture, little or no watering will be required unless a long drought occurs.

Ornamental Peppers as Pot Plants. Certain varieties of Pepper, when grown in pots, are very decorative in fruit and are especially useful as ornamentals in fall and early winter and for Christmas. Those most suitable for this purpose are Capsicum frutescens cerasiforme, the Cherry Pepper, and C. frutescens conoides, the Cone Pepper. The varieties of these kinds have red, purple or cream-colored fruits displayed attractively above the rich green foliage.

Culture. To secure good plants for early winter and for the Christmas season, sow the seeds in July, and treat them as recommended above for Peppers raised from seeds for planting in the vegetable garden. The only exception is that the seedlings should always be transplanted individually directly from the seed pot into small pots, and later be transplanted to larger pots as the needs of growth make necessary.

Any good potting soil that is porous and well drained is suitable. Excessive fertilization is to be guarded against, but an occasional application of liquid fertilizer may be needed to keep the foliage from yellowing because of lack of sufficient nitrogen. Avoid, too, overwatering; by keeping the soil slightly on the dry side, more compact and bushier plants are obtained. The plants should not require pinching, but if any shoots tend to run up too long they may be pinched.

At all times Peppers must have full sun. During the hot weather they may be kept in the greenhouse or may be buried to the rims of their pots outdoors in a bed of ashes or sand. They must, of course, be brought into a warm greenhouse before the cold nights of fall arrive. Low temperatures cause the foliage to turn yellow and the leaves to fall off.

Although these plants are technically perennials, they are not worth keeping after they have fruited once; it is better to start with new plants each year. Ornamental Peppers do not make satisfactory permanent house plants.

PEPPERBUSH, SWEET. Clethra alnifolia, which see.

PEPPER, CAYENNE. The produce of several varieties of Capsicum annuum. See Capsicum and Pepper.

PEPPERIDGE. Nyssa sylvatica, which see.

PEPPERMINT. The common name used for Mentha piperita. There are two principal forms of Peppermint: Mentha piperita variety officinalis and M. piperita variety vulgaris, the former called Black Peppermint and the latter White Peppermint by reason of the purplish-brown and green stems respectively.

The Black Peppermint is regarded as being rather hardier than the White and has a higher oil percentage; the White makes up for the deficiency by producing a finer quality oil. It does not matter much which form is grown, but they should not be mixed. Both are selected strains of the wild M. piperita.

Rich and well-worked ground is selected for Peppermint fields and, when a new field is to be planted, young shoots 4-5 in. long are taken from old stocks and dibbled into the ground about 1½ ft. apart. They grow rapidly and soon cover the ground with runners if it is permanently moist without being water-logged. The full-grown shoots are cut when dry, just before flowering time, and may be allowed to lie and wilt a little before distillation, or they may be taken direct to the still.

By careful manuring, the same field will yield a satisfactory crop for three or four seasons; but as soon as it begins to deteriorate, new beds should be planted and the old field placed under a different crop.

Peppermint oil has many uses. It is used in the preparation of crème de menthe and other liqueurs, as a flavoring agent in confectionery and in medicine and perfumery; it is also of medicinal value in cases of coughs, colds, etc., and is the chief source of menthol, for which there are many medicinal uses.

PEPPER TREE. Schinus, which see.

PEPPER VINE. Schinus, which see.

PEPPERWORT. Marsilea, which see.

PEPUL TREE. See Ficus.

PERENNIAL. A perennial plant is one that lives on from year to year; the word is derived from the Latin *perennis,* meaning lasting through the years. The word perennial is often used as though it referred only to those herbaceous plants which live on from year to year. Trees and shrubs are, of course, perennials; they are woody or shrubby perennials; that is to say, not only the roots but the branches persist from year to year. The familiar hardy border plants—Delphinium, Phlox, Erigeron, Peony, and many more are herbaceous perennials; although the rootstock lives on from year to year the leafy or herbaceous top growth usually dies down annually and fresh growth appears in spring.

In common garden usage the word perennial is restricted to nonwoody kinds; that is to say, to herbaceous perennials. These, of course, include bulbous kinds such as Lilies, Daffodils and Tulips as well as nonbulbous plants.

Some kinds of border perennials are evergreen—the top growth does not die down in autumn, but persists throughout the year. They are correctly termed evergreen herbaceous perennials. Familiar examples are Thrift or Armeria, Border Carnation and Pink.

Some plants which are true perennials in nature, and in gardens also when they are grown under conditions which suit them, are commonly treated as annuals or biennials by gardeners, because, when raised fresh every year from seeds or cuttings, they yield finer blooms and generally prove more reliable than old plants.

A Selection of Reliable Hardy Perennial Plants

Name	Color	Height (feet)	Season
Achillea Millefolium Fire King	cerise-red	2	June–Sept.
Achillea Ptarmica Perry's Giant White	white, double	2½	July–Sept.
Achillea Taygetea	pale yellow	2	July–Aug.
Aconitum Fischeri Wilsonii	violet-blue	5	Aug.–Oct.
Aconitum Napellus Spark's variety	violet-blue	5	July–Aug.
Anchusa azurea (italica) Loddon Royalist	purple-blue	4	June–July
Anchusa azurea (italica) Opal	pale blue	4	June–July
Anemone japonica alba	white	2–3	Aug.–Sept.
Anemone japonica September Charm	pink	2–3	Aug.–Sept.
Anthemis tinctoria Grallagh Gold	golden-yellow	2½	June–Aug.
Anthemis tinctoria Moonlight	sulphur-yellow	2	June–Aug.
Aquilegia Long-spurred Hybrids	mixed	2½	May–June

A Selection of Reliable Hardy Perennial Plants

Name	Color	Height (feet)	Season
Armeria maritima Laucheana	rose-red	½	May–June
Armeria maritima Royal Rose	bright pink	1½	May–June
Artemisia lactiflora	white	5	Aug.-Sept.
Aster (Michaelmas Daisy) varieties	many shades	1–6	Aug.–Oct.
Aster Frikartii Wonder of Staffa	violet-blue	1½	July–Oct.
Astilbe Betsy Cuperus	pale pink	2½	July
Astilbe Fanal	deep red	2	July
Astilbe Deutschland	white	2½	July
Astilbe Salland	bright red	2½	July
Campanula glomerata dahurica	deep purple	1½	June–July
Campanula lactiflora	pale blue	4	July
Campanula persicifolia grandiflora caerula	blue	2½	June–July
Campanula persicifolia grandiflora alba	white	2½	June–July
Catananche caerulea	blue	2½	July–Aug.
Centaurea montana	violet-blue	2	June–July
Chrysanthemum maximum Mount Shasta	white, double	2	June–Aug.
Chrysanthemum maximum Majestic	white	3	June–Aug.
Chrysanthemum maximum Thomas Killin	white	3	June–Aug.
Cimicifuga racemosa	ivory-white	3–4	Aug.–Sept.
Coreopsis grandiflora	golden-yellow	3	June–Sept.
Coreopsis verticillata	golden-yellow	2	July–Aug.
Delphinium hybrids	mauve, blue, white	4–6	June
Delphinium Belladonna Clivedon Beauty	blue	3	June–July
Delphinium Bellamosa	dark blue	3	June–July
Echinacea (Rudbeckia) purpurea The King	red-purple	3½	July–Aug.
Echinops Taplow Blue	silver-blue	5	July–Aug.
Erigeron speciosus Sincerity	lavender-blue	2	July–Aug.
Eryngium amethystinum	rich blue	2½	Aug.–Sept.
Gaillardia Mr. Sherbrooke	yellow	2	June–Sept.
Gaillardia Ruby	ruby-red	2	June–Sept.
Geranium grandiflorum	violet-blue	1½	June–July
Geranium ibericum	violet-blue	1½	June–July
Geum Fire Opal	scarlet	2	June–Sept.
Geum Lady Strathedon	golden-yellow	2	June–Sept.
Gypsophila paniculata flore-pleno	white, double	3	July–Aug.
Gypsophila Rosy Veil	pale pink	1½	June–Aug.
Helenium autumnale pumilum magnificum	yellow	2	July–Aug.
Helenium Chipperfield Orange	rich orange	4	Aug.–Sept.
Helenium Moerheim Beauty	brown-red	3½	July–Sept.
Helenium Butterpat	yellow	3½	July
Helianthus decapetalus (multiflorus) flore-pleno	yellow	4	Aug.–Sept.
Heliopsis scabra Gold Greenheart	yellow & green	3–4	Aug.–Sept.
Heliopsis scabra incomparabilis	orange-yellow	3–4	July–Aug.
Hemerocallis varieties	yellow, red	1–3	June–Sept.
Heuchera Rosamondii	pink	1½	June–July
Heuchera sanguinea	bright red	1½	June–July
Hollyhock, single and double	various	6–8	July–Sept.
Hosta caerulea	lavender-blue	3	July–Aug.
Hosta Sieboldiana	pale lilac	2	July
Iberis sempervirens	white	1	April–May
Iris sibirica Perry's Blue	sky-blue	2½	May–June

A Selection of Reliable Hardy Perennial Plants

Name	Color	Height (feet)	Season
Iris sibirica Snow Crest	white	2½	May–June
Iris Tall Bearded varieties	various	3–4	May–June
Kniphofia (Tritoma) Coral Sea	coral-red	2½	June–July
Kniphofia Springtime	yellow & red	3	July–Aug.
Liatris pycnostachya	rosy-purple	3	Aug.–Sept.
Liatris scariosa White Spire	white	5	Aug.–Sept.
Liatris September Glory	rosy-purple	5	Aug.–Sept.
Limonium (Statice) latifolium	lavender-blue	2	Aug.–Oct.
Lupinus Russell Hybrids	rich & varied	3–4	May–June
Lychnis chalcedonica	scarlet	3½	June–July
Lychnis Viscaria flore-pleno	rose-red, double	1½	May–July
Lythrum Morden's Pink	rose-red	3½	July–Aug.
Lythrum Robert	deep rose	3	July–Aug.
Macleaya (Bocconia) cordata	pale pink	6	July–Aug.
Monarda didyma Cambridge Scarlet	rich red	3–4	July–Aug.
Monarda didyma Croftway Pink	light pink	3–4	July–Aug.
Nepeta Blue Beauty	deep mauve	2	June–Sept.
Nepeta Mussinii	mauve	1	June–Sept.
Oenothera fruticosa Youngii	bright yellow	2	June–Aug.
Paeonia, single and double varieties	various	2–3	May–July
Papaver orientale	scarlet	2½	May–June
Papaver orientale Watermelon	bright-pink	3	May–June
Papaver orientale Salmon Glow	salmon-orange	3	May–June
Phlox in variety	various	2–4	July–Sept.
Physostegia virginiana Vivid	deep rose-pink	2	Sept.–Oct.
Platycodon grandiflorum	blue	2	June–Sept.
Platycodon grandiflorum album	white	2	June–Sept.
Potentilla Warrensii	yellow	2½	June–Sept.
Rudbeckia laciniata Goldquelle	yellow, double	3	Aug.–Sept.
Rudbeckia White Lustre	white	2	Aug.–Sept.
Salvia Pitcheri	blue	3–4	July–Aug.
Salvia Sclarea turkestanica	blue-pink	3	July–Aug.
Salvia virgata nemorosa	purple	2½	July–Aug.
Scabiosa caucasica Clive Greaves	lavender-blue	2	July–Oct.
Scabiosa caucasica Miss Willmott	white	2	July–Oct.
Sidalcea Elsie Hugh	rose-pink	3½	July–Sept.
Stachys (Betonica) grandiflora	purple-violet	1½	June
Thalictrum aquilegifolium	mauve	3½	July–Aug.
Thalictrum dipterocarpum	violet-mauve	5	July–Aug.
Thalictrum glaucum	pale yellow	5	June–July
Tradescantia Purple Dome	purple	1½	June–Aug.
Trollius Goldquelle	golden-yellow	2	May–June
Trollius Ledebouri	orange-yellow	3	June
Trollius Lemon Queen	lemon yellow	2½	May–June
Trollius Orange Globe	orange-yellow	2½	May
Verbascum Cotswold Gem	bronze-salmon	4	June–Aug.
Verbascum Bridal Bouquet	white	4	June–July
Verbascum Pink Domino	rosy-pink	4	June–July
Veronica maritima (longifolia) subsessilis	clear blue	2	July–Sept.
Veronica spuria (amethystina) Blue Peter	rich blue	1½	June–July
Veronica spuria (amethystina) Royal Blue	bright blue	3	June–July

PERENNIAL BORDERS
How to Plan, Plant and Maintain These Attractive Features

There are so many beautiful and easy-to-grow hardy herbaceous perennial plants available, at comparatively small cost, that a border devoted to them, or to them and selected annuals and biennials, is a sound proposition both economically and aesthetically. And the range of plants is so great that few sites cannot be made colorful and interesting by their use. They are, indeed, the standby of the amateur gardener for maintaining a continuous display from spring until late autumn.

While selections of perennials can be made that provide bloom from earliest spring until killing frost or even somewhat later, mixed borders, consisting of perennials, annuals and biennials, provide a more colorful, continuous display than borders devoted entirely to perennials. This is because most perennials, as compared with most annuals, have comparatively short periods of bloom and so a border filled with them is likely to have only a small proportion of its total area in flower at any one time.

When arranging mixed borders it is important to leave definite areas, each a square yard or more in extent, between the groups of perennials to receive the annuals and biennials and these areas should be dug over deeply and fertilized before each new planting of annuals and biennials. Both the perennials and the more temporary plantings suffer if the latter are just stuck among the perennials without special patches being allotted to them and prepared for them.

Planning the Border

Choosing the Site. If a wide selection of

In this border at The New York Botanical Garden biennials such as Canterbury Bells and Foxgloves are interplanted with perennials.

Groups of Hyacinths are planted at the front of this perennial border to bloom in early spring.

incongruous effect. Thus a width of 12 feet or more is the ideal for creating a really bold display, with generous use of Delphiniums, perennial Sunflowers (Helianthus), and other really tall growers, although such a width is not always practicable in gardens of less, say, than one-quarter of an acre in size.

Favorite and practicable sites for herbaceous borders are beside main paths, flanking a lawn, or in the foreground of shrub plantings, the shrubs providing an excellent background for the herbaceous plants.

Whether the front of the border is straight or curved matters little, provided it conforms to the general layout of the garden, but curves, if they are bold and sweeping, not small and acute, allow the more free use of tall plants to avoid formality and solidness.

A Plan Is Essential. Having decided upon the site of the perennial border, and fixed its width, length and shape, the next step is to draw a plan of it to scale, then mark in the positions to be occupied by the plants already available, or to be ordered from reliable nurseries.

different kinds of plants is to be grown, the border should be open and sunny. It should be as wide as practicable in conformity to the size and general layout of the garden—and it is with bearing in mind that the wider the border, the greater range of heights will it be possible to use without

To transform unplanted land into a perennial garden such as this, a working plan is desirable. The perennial borders here are without background plantings.

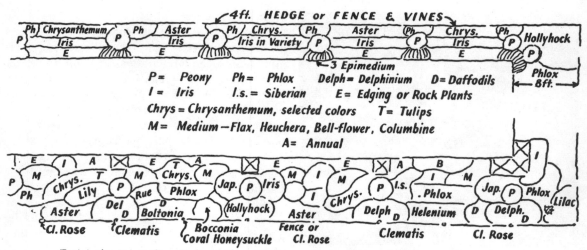

(Top) A plan to provide succession of bloom in a narrow border. (Bottom) A plan to provide succession of bloom in a wider border. The greater space permits greater variety, and regularly spaced perennials are used to give a formal touch.

In this way the positions of the individual plants of each variety can be fixed, spacing them from 9 or 12 in. apart in the case of the dwarf subjects, to 18 in. or more for the taller, clump-forming Michaelmas Daisies, Heleniums, Delphiniums, etc., and allowing somewhat greater distances between the groups. It is also possible, by this means, to ascertain the exact number of plants required to fill the border.

Planning Pointers. Generally, the subjects should be arranged according to height from front to back, but to avoid a too solid effect this method of arrangement should not be adhered to rigidly. Taller plants may be brought forward to the middle of the border occasionally, and medium-height plants, especially those of bushy growth, to the front, to break any flatness in the arrangement and create an informal effect.

Season of flowering must also be considered carefully. Too many early- or late-flowering subjects should not be planted in close association; bear in mind that they will be flowerless for long periods. An attempt should also be made to screen the early-flowering plants, as for instance Lupines, Anchusa, Irises and Oriental Poppies, with later subjects of similar or greater height.

Color arrangement is equally important. No hard and fast rule is possible on this subject, as so much will depend on the individual taste and artistic ability of the planner, but generally it is best to try to arrange the plants in a series of

color blends, with perhaps an occasional contrast, but not of a violent nature.

White-flowered plants may be used effectively as links between the various color arrangements, or as foils for almost any shade. Free use should also be made of gray and silvery leaved herbaceous plants.

To avoid a "spotty" effect, each subject, no matter how small the border, should usually be represented by not fewer than three plants, a larger number than this being desirable for most

An informal background of trees and shrubs, including evergreens, makes a perfect foil for a perennial garden.

A closely clipped hedge serves as a formal background for this perennial border.

of the dwarf subjects at the front of the border. If single plants of choice subjects have to be included, on the score of cost, an early attempt should be made to propagate them.

Backgrounds. Probably the ideal background for a herbaceous border is one of ornamental shrubs and small trees, including a number of evergreens, but to be really attractive these must be in sufficient depth to give a banked effect, with forward plantings here and there to break the line of the back row of herbaceous plants.

Closely clipped hedges of Yew or Hemlock make attractive backgrounds to flower borders. When planting is done, a space of at least 2 ft. should be left between the back-row plants and the hedge to allow for soil cultivation and clipping. This is particularly important when borders are planted in proximity to Privet, Hornbeam and other heavy feeders.

Backgrounds of Roses. For a light but colorful background to the herbaceous border, Rambler Roses trained to tall posts connected by wooden top pieces or wires can be delightful. The posts are set a foot or so in from the back edge of the border, and the taller herbaceous plants grouped boldly between them. In large herbaceous borders, with a width of not less than 12 ft., pillars of Rambler and Climbing Roses, or of Clematis, set at regular intervals towards the back, may also add to the attractiveness of the border.

Borders Without Backgrounds. If the border occupies a position where it can be viewed from both sides, as for instance when flanked by a path on one side and the lawn on the other, the arrangement of the plants calls for very careful consideration. Except where sufficient width is available to justify their use in the center of the border, very tall plants should be omitted. Indeed, in all such borders the height of the plants should be governed by the width of the border if the result is not to be incongruous. Thus, with a border 6 ft. wide, it would be wise to limit the height of the tallest plants to about 4 ft., and not to use too many of these.

Planting the Border

Preparing the Ground. The majority of the never-fail, hardy perennial plants, which should form, as it were, the foundation of the herbaceous border, do appreciate generous feeding and, indeed, need it if they are to remain vigorous and flower freely each year. For this reason the ground should, if practicable, be deeply dug and plenty of decayed vegetable matter mixed with the subsoil to help hold moisture in summer and supply a reserve of food for the deep-rooting subjects.

Even if such deep cultivation is not possible, the border should be dug thoroughly and an abundance of manure or compost buried beneath the top. It is almost impossible to mix too much compost, leaf mold and well-rotted old manure with the topsoil.

Final Preparation for Planting. A dressing of 3 oz. of bone meal and 4 oz. ground lime per square yard is recommended. To prepare the soil for planting, it should be forked through carefully with a view to removing all perennial weed roots; if these are left in the ground they are sure to grow up among the perennial plants and give a lot of trouble later. If, after this fork-ing, there is not time to allow the soil to settle naturally, tread it lightly.

Setting Out the Plants. It is always a good plan to label the occupants of the herbaceous border, not only for easy reference to their names, but also to prevent any confusion later if alterations or replantings have to be carried out. And if the labels are prepared in advance, this will save a lot of time and trouble when it comes to setting the plants in position.

Working according to plan, the labels can be inserted to mark the positions of the groups, the outlines of which can be marked on the soil with a pointed stick.

Planting. Except for small pot-grown plants, a spade will generally be found the most convenient tool for planting herbaceous subjects. Holes should be made wide and deep enough to take the roots comfortably, so that the crowns of the plants will be just showing through the surface when planting is finished. If the plant is held in position in the hole, sufficient soil can be pushed in with the foot to anchor it, after which the remainder can be shoveled in with the spade. Tread all plants in firmly, then level off with a fork and insert the label close to the front plant of the group, where it will not be pushed over or broken when hoeing is done.

The best effect is obtained when young perennials are set out in groups.

When to Plant. The majority of hardy herbaceous flowers may be put in any time when the ground is not sodden or frozen in autumn or early spring; but spring is the most satisfactory period for fleshy-rooted subjects, like Anchusa italica varieties, Oriental Poppies, Eryngiums, Gypsophila Bristol Fairy, and subjects which take a year to become established or do not stand the winter well until they have obtained a good root hold.

Also best planted in the spring are Border Carnations and Pinks, Violas from cuttings, Michaelmas Daisies of the Aster Amellus type, Hardy Chrysanthemums, Scabiosa caucasica varieties, Coreopsis grandiflora varieties, Gaillardias, Poker Plants (Kniphofias), Penstemons, Pyrethrums, Salvias, and Catmint (Nepeta Mussinii).

Most hardy bulbs, such as Narcissi, Tulips, Hyacinths, Scillas and Crocuses are planted in fall. Lilies may be planted in fall or spring.

Maintaining the Border

Thinning and Staking. Although the majority of hardy perennial herbaceous plants may be allowed to grow naturally, with some of the taller kinds, like Delphiniums, Heleniums, Michael-

mas Daisies, and the giant-flowered perennial Sunflowers, it certainly pays to thin out the weakest shoots at an early stage if large heads of flowers are desired. Phloxes also respond well to light thinning of the young shoots.

There are various methods of staking hardy border flowers, but for the taller-growing kinds strong stakes are undoubtedly most satisfactory. These should be set behind the plants and the growths tied loosely to them, although occasionally one stake may be made to serve two plants by setting it between them. The stakes should be tall enough to support the mature growth but be hidden from view when the plants are in bloom. With Michaelmas Daisies, by staking skilfully it is often possible to spread the growths forward and sideways to hide partially neighboring subjects that have gone out of bloom.

Plants of medium height and bushy habit may be supported very satisfactorily by inserting brushwood among and around them and breaking the tops over to interlace them and form, as it were, a cat's cradle, through which the flowering shoots will grow to hide them. Pieces of wide-meshed chicken wire fixed horizontally over the plants and supported by stakes at about half the final height of the plants, will serve the same

The perennial border needs periodic attention from spring to fall to keep it in good condition. Staking and tying, thinning of overcrowded shoots, watering, weeding and the removal of dead flowers and foliage must all receive attention.

purpose. Though Phloxes and other sturdy growers of similar height do not normally require staking, in exposed gardens it may pay to give some support by setting short stakes at the corners of the groups and connecting these with binder twine or coarse string.

The Spring Checkup. Soon after new growth has begun in spring, established borders of hardy flowers should be checked over for gaps, and these filled with suitable plants. Hardy annuals may be used, also biennials, young perennials, and summer-flowering bulbs and tubers such as Gladioli and Dahlias.

Summer Management. During the spring the soil between the plants should be stirred occasionally with a hoe or hand cultivator, to prevent weeds and promote growth. During dry weather watering will benefit all of the plants, provided it can be done heavily enough to soak the soil thoroughly at least several inches deep. Mulching the soil during summer is very beneficial; it conserves moisture and promotes growth.

As the plants finish flowering, the spent heads and spikes should be removed to prevent seeding, but as much foliage as possible should be left.

Fall Work. After frost has killed most of the foliage, old stems should be cut down and dead

A hand cultivator is useful for stirring the soil at the front of the perennial border.

foliage removed. In cold climates, winter protection in the form of a light covering of salt marsh hay or of evergreen branches should be laid over perennial beds after the ground has frozen to a depth of an inch or two.

Easy to Raise from Seed. Among first-class border plants which are easy to raise from seed sown early indoors, or in a cold frame or a prepared bed in the open in spring, to give plants for flowering the following year, special mention may be made of Delphiniums, Anchusa italica, long-spurred Aquilegias, Coreopsis grandiflora, Gypsophila, Salvia Sclarea and other hardy kinds, and Verbascums.

Kinds of Borders

A Scented Border. A border filled with fragrant flowers and herbs, close to the house, or a small garden of formal beds edged with clipped hedges of Lavender, can be very attractive and are worth considering where space permits. The company would include a variety of herbs, like Bergamots (Monarda didyma Cambridge Scarlet and Croftway Pink), Hyssop, Balm, Pennyroyal, various Mints, with fragrant Dianthus, Sweet Rocket (Hesperis), Lily of the Valley, Tree Lupines (Lupinus arboreus), Peony, Madonna Lily (Lilium candidum), and Regal Lily (L. regale).

A few shrubs could be included, especially Lavender, Rosemary, Lemon-scented Verbena (Lippia citriodora), Daphne Mezereum, Old Man or Southernwood (Artemisia Abrotanum), while fragrant Hyacinths, Stocks, Wallflowers, and annual flowers like Mignonette, Sweet Peas, Sweet Scabious and Sweet Sultan, would add their rich perfumes in their respective flowering seasons.

Colorful Edging Plants. For continuous edgings to herbaceous borders and beds of hardy flowers, specially suitable subjects on account of their growth and wealth of flowers are Mauve Catmint (Nepeta Mussinii), white and colored Pinks, the dwarf Hybrid Asters, Thrift (Armeria), Lychnis Viscaria, Campanula carpatica and C. Portenschlagiana (muralis), double white Arabis, Aubrietas, Golden Alyssum, Mossy Saxifrages and Violas.

For Partly Shaded Borders. Hardy herbaceous

Bergenia crassifolia is a splendid hardy perennial plant for a partly shaded location. It prefers moderately moist soil.

plants which grow and flower well in partly shaded borders, provided they receive a fair amount of light, include Japanese and Wood Anemones, Peonies, Astrantia major, Astilbes and Spiraeas, Campanula lactiflora, Ajuga, Dicentra spectabilis, Plantain Lily (Funkia or Hosta), Primulas, Phloxes, Christmas and Lenten Roses (Helleborus), Lily of the Valley, Omphalodes verna, Ranunculus aconitifolius, Mossy and Bergenias (Megaseas), Trilliums, Primroses, Polyanthuses, and Violas, with various spring bulbs.

Hardy Ferns in variety are excellent for planting in cool, shady places in soil containing plenty of leaf mold or peat, especially the Lady Fern (Athyrium), hardy Maidenhair Fern (Adiantum pedatum), Blechnum spicant, Sensitive Fern (Onoclea), Male Fern (Dryopteris), Common Polypody (Polypodium), and Hart's-tongue (Phyllitis Scolopendrium).

Best Moisture-loving Plants. Especially lovely subjects for moist positions, where they may be left undisturbed for many years, are Aconitum (Monkshood), Astilbes, double Caltha palustris, Cimicifuga, Dicentra spectabilis (Bleeding Heart), Hosta (Plantain Lily), Hemerocallis (Day Lily), Iris Kaempferi (Japanese Iris) and others, Lobelia cardinalis hybrids, Lysimachia clethroides, Lysichitum (Yellow Skunk Cabbage), Lythrum (Loosestrife), Mimulus (Monkey Flower), Physostegia (Obedient Flower), Rodgersia, Primula denticulata and others, Saxifrage peltata, Spiraea, Trillium and Trollius (Globe Flower).

PERENNIAL PEA. Lathyrus latifolius, which see.

PERENNIAL RYE GRASS. Lolium perenne, which see.

PERESKIA (Peresk'ia). Tender, evergreen, flowering trees and shrubs which belong to the Cactus family, Cactaceae, and are natives of South America, Central America, the West Indies and Mexico. They have long slender branches and ovate or oblong leaves, 2-5 in. long, in the axils of which large spines are produced. The flowers are rotate (roundish), many-petaled and 1½ in. in diameter. They are yellow, white or red, and are followed by large, edible fruits.

These plants are often grown as stocks on which Epiphyllum and other Cacti are grafted. The name Pereskia commemorates Nicholas de Peiresc, a French botanist.

For a Warm Greenhouse. These plants require a minimum winter temperature of 55 degrees and a soil compost of equal parts of loam, peat and sand. When grown as specimens, they are planted in large pots or set in a prepared border and the shoots tied to stakes or wires. The pots are well drained with crocks, and these are covered with coarse leaves.

To prepare the bed for planting, a hole 2 ft. square is taken out, 6 in. of drainage is placed in the bottom, and covered with leaves or grass sod turned upside down. Sufficient soil is then placed in the pot or bed and the plant is put in position. Then the remainder of the soil is added and made firm.

Once potted in a large pot or set in a bed, the plants need not be disturbed for many years. An occasional top-dressing of new soil is sufficient to keep them healthy.

After planting, the soil should not be watered until it becomes quite dry, and then it must be thoroughly soaked. During the summer the soil is kept moist, but throughout the winter it is maintained on the dry side, sufficient water only being given to prevent the leaves from shriveling.

When to Take Cuttings. Small side branches

are taken off in spring, the lower leaves removed and a cut made below the bottom joint. The branches are inserted in pots of sandy soil and placed in the greenhouse until roots are formed. No water is given until the soil becomes moderately dry and then it is thoroughly soaked. This method of watering is continued until roots are formed, when the cuttings are potted separately in 3-in. pots, and later in 5-in. pots from which they are placed in large pots or in a prepared bed of soil in the greenhouse.

If required as stocks for grafting, the central shoots are tied to stakes as soon as the plants are potted in 3-in. pots, and all side shoots are cut off. When 12 in. or taller, if required, shoots of Epiphyllum or other Cacti are grafted on them (see Cacti).

Outdoor Culture in Warm Regions. In warm climates such as that of southern California, Arizona and Florida, Pereskias can be grown outdoors in well-drained soils and sunny locations.

The chief kinds are P. aculeata, the Barbados Gooseberry or Lemon Vine, with stems to 30 ft. long, and white, yellow or pinkish flowers (this is the kind chiefly used as a stock for grafting); P. aculeata variety Godseffiana, with leaves variegated with yellow, red and green; P. Bleo, tree to 20 ft. tall, flowers pink; P. grandifolia, 15 ft., rose or white with sepals green; P. lychnidiflora, 4 ft., flowers apricot-yellow; P. tampicana, shrub, flowers white or pink.

PERESKIOPSIS (Pereskiop'sis). A group of shrubby or treelike Cacti that differ from most Cacti in that they produce true leaves. In general appearance the plants resemble Pereskia; their flowers are similar to those of Opuntia. Pereskiopsis belongs to the Cactus family, Cactaceae. The name is derived from Pereskia, a genus of Cacti, and *opsis*, which means like. They are natives of Mexico and Guatemala.

Pereskiopsis require the same treatment as Pereskia, which see. See also Cacti.

Kinds include P. Chapistle, 16 ft., flowers yellow; P. Gatesii, 4 ft., flowers deep rose; P. Porteri, 4 ft., flowers yellow; P. spathulata, 6 ft., flowers red; P. velutina, 4 ft., flowers bright yellow.

PEREZIA (Pere'zia). Perennial plants which belong to the Daisy family, Compositae. They

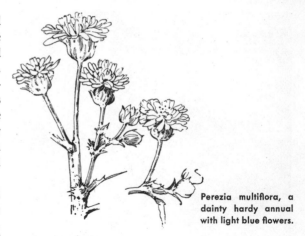
Perezia multiflora, a dainty hardy annual with light blue flowers.

are natives of South America and of North America, including the western and southwestern United States. The name Perezia commemorates Lazarus Perez, a sixteenth-century Spanish chemist.

These plants are not common in cultivation. The most familiar kind is Perezia multiflora, a native of Brazil, which reaches a height of 2-3 ft. and bears light blue, somewhat star-shaped, flowers in summer. It thrives in ordinary well-cultivated soil, in a sunny position in the garden, and is suitable for the border. It may be grown as an annual. The seedlings may be raised by sowing seeds in a pan of fine soil in a frame or greenhouse in March and planting the seedlings out of doors in May, 10-12 in. apart. Or the seeds may be sown out of doors in April, the seedlings being thinned out gradually until they are 10-12 in. from each other. Perezia viscosa, from Chile, bears purple flowers.

PERGOLA. Pergolas have been features of gardens from very ancient times. They were apparently common in Egyptian gardens, for in the tomb paintings grapes are depicted growing over pergolas, the latter consisting of painted wooden pillars. In ancient Roman gardens they were conspicuous features, and numerous pergolas are depicted in Pompeian frescoes.

In medieval and Tudor times in England, pergolas were called "herbers," and those constructed along a wall were called "wall-herbers." In the sixteenth century great attention was paid to walks, and shady alleys under herbers were popular. The thick-pleached alley where Antonio

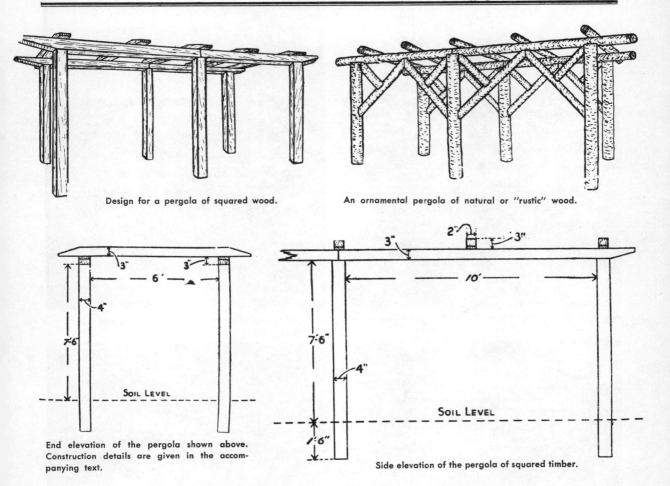

Design for a pergola of squared wood.

An ornamental pergola of natural or "rustic" wood.

End elevation of the pergola shown above. Construction details are given in the accompanying text.

Side elevation of the pergola of squared timber.

saw Don Pedro and Claudio walking (*Much Ado About Nothing*) was doubtless an herber of this type, and Bacon describes a similar type, "a covert alley upon carpenter's work about twelve feet in height, by which you may go in shade into the garden."

The "galleries" of Tudor times were in reality very substantial pergolas, and they were frequently enlarged at the corners into arbors. These galleries were often made leading to the church or the chapel. For instance, at Thornbury Castle, in Henry VIII's reign, there was a gallery "conveying both to the chapel and parish church." In Vriedeman de Vries' pictorial plans, pergolas are shown sometimes extending all around the garden. In those days wealthy folk liked to have "privy ways" whereby any part of the garden could be visited without inconvenience in bad weather.

Pergolas fell into disfavor during the supremacy of the early landscape school, for they condemned everything that was not natural. They came back into favor about the middle of the nineteenth century, and are now sometimes featured in even small gardens.

Where to Place a Pergola. A pergola adds charm to a garden if it is rightly placed. Unfortunately the pergolas in many gardens are wrongly placed; they are set up merely as a support for climbing plants and often detract from, rather than add to, the beauty of the scene. There should always be a good reason for putting up a pergola: it should lead somewhere—to a garden seat, an arbor or summerhouse, form a connecting link between two definite places in the garden. But to set it up in the middle of a plot of ground, without its serving any useful purpose, is entirely wrong.

A pergola built of milled lumber used to support Grape vines.

Climbing Roses decorate this rustic log pergola.

This elaborate pergola has masonry on one side and elaborate wooden supports on the other.

A short pergola built of stone provides a passageway between massive hedges of Hemlock.

A pergola built of squared posts set in short brick pillars, or in concrete, will last indefinitely and looks well. One built of brick pillars with crosspieces of squared oak is even more attractive but expensive to build. A cheaper way is to build the pillars of concrete; they look rather out of place at first but vigorous climbing plants soon veil them almost completely with leaf and flower.

Squared wood is to be preferred to rustic poles whether used for the uprights and crosspieces or both; but it costs more.

Whether squared wood or rustic poles are used for the uprights of a pergola, it is a good practice to embed them in cement or concrete and to continue the latter above the soil level, for it is at this point that decay of the posts sets in.

It is a simple matter to dig a hole about 18 in. deep, fill it with a mixture of half cement and half sand and embed the post in it; it is well worth while, for the wood will then remain sound indefinitely.

How to Make a Pergola. It is not difficult to construct a pergola, as the joints are easily made, and very little cutting is necessary if the wood is bought ready sawed to size. Two designs are shown, one of square wood and the other rustic. The instructions are applicable also to a rustic pergola of similar dimensions.

The uprights are 9 ft. high, 18 in. being below soil level and 7 ft. 6 in. above. They are made of wood 4 in. square; this should be well treated with a wood preservative for the bottom 24 in. before being set in the ground. The uprights should be placed 10 ft. apart, the path beneath

Perilla frutescens crispa.

ought to be 6 ft. wide. The side runners for each end section are cut from wood 4 in. by 3 in., and are 11 ft. 6 in. long, to allow for an overhang of 12 in. at the ends. For the middle sections the runners are 10 ft. 4 in. long, the joints coming in the middle of a side pillar as shown.

The crossbars on top are cut from wood 3 in. by 2 in., and are 8 ft. 8 in. long, giving an overhang of 12 in. at each side. The ends are cut to slope in a similar manner to the side runners, as shown in the diagram.

The rustic pergola has additional pieces at the sides, which may be omitted or varied as desired, and the sides may also be embellished by partly filling them in with trelliswork. Both pergolas shown are 20 ft. long, but any number of 10-ft. sections may be used.

Among long-lasting woods that are suitable for the construction of pergolas are redwood, cypress, oak and locust. If good pine posts are used and thoroughly creosoted at the base they will last a long time. The bottom may be charred in a bonfire as an alternative to tarring, or may be set in concrete—the best of all ways. All joints should be cut square. Cut nails should be used, as these give a stronger hold than wire nails.

Favorite Plants for Pergolas. Some climbing plants are specially suitable for covering a pergola. Among them are Rambler Roses, Akebia quinata, Aristolochia, Clematis, Jasminum, Lonicera (Honeysuckle), Polygonum baldschuanicum, Vitis Coignetiae, Grape vines, and Wisteria.

PERIANTH. The botanical term for that part of a flower which surrounds the pistil and stamens; it generally consists of green sepals and colored petals.

PERILLA (Perill'a). Of this group of plants, which consists of a number of annuals, only one is seen in gardens. That is P. frutescens variety crispa, 2-3 ft. high, grown for the sake of its ornamental leaves, which are large and of dark-purplish coloring. This plant is a native of India and China, and belongs to the Mint family, Labiatae. Perilla is the Hindu name for the plant.

Perilla frutescens crispa (nankinensis) is used for setting in summer flower beds as a dot plant, or in beds which are devoted to plants valued for their colored leaves; it looks especially well as a contrast with various gray-leaved plants—for example, Cineraria maritima and Artemisia ludoviciana.

When to Sow Seeds. Plants are easily raised from seeds sown in a warm greenhouse, temperature 55-60 degrees, early in March. These are sown in a pot of sifted compost consisting of loam and leaf mold, with a scattering of sand. If the seeds are lightly covered with similar soil, and then with a piece of glass, and kept moist, they will soon germinate, and the seedlings grow quickly. Before they become crowded in the seed pot, the seedlings should be potted separately in 3-in. pots in a soil mixture similar to that used for raising the seedlings, except that it should be coarser.

When established in pots, the plants must be hardened off in a cold frame and planted out of doors after the weather is warm and settled. In warm, moist, summer weather, the plants grow very freely and may become so tall that they spoil the appearance of the flower bed unless the tops are pinched off. Seeds of Perilla may also be sown directly outdoors in spring; often self-sown seedlings appear near where plants were grown the previous year.

PERIPLOCA GRAECA—*Silk Vine* (Peri'ploca; Periplo'ca). A climbing shrub which is found wild in the Near East and belongs to the family Asclepiadaceae. The name is derived from *peri*, around, and *ploke*, twining.

A Quick-growing Climbing Plant. This vigorous vine is not often seen in gardens, though it has long been in cultivation. It grows to a height of 40 ft. but not in the North. Although hardy as far north as lower New England, it benefits from some winter protection there. It grows quickly and is attractive when its slender leafy shoots, which bear purplish-brown flowers in summer, are well developed.

Planting and Pruning. Periploca thrives in ordinary, well-tilled garden soil; if the ground is clayey, a hole 2 ft. or so deep and 2 ft. wide should be excavated and sand and good compost should be mixed with the soil before the hole is filled in. Planting should be done in early fall or spring. This climbing shrub forms a suitable covering for a trellis in the open garden or for a sheltered wall where winters are a little too severe

for it to succeed without some protection. Little pruning is required, but if it becomes necessary to cut back any shoots which are too vigorous, or which have grown beyond the support, this should be done in autumn or spring.

Layering and Taking Cuttings. Propagation is by layering the branches in August-September, or by cuttings, about 4 in. long, made from firm shoots in July or August and inserted in a cold frame. Except for a brief daily airing, the frame must be kept close for several weeks to assist the cuttings to form roots. In the following spring the rooted cuttings may be planted out of doors in a nursery border.

PERISTERIA — *Dove Orchid* (Perister'ia). Summer-flowering Orchids which are found wild in Central America. All have evergreen leaves and large pseudobulbs, from the base of which the erect or pendent flower spike is produced. The flowers are 2-3 in. across, fleshy and somewhat globular.

The name Peristeria is derived from *peristera*, a dove. This Orchid is so named from the resemblance of the flower column to a dove—this is particularly the case with P. elata, in which the ascending side lobes of the lip have the appearance of wings.

Orchids for a Hothouse. Peristeria enjoys abundant heat and a moist atmosphere when in full growth; a greenhouse in which the temperature is tropical in summer is needed for its cultivation. The fleshy roots and hard pseudobulbs are able to withstand dry conditions when dormant, so a minimum winter temperature of 60 degrees is high enough, and an occasional fall in temperature does no harm.

P. elata may be treated as a terrestrial Orchid and grown in a mixture of fibrous loam with a little sphagnum moss and finely broken crocks. If the loam is heavy, a little cut osmunda fiber should be added. Those kinds which have pendent flower spikes should be grown in a compost of half fibrous loam and half osmunda fiber.

When to Repot. The flower spikes are usually produced at the same time as the young growths; thus, if repotting is necessary, it should be done early in the year. P. elata is a vigorous plant and needs a large pot. P. aspersa and P. cerina, which have pendulous flower stems, should be grown in baskets or, if in pots, the compost should be raised above the rims of the pots.

When growth commences, shading becomes necessary, but the shading must be removed early in autumn. The plants need a good deal of water when in full growth, but very little in winter.

The chief kind is P. elata, the Holy Ghost Flower, from Panama. It has erect stems 4-5 ft. high. The fragrant flowers, which open in June or July, are cream-white, the base of the lip spotted with purple.

PERISTROPHE (Peri'strophe; Peristroph'e). Tender, herbaceous, winter-flowering plants from India, which belong to the Acanthus family, Acanthaceae. The only kind commonly cultivated, P. speciosa, grows 2-3 ft. in height and forms a bushy plant with smooth, green stems, clothed with entire (undivided) ovate leaves, 2 in. in length.

The flowers, which open in winter and early spring, are in small clusters on the ends of the branches. They have long, slender tubes and spread out at the tips into two large petals, which are violet-purple. The name Peristrophe is derived from *peri,* around, and *strophos,* belt, and refers to the involucre (belt of leaves around the inflorescence).

A Winter-flowering Plant for a Warm Greenhouse. This plant requires a minimum winter temperature of 55 degrees and a soil compost of two parts loam and equal parts of well-decayed

Peristrophe speciosa, a winter-flowering plant for the warm greenhouse, with flowers of violet-purple.

manure and leaf mold or peat moss with a free sprinkling of sand. The best results are obtained by raising young plants annually.

For this purpose, shoots 3 in. in length are taken off in March-May. The leaves from the lower half of the stems are removed and a cut is made below the bottom joint to prepare the shoots as cuttings.

Inserting the Cuttings. The cuttings should be inserted in a bed of sand or vermiculite in a propagating case in the greenhouse. By keeping the case close, a moist atmosphere is maintained and the leaves are prevented from wilting. To prevent the decay of the shoots, however, the top of the case is raised for a few minutes each morning and the surplus moisture is wiped from the underside of the glass.

When roots are formed, more air is admitted each day, and at the end of a week the cuttings are exposed to maximum ventilation for a few days to inure them to the atmosphere of the house before disturbing the roots.

The plants are then potted singly in 3-in. pots and, when well rooted in these, are potted in 5-in. and later on in 7-8-in. pots in which they will bloom.

Pinching the Shoots. To obtain bushy plants, the tips of the main shoots are removed and the subsequent side branches are treated similarly. Until they become well rooted, the plants are watered sparingly, but when they are established the soil is kept moist until the flowers have faded. When well rooted in the final pots, they are placed in a well-lighted position and dilute liquid fertilizer is applied to the soil once a week.

After the final potting the plants may be kept in the greenhouse or be plunged to the rims of their pots in a sand or ash bed in a sunny place outdoors. If the latter plan is followed, they must be brought indoors before frost.

Winter Management. During the winter less water is required, but the soil must not be allowed to become dry until the flowers have faded. To rest them, or give them a period of comparative inactivity of growth, as is necessary for many kinds of plants, place them in a cooler house and keep the soil on the dry side until time for taking cuttings. The shoots are slightly shortened and frequently syringed until they break into new growth; then the soil is saturated and, when the side shoots are long enough, the cuttings are taken.

If desired, large plants can be obtained by potting one-year-old plants in 10-in. pots and growing them in the manner described.

The chief kind is P. speciosa, violet-purple (sometimes grown in gardens as Justicia speciosa).

PERIWINKLE. See Vinca.

PERLITE. This light-weight inorganic material is used as a propagating medium and also as an ingredient in some planter mixes and soil composts. Perlite is prepared from a volcanic lava by crushing and then subjecting it to great heat. The heat causes the rock particles to expand so that after treatment each contains a labyrinth of air spaces. Perlite weighs about 7½ lbs. per cubic foot.

PERMANGANATE OF POTASH. This chemical, also known as potassium permanganate, consists of dark-purple, rhombic prisms which appear red by transmitted light. They dissolve readily in water, forming a rich, purple solution.

In the garden, potassium permanganate is sometimes used for disinfecting soils and for eradicating spores of disease and fungi on plants. A pinch of crystals is stirred into a gallon of water or one ounce is dissolved in 6 gallons of water; this is enough to make a rich solution which is not harmful to plants. To disinfect soil before crops are sown or planted, soak it thoroughly with the solution and let it stand for a week or so.

It is only moderately effective in this respect and in recent years it has given place to other and more efficient fungicides. Potassium permanganate, either alone or mixed with sand or grit, can be sprinkled around plants to keep off slugs. Watering the lawn with a solution of permanganate of potash will bring worms to the surface. To eradicate worms from pot plants, stand the pot to the brim for an hour in a pail of the solution.

PERNETTYA MUCRONATA (Pernett'ya). An evergreen shrub of dense habit, 2-5 ft. high, bearing small, leathery, dark green leaves, attractive white flowers in May, and showy berries of

Fruiting branches of the evergreen Pernettya mucronata, an interesting shrub for peaty soils. The berries range in color from white to deep purple and crimson.

various shades of red, lilac, purple or white. The berries ripen in early autumn and remain on the plants all winter unless they are injured by severe frost.

A Beautiful Berried Shrub. The shrub is common in the extreme south of South America and is one of the hardiest shrubs from the region about the Strait of Magellan; however, it is not reliably hardy outdoors north of Philadelphia. It belongs to the Heath family, Ericaceae, and was named in honor of A. J. Pernetty, who accompanied Bougainville in his South American travels and wrote a book on a voyage to the Falkland Islands.

Pernettya mucronata may be increased by means of seeds, cuttings, division and layers. Selected varieties must be propagated by cuttings, layers or division.

Taking Cuttings. Cuttings of short shoots may be taken in July and inserted in sandy peat beneath a bell jar or in a cold frame. Plants may be divided in early autumn or spring and branches can be pegged down into sandy soil in spring.

Thrive Best in Peaty Soil. These plants require moist, peaty soil, or, if planted in loam, then peat or leaf mold should be added to the soil at planting time. As a rule, very little pruning is necessary, but if the plants are loose in habit they may be cut back in spring. P. mucronata fruits more abundantly in a sunny position than when planted in shade.

Of selected varieties the following are all at-tractive (the description refers to the color of the berries): coccinea, bright red; lilacina, lilac; purpurea, purple; alba, white; atrococcinea, deep reddish-purple; speciosa, crimson; Bell's Seed-ling, crimson, very large berries.

PEROVSKIA ATRIPLICIFOLIA — *Azure Sage* (Perovs'kia). This is a leaf-losing, sub-shrubby plant suitable alike for the perennial border and shrubbery, or for massing under semiwild conditions. It is a native of the Himala-yas and is widely distributed in Afghanistan and Baluchistan. Growing 3-4 ft. high, it forms a wide, spreading bush. The stems are covered by dense grayish down and the leaves also are downy. The coarsely-toothed gray-green leaves are 1-2 in. long and up to 1 in. wide. The long-branched inflorescences of violet-blue flowers are produced from the ends of the shoots in August and September; though the individual flowers are small, collectively they are very attractive, more particularly as all the stalks are white by reason of a dense felt of hairs.

Planting, Propagation and Pruning. Propaga-tion is usually by short side shoots inserted in sandy soil in a frame in July. They should be planted in a sunny position in well-drained

Fruits of Avocado, Persea americana.

loamy soil; the old flower heads should be trimmed off in autumn.

The name Azure Sage refers to the color of the flowers and the sagelike odor of the bruised leaves. Perovskia belongs to the Mint family,

Labiatae, and the name commemorates V. A. Perovski, a Russian official.

PERSEA (Pers'ea). Small evergreen trees that belong in the Laurel family, Lauraceae; one, the Avocado, is cultivated for its delicious, edible fruits. The name is an old Greek one by Theo-phrastus for an Egyptian tree and later used in its present sense. Most Perseas are natives of South and Central America but the genus is also represented naturally in the Canary Islands and in southeast Asia. P. Borbonia, the Red Bay or

A young Avocado grown in a pot as a house plant.

Bull Bay, is a native of the United States from Delaware to Florida and is sometimes planted for ornament. P. palustris, the Swamp Red Bay, oc-curs as a native from North Carolina to Florida and Texas.

The ornamental species of Persea require no special culture; they grow readily in a variety of soils. They may be propagated by seeds, cuttings and by layering.

Culture of the Avocado. The cultivation of the Avocado, Persea americana, is confined to the warmest parts of the United States such as

When Avocado seeds are planted to produce house plants they should be about half covered with soil. This one has just germinated. The young stem is seen emerging from the seed.

southern Florida, southern California and to the Rio Grande Valley of Texas. The degree of sensitiveness to cold varies considerably according to variety. Trees belonging to the West Indian race of Avocados are most tender—they are injured if the temperature drops to 27 degrees and are killed if it drops to 24 degrees. Guatemalan varieties are not killed unless the temperature drops to 21 degrees, and certain Mexican varieties can stand temperature as low as 18 degrees F.

The soil requirements of this tree are not exacting. It flourishes in muck soils and also in sandy and limestone soils. Good drainage it must have. The trees will not prosper if the soil is wet or waterlogged. They are sensitive even to temporary flooding of the soil and will succumb to as little as two days of this.

In exposed places Avocado trees should be sheltered from sweeping winds by a shelter belt or windbreak of other trees.

Planting. The best time to plant Avocados is during spring, although they can be successfully set out at other times if precautions are taken to ensure their speedy establishment, such as regularly watering them during dry weather, shading them against strong summer sunshine and protecting them against winter cold.

The distances between trees should depend upon the variety of the Avocado and the type of soil. Somewhat wider spacing should be allowed

on rich soils than on poor soils. A distance of 25-35 ft. between trees is about right.

Interplanting to Ensure Fruiting. Although the flowers of Avocados contain both functioning male and female elements, they are not ordinarily self-pollinating because the stigma (female part) of each flower matures before the stamens (male organs) of the same flower produce their pollen, and the stigma ceases to be receptive before the pollen is ripe. Furthermore, because the condition of stigma and pollen is the same for all trees of each variety at any one time, all the trees of a variety are either functioning as fertile males or fertile females at one time but not as both at the same time.

To ensure satisfactory pollination and fertilization, which alone can result in good fruit crops, it is usually necessary to avoid planting solid blocks of the same variety, but, instead, to interplant varieties that pollinate each other satisfactorily. Consult the Agricultural Experiment Station of the state where the planting is to be done for recommendations regarding this important matter. Many excellent named varieties are available.

Cultural Care. Newly set-out trees should be kept well watered and should be shaded at first against strong sunshine. Avocados are heavy feeders and respond well to generous fertilization either with animal manures or fertilizers. Keeping the soil about the trees covered with an organic mulch is a most excellent practice. Care must be taken that excessive use of nitrogenous fertilizer does not result in too much vegetative growth at the expense of fruit production.

Fruit is not usually borne by seedling trees until they are 5-7 years old, but trees propagated by budding and grafting will fruit much sooner. Most trees tend to bear heavier crops every two years than they do in the alternate seasons. When the fruits of Avocados are picked, the stem of the fruit should always be taken with each fruit.

Propagation. Avocados are often propagated by seeds, but because this method produces great variation in the quantity and quality of fruit and the time of fruiting of individual trees, it is better to bud or graft scions from a tree having the qualities desired, on to seedling understocks. Budding and grafting are usually performed in midwinter, December and January being favored months.

As House Plants. Young Avocado plants are interesting and attractive when grown in pots in the house. They are easily raised from seeds. All that is necessary is to remove the single large seed from the center of an Avocado fruit and plant it, either vertically with its pointed end up or horizontally, in a well-drained 4 in. or 5 in. pot containing a porous fertile soil. The top of the seed may just show above the soil surface. In a temperature of 60-70 degrees or thereabouts, if the soil is kept moderately moist but not constantly saturated, growth soon begins and a decorative, leafy plant develops that under favorable conditions will be attractive for several years.

Avocado plants grown in pots indoors prosper in sun or in good light without direct sun but not in poorly lighted locations. When they have filled their containers with healthy roots they should be potted on into larger ones. Potting, for preference, should be done in spring. At other times of the year well-rooted specimens benefit from being given dilute liquid fertilizer every week or two. Watering should be done at intervals that assure that the soil will never become really dry nor remain for long periods in a soggy, waterlogged condition.

After a few years pot-grown Avocado plants frequently develop a condition which causes the leaves to be spotted and blotched and to develop a general unhealthy appearance. It is scarcely worthwhile attempting to nurse such specimens back to health. It is easier and simpler to raise new plants from seeds.

Avocado seeds may also be started into growth in water but unless the young plants are transferred to soil within a few weeks or months they deteriorate. To start a seed in water, stand it, pointed end up, with its base in the neck of a jar containing water and, if possible, a few pieces of charcoal. The water should just touch the bottom of the seed and should be kept at that level by replenishment when necessary. If the neck of the jar is so big that the seed slips into the container this may be prevented by sticking three stout toothpicks or similar slivers of wood horizontally into the sides of the seeds and resting these on the rim of the jar.

PERSIAN CANDYTUFT. Aethionema, which see.

PERSIAN LILAC. Syringa persica, which see.

PERSICIFOLIA. A botanical term used in describing plants with leaves which resemble those of the Peach. A familiar example is the Peach-leaved Bellflower, Campanula persicifolia.

PERSIMMON. Persimmons consist of two species of importance. The first is the American Persimmon, Diospyros virginiana, which is native from southeastern New York and Connecticut, southward to Florida and westward to Kansas and Texas; the second is the Oriental or Japanese Persimmon, Diospyros Kaki, a native of China and Korea.

The Common Persimmon or native American Persimmon is a fine fruit that in its best forms is well worth growing as a home-garden fruit as far north as the southern shores of the Great Lakes.

This handsome tree grows up to 50 ft. in height and has lustrous, large, dark green leaves. The greenish-yellow urn-shaped flowers are inconspicuous, with the male and female flowers borne on separate trees. The fruits vary in size, with the largest about 2 in. in diameter, yellow or orange in color with a reddish cheek. Large seeds are embedded in the soft flesh. The fruits in different varieties ripen from early September until January. The flesh is very astringent until fully ripe, when it becomes sweet and rich in the best varieties.

A number of varieties have been introduced from time to time but only a few are available from nurseries. Garrettson, Early Golden, Kansas and Killen are among the best in quality. Others are Josephine, Hicks, Lambert, Miller and Ruby. These varieties will ripen at Geneva, New York, in most seasons. Frost is not necessary to ripen Persimmons; in fact, a hard frost before the fruits are ripe will ruin them. They are not injured by freezing when fully ripe.

American Persimmons are propagated by root cuttings, hardwood cuttings of 2- or 3-year-old wood, and by budding or grafting on seedling rootstocks. Cleft grafting (which see) and complete waxing of the scion offer a simple, satisfactory method for the amateur.

The seeds require stratification if they are to be kept until spring for planting, but they may be planted in the fall, immediately after harvesting, and mulched with leaves or sawdust.

Persimmons are not particular as to soils, provided they are well drained, and they respond to the same care given to most other woody plants. Nitrogen fertilization, weed control and light, corrective pruning are the principal cultural requirements. The trees should be set in their permanent location while young, as the long taproot makes transplanting difficult.

The Japanese or Oriental Persimmon is a tree for the Cotton Belt. It is grown commercially in California and Florida, and occasionally elsewhere northward as far as Washington, D. C., although it may experience winterkilling there during severe winters. As the fruit becomes better known, the culture of this tree is increasing. Its freedom from serious diseases and insect pests, its handsome, glossy foliage and large, brilliantly colored fruits make the Japanese Persimmon an excellent home-garden fruit.

Japanese Persimmons fall into three groups, according to their flower types:

Group I varieties produce only pistillate (female) flowers, and these varieties are called pistillate constants. Hachiya, Tanenashi and Tamopan, important commercial varieties, are in this group. They commonly bear seedless fruits without pollination.

Group II varieties bear both staminate (male) and pistillate flowers regularly and are called staminate constants.

Group III varieties bear pistillate flowers and occasionally staminate flowers, and this group is known as staminate sporadics.

Varieties are divided into two groups according to their flesh color. In the group called pollination constants, the varieties are light-fleshed, whether seedless or seedy. The varieties are Hachiya, Tanenashi, Tamopan, Fuyu, Costata, Triumph and Tsuru.

In the other group—pollination variants—the fruit is light-fleshed when seedless, dark-fleshed when seedy. These varieties are Gailey, Godbey, Hyakume, Okame, Yeman, Yeddo, Ichi, Zingi, Taber 23 and Taber 129. Gailey is a profuse pollen producer and is used principally for interplanting with varieties requiring cross-pollination.

The Japanese or Oriental Persimmon is commonly grown on Common Persimmon rootstocks in the South and to some extent in California. Oriental Persimmon seedlings and seedlings of Diospyros Lotus, another Asiatic Persimmon, are also used as rootstocks in California. Grafting in early spring and budding in late summer are both practiced in the nursery, but grafting is more successful. Native Common Persimmon trees may be top-worked to the Oriental varieties successfully by cleft grafting.

Oriental Persimmons do well on reasonably fertile, well-drained soils and are sometimes grown on rather poor soils, where the Common Persimmon is found.

One-year-old trees are preferable to the 2-year trees, as the latter have a long tap root that makes digging difficult. Trees are planted about 20 ft. apart each way. The planting may be done at any time during the dormant season.

Care of the Oriental trees is similar to the care given to other fruit trees: namely, weed control by tillage or mulching, and the application of commercial fertilizers as needed. Pruning should be very light, as the trees do not make very dense tops. Dead branches and any that are crowding main branches should be removed as necessary.

PERUVIAN DAFFODIL. Hymenocallis calathina, which see.

PERUVIAN LILY. See Alstroemeria.

PERUVIAN MASTIC TREE. See Schinus.

PESTS AND DISEASES. See page 2492.

PETAL. One of the floral leaves which combine to form the perianth of a flower.

PETALOID. A botanical term meaning petal-like.

PETALOSTEMUM—*Prairie Clover* (Petalostem'um). A group of mostly perennial herbaceous plants and subshrubs that are natives of North America and are sometimes grown in wild gardens, flower borders and rock gardens. They belong to the Pea family, Leguminosae. The name comes from *petalon,* petal, and *stemon,* stamen.

These plants thrive in sunny positions in thoroughly drained soils. They are propagated by seeds sown as soon as ripe or in spring, or by division in early spring.

The chief kinds include: P. candidum, 1-2 ft., white; P. oligophyllum, 2-2½ ft. tall, white; P. purpureum, 2-3 ft., violet or purple; P. villosum, 2 ft., rose-purple or white.

PETASITES—*Butterbur* (Petasi'tes). Hardy perennials which are found wild in various parts of Europe, Asia and North America. With few exceptions they have little or no garden value. They belong to the Daisy family, Compositae. The name is derived from *petasos,* an umbrella, because of the large leaves of some kinds.

The white, sweet-scented Winter Heliotrope, Petasites fragrans.

With Fragrant Flowers. Petasites fragrans, called Winter Heliotrope, is the chief kind to be recommended for planting in gardens, and even this is suitable only for informal, semiwild areas, for it may spread and become a troublesome weed. It thrives in ordinary soil, grows 6-8 in. high and bears fragrant, white flowers in late winter or early spring. Pieces may be dug up and replanted in October. Plants grown in pots for winter bloom are welcome for their fragrance.

The Japanese Butterbur, Petasites japonicus, grows to 6 ft. tall and is sometimes planted in moist soil.

PETIOLE. A botanical term used in describing the stalk of a leaf.

PETREA—*Purple Wreath* (Petre'a). Tender climbing plants with ornamental flowers. They are natives of tropical America, and belong to the Verbena family, Verbenaceae. These beautiful twining plants have opposite, elliptic (oval), leathery leaves, and bear long pendent racemes of attractive flowers, each of which is composed of a star-shaped lilac calyx surrounding the violet or purplish five-petaled corolla. The name Petrea commemorates Robert James, Lord Petre, a patron of botany in the early eighteenth century.

Petrea volubilis is a commonly planted vine in the lower South where there is no danger of frost. It is also a good vine for the greenhouse. When grown in greenhouses, Petreas require a minimum winter temperature of 55 degrees and a compost of equal parts of loam, peat and leaf mold, with sand freely added. These plants do not flower in a small state and are therefore grown in large tubs or pots, or are planted out in a bed in the hothouse.

Cultivation. The pots or tubs are prepared by draining them with crocks, over which a layer of the rough siftings from the soil compost is placed. Enough of the compost is then put in so that when the plant is set in position the top of the ball of soil is 2 in. below the rim of the vessel. The plant is knocked out of the pot, the crocks and loose soil are removed from the roots, and the plant is set in the pot or tub with the roots well spread out. The remainder of the compost is then added and made firm.

To prepare a bed of soil in the greenhouse, a hole 30 in. in depth is taken out, and a 9-in. layer of broken bricks placed in the bottom. These are covered with rough siftings from the compost and the remainder of the space is filled with the prepared soil. A few days are allowed for the soil to settle.

A hole is then taken out large enough to allow the roots to be spread out and deep enough for the uppermost roots to be covered with an inch of soil; the plant is set in position and the soil made firm. Wires are fixed to the wall or roof of the greenhouse to support the twining shoots. Plants growing in pots can also be trained in this way, or to a tripod of stakes or a balloon-shaped structure made of wire, fixed in the pots or tubs.

Watering. After potting or planting, the soil is not watered until it becomes moderately dry, but the atmosphere is kept moist and the foliage frequently syringed to assist root action.

When the plants are well rooted the soil is kept moist during the summer. As autumn approaches less water is needed.

Pruning, which is done in February, consists of thinning out weakly shoots and slightly shortening the side branches.

Propagation Is by Cuttings. Shoots 2 in. in length are taken off the plant and prepared by removing the leaves from the lower half of the stem and making a cut just below the bottom joint. The cuttings are inserted in well-packed sand or sand and peat moss in a propagating case or under a bell jar. Every morning the inside of the glass must be wiped dry. This treatment is continued until roots are formed, when the bell jar is removed.

After a few days have been allowed for the shoots to harden and become acclimatized to the atmosphere of the greenhouse, the plants are potted singly in 3-in. pots. When well rooted in these, they are transferred to 5-in. pots.

The chief kinds are P. racemosa, 12 ft., purple; P. volubilis, 20 ft., violet or lilac; P. arborea, 12 ft., violet; and P. Kohautiana, 30 ft., lilac-blue to purple. All bloom in midsummer.

PETROCALLIS PYRENAICA (Petrocal'lis). This plant from the European Alps is closely related to Draba, and was previously included in that genus. The name is from *petros*, rock, and *callis*, beauty.

This beautiful little plant delights in full sun, in well-drained, stony soil, moraine or scree, surfaced with limestone chips. It forms a dense cushion, as much as 12 in. across in a good specimen, the downy shoots furnished with tiny, wedge-shaped leaves, and producing small white, lilac-tinted, fragrant flowers on 2-3 in. stems in April–May. Cuttings of small pieces of growths can be rooted in sand in a frame in late summer.

PETROCOPTIS (Petrocop'tis). A small genus of alpine plants from the Pyrenees. They are closely related to the genus Lychnis, in which they were previously included. They belong to the Pink family, Caryophyllaceae.

For the Rock Garden. P. Lagascae, a native of the Pyrenees, is an old and deservedly popular rock plant. It is tufted, branched and wiry, with rather glaucous leaves and numerous bright, rose-pink flowers, each about ½ in. in diameter. The height of the plant, which is perennial, is 3-4 in. It should be grown on sunny slopes of light soil in the rock garden, where it flowers profusely in late summer, at which time of year there is otherwise rather a lack of bright alpines.

P. pyrenaica is superior to it, having rather larger flowers of a more pleasing color. It requires the same treatment as P. Lagascae, both as to soil and situation in the garden.

These plants are seldom long-lived, but are easily raised from seed sown in pots of sandy soil in a frame or greenhouse in spring, the seedlings being grown on in small pots for planting out the following spring.

PETROCOSMEA NERVOSA (Petrocos'mea). A rare alpine plant from Yunnan, requiring treatment similar to that given Ramonda, but perhaps safest with the protection of an alpine house or frame. It belongs to the family Gesneriaceae, and the name is from *petros*, rock, and *kosmos*, ornament.

This choice plant is a perennial, with obovate or rounded leaves about 2 in. across, and blue, two-lipped flowers in loose cymes on stems 2-4 in. tall, the lower lips of the flowers being deeply 3-lobed. It can be raised from seed or by careful division in early spring.

PETROPHYTUM (Petro'phytum; Petrophy'tum). Hardy, low-growing, evergreen shrublets that are natives of North America and are suitable for cultivation in rock gardens. They belong to the Rose family, Rosaceae. The name is derived from *petros*, rock, and *phyton*, plant, and refers to the fact that these plants naturally inhabit rocky places.

These plants are propagated by seeds sown in fall or early spring and by careful division in spring. They need a gritty, well-drained soil and a sunny situation. It is an advantage if the soil contains a good proportion of crushed limestone.

Kinds include P. caespitosum (Spiraea caespitosa), which forms mats to 3 ft. across and has white flowers, and P. Hendersonii (Spiraea Hendersonii), a somewhat less hardy, mat-forming kind, also with white flowers.

PETROSELINUM (Petroseli'num). A genus of annual and biennial herbs, family

[8—12a]
Phlox paniculata variety

[8—12]
Pereskia grandiflora

[8—12b]
Phlox Drummondii

[8—12c]
Picea pungens, narrow variety

Collection of Philodendrons

Umbelliferae, of horticultural importance on account of one species, Petroselinum crispum, the Parsley, which see for details of cultivation.

PETUNIA (Petu'nia). Tender perennial plants, natives of South America, belonging to the Nightshade family, Solanaceae. The word is derived from *Petun,* a local name for tobacco or Nicotiana, to which Petunia is related, for the Tobacco Plant also belongs to the family Solanaceae.

Petunias are exceptionally showy flowers, useful alike for the summer flower beds and for cultivation in pots in the greenhouse, or in window boxes. The modern varieties are of two types, one having large, double or single blooms which exhibit a remarkable range of coloring; the other small-flowered and compact and bearing large numbers of flowers.

Sun-loving Plants. Petunias are essentially sun-loving plants and are useless in heavy shade. There they will grow, but they will not bloom satisfactorily. They thrive much better in well-drained, rather light soil than in clayey ground, for they like warmth. Petunias are admirable

Bedding Petunias are almost indispensable annuals. They prefer full sun but can stand a little shade. The beginner should buy plants, for seeds must be started in heat in late winter, and transplanting requires skill.

Single-flowered Petunias may be had in a variety of colors. They bloom freely throughout the summer.

plants for cultivation and display in window boxes.

Although Petunias are tender perennial plants, they are generally treated as annuals, and raised from seeds sown under glass in spring. Double varieties do not come perfectly true, but a good proportion of them will bear double flowers, and those which are single will yield large and showy blooms.

The improvement in the colors of Petunia is very marked in the modern varieties. The flowers of some varieties are attractively fringed, others are striped with colors which contrast with the ground color.

Raising Plants from Seed. To provide plants which will be large enough to plant out of doors in the flower beds and borders when danger of frost has passed, seeds are sown under glass towards the end of February or early in March. Flats or flower pans should be filled with finely sifted seed soil (a mixture of loam, peat moss or leaf mold and sand is satisfactory). The seeds are sown thinly and covered with merely a sprinkling of the sifted compost. A piece of glass is placed over the seed pan or flat, and brown paper set on the glass provides the necessary shade.

The seedlings should be raised in a tempera-

ture of 55-60 degrees. It is necessary to keep the soil always moist, but it must not be overwatered or the seedlings will damp off very quickly.

As soon as the seedlings are 1 in. or so high—large enough to be handled conveniently—they should be transplanted 2-3 in. apart in flats or potted separately in 3-in. pots filled with the same kind of soil as used for the seeds, but passed through a sieve with a larger mesh.

Save the Smallest Seedlings. In transplanting seedlings there is always a temptation to select the largest and finest and, if there are more than are wanted, to destroy the smaller, weaker ones. If this is done when dealing with seedlings raised from seeds of double-flowered Petunias it may be found that most of them will produce single blooms. The largest percentage of double flowers is produced by the smallest seedlings.

As a matter of fact, this detail is of less importance in the cultivation of Petunias for planting out of doors than of those to be grown in pots under glass, for the single-flowered varieties are generally to be preferred for filling beds and borders, the double ones for the greenhouse and window garden. Nevertheless, the smallest seedlings, even of single Petunias, are said to often bear the most brilliantly colored blooms, so they should not be discarded in favor of the large, vigorous ones.

Double-flowered Petunias are very handsome. They do not stand wet weather as well as the single-flowered varieties.

As soon as the seedlings have become well rooted in the pots of soil to which they were moved, they should be placed in a cold frame, provided the weather is mild. There they will remain until planting-out time.

Growing Petunias in Pots. Petunias intended to be grown in flowerpots for greenhouse, terrace or window decoration during the summer months are raised from seeds sown in a warm greenhouse during February. When the seedlings are large enough to be moved, they are potted separately in 3-in. pots in a compost of half loam and half leaf mold with a free scattering of sand.

As the seedlings make progress, they must be grown in a lower temperature—50 degrees at night is high enough. If kept moist and warm, they will be weakly and will develop into ungainly plants. Repotting must be done as it becomes necessary; as soon as roots in quantity reach the sides of the small pots the plant must be repotted, preferably in 7-in. pots, in which they will grow into splendid specimens.

For the final potting a compost consisting of half loam and half leaf mold and thoroughly decayed manure should be used, scatterings of sand and of bone meal being added. The pots must be well drained. Again, watering must be done with care until the plants are well rooted in the larger pots. Later on, when the plants are coming into bloom, occasional applications of weak liquid fertilizer will be beneficial.

Propagating Petunias by Cuttings. Choice varieties of Petunias, such as particularly good double varieties, may be propagated by means of cuttings taken in August and inserted in a cold frame or under a bell jar outdoors. If this is kept close and shaded for a few weeks, the cuttings will soon root. When well rooted, the cuttings must be potted separately in small pots, in which they will pass the winter. Before cold weather sets in, the Petunias must be placed in a greenhouse or brought into a sunny window in a cool room having a minimum temperature of 50 degrees.

In February, when the plants begin to make fresh growth, they are repotted in 5-in. pots in the compost advised for pot plants grown from seeds. Later on, they will need to be repotted once more, this time in 7-in. or 8-in. pots, in which they may be left until they flower.

By pinching out the tips of the shoots occasionally in spring and early summer, large, well-branched plants are obtained which will yield a profusion of bloom. If a further stock of plants is needed, it can be obtained in spring by taking off the tops of the cuttings rooted in autumn and rooting them beneath a bell jar or in a propagating case in the greenhouse.

Petunias in Window Boxes. Petunias used for the decoration of window boxes should be planted there about the time it is safe to plant tomatoes outdoors. Either double- or single-flowered varieties may be used for this purpose.

Seeds of Petunias are sold in mixture as well as in separate colors, and many fine named varieties that come reasonably true to type and color are offered.

Seedsmen offer magnificent strains of both large- and small-flowered Petunias. The latter are especially valuable for summer bedding and window boxes, particularly the dwarf compact types in white, purple, mauve, pink, salmon, scarlet, violet and rose.

PEYOTE. See Lophophora.

pH. See Soil Testing.

PHACELIA (Phace'lia). A group or genus of hardy annuals and perennials, comparatively few of which are grown in gardens. They are natives of North and South America and belong to the family Hydrophyllaceae. The word Phacelia is derived from *phakelos,* a bundle or fascicle, and refers to the way in which the flowers are arranged.

The favorite kind is Phacelia campanularia, which is found wild in California. It is an annual, 9-10 in. in height, which bears bunches of rich blue, bell-shaped flowers in the summer. This is one of the loveliest of all hardy annuals, and especially well suited to cultivation in sunny gardens in which the soil is well-drained or light. It is not usually a success on heavy, ill-drained land, and there the germination of the seeds is often disappointing.

This plant needs a rather light soil, or, at any rate, one which is well drained and does not become sodden in rainy weather. It also requires the sunniest possible exposure. Unfortunately these annuals do not thrive in really hot weather;

The blue hardy annual Phacelia campanularia.

where really hot summers prevail they are best suited for late spring and early summer bloom only.

When to Sow. The seeds should be sown early in spring, and in the place where the plants are to bloom, for it is not advisable to transplant the seedlings. Moderately thick sowing is recommended, for the seeds sometimes do not germinate freely. The seedlings ought to be thinned out until they are 5-6 in. apart from each other to give them full room for development.

In regions of mild winters the seeds of Phacelia may be sown in early September; there may be losses among the seedlings in winter, but those that survive will develop into finer plants than others raised from seeds sown in spring.

A Good Bee Flower. Several other kinds are sometimes grown in gardens, though none of them is such a favorite as Phacelia campanularia. Phacelia viscida, which is perhaps better known as Eutoca viscida, reaches a height of 9 in. and bears flowers of vivid blue coloring. Bees are very fond of the blooms of this plant, and those who keep bees in the garden should certainly sow seeds of it every spring.

Other kinds are P. congesta, 12 in., with flowers of mauve-blue shade; P. divaricata, 12 in., violet-purple; P. tanacetifolia, 18-24 in., pale mauve or rose-mauve; and P. Whitlavia, erect, 6-12 in., with blue, bell-shaped flowers in many-flowered clusters. The last-named is commonly

listed under the name of Whitlavia grandiflora; a variety of it with blue flowers with white centers is called W. grandiflora gloxinoides or, more properly, Phacelia Whitlavia gloxinoides.

All of these are annuals which are usually raised by sowing seeds out of doors in spring where the plants are to bloom, the seedlings being thinned out, not transplanted; they may, however, be sown in a sunny, sheltered border late in August and early in September to provide plants which will come earlier into bloom than those sown in spring. If some of the seedlings raised in August are potted, they will prove useful for the decoration of the greenhouse during spring.

PHAEDRANASSA — *Queen Lily* (Phaedranass'a). Tender bulbous plants, from Costa Rica and Colombia, which belong to the Amaryllis family, Amaryllidaceae. They have large tunicated (scaly coated) bulbs, 2-3 in. in diameter, from which are produced bright green, lanceolate leaves, 12 in. in length. The flowers, which are in clusters on the ends of stout stalks, 12-24 in. long, are tubular, 1-2 in. long, scarlet with green tips. The name Phaedranassa is from the Greek *phaidros*, gay, and *anassa*, queen, and refers to the beauty of the flowers.

Bulbs for the Greenhouse. The cool greenhouse kinds require a minimum winter temperature of 45 degrees and the warm greenhouse kinds one of 55 degrees. The best potting compost consists of equal parts of loam and leaf mold with a scattering of sand. Repotting is done in February or March, or as soon as the plants show signs of making new growth. The bulbs, which are rested during the winter by keeping the soil dry, are then taken out of their pots, the crocks and all loose soil are removed from the roots. The new pots, well-drained with crocks, should be one size larger if the roots are in a healthy condition, or the same size as those from which the bulbs were removed, if the roots are much decayed. Potting is done firmly and the bulbs are buried to half their depth.

Summer and Winter Management. After potting, the bulbs are lightly syringed several times daily. No water is applied to the soil until it becomes moderately dry; it is then thoroughly moistened. This treatment is continued until roots have formed freely, and then the soil is kept moist during the summer.

After the flowers have withered, watering is continued until the leaves begin to turn yellow, when it is gradually discontinued. When the leaves have completely withered, the soil is kept quite dry, the pots being laid on their sides during the winter.

Propagation. The small bulbs which are found clustering around the parent bulbs are removed and potted in small pots. They are treated as advised for the larger bulbs and grown on until they reach flowering size.

The Chief Kinds. *For the warm greenhouse:* P. Carmiolii, red, tipped green; P. Lehmannii, scarlet. *For the cool greenhouse:* P. chloracra, purple and rose, tipped with green.

PHAEDRANTHUS (Phaedran'thus). The plant commonly grown as Bignonia buccinatoria is now classified as constituting a separate genus, under the name of Phaedranthus buccinatorius. It is a very showy evergreen climber from Mexico, which in summer produces terminal racemes of drooping trumpet-shaped flowers, rich blood-red, yellow at the base. It belongs to the family Bignoniaceae, and the name is derived from *phaidros,* gay, and *anthos,* flower, on account of the rich colorings of the flowers. Cultivation outdoors is restricted to the far South; it is also grown in warm greenhouses. It needs well-drained soil and a sunny position. Prune in the same way as Bignonia.

PHAENOCOMA (Phaenoco'ma). Tender evergreen flowering shrubs, from South Africa, which belong to the Daisy family, Compositae. The only kind in cultivation, P. prolifera, forms a branching shrub, 2 ft. high. The stems are clothed with small, stiff, closely set leaves, and the young shoots are tomentose (hairy). The flowers are solitary (borne singly on the ends of the stems), 1 in. in diameter, rosy-purple, and are surrounded by an involucre of crimson bracts; this adds very considerably to their attractiveness.

This plant is closely allied to the Helichrysum (Everlasting Flower), in which genus it is included by some botanists. The name is from *phaino,* to shine, and *kome,* hair, in reference to the hairs on the young stem.

Everlasting Flowers. When grown in a greenhouse these shrubs require a minimum winter temperature of 45 degrees and a soil compost of two parts peat, one part sand, and a sprinkling of crushed charcoal. Repotting is done in March. The shoots are first shortened to one half or one third, according to their vigor; when new side shoots commence to form, the plants are set in slightly larger pots. Crocks and all loose soil are removed from the roots before repotting.

After repotting, the soil is not watered until it becomes quite dry. This method of watering must be adhered to until the plants are well rooted, as a waterlogged condition is fatal. For the rest of the summer the compost should be kept moist; in autumn the water supply must be gradually lessened, and throughout the winter very little water is required, enough only being given to prevent the stems from shriveling. These plants do not require shading, and a light syringing once a day in summer is sufficient.

As the flowering shoots elongate, they must be fastened lightly to a central stake thrust into the center of the pot. When fully expanded, the flowers may be cut and dried and used in the winter as everlasting flowers.

In California and similar mild climates this shrub may be grown outdoors.

Propagation is by cuttings of side shoots 2 in. long, taken with a heel and inserted in a greenhouse propagating frame. When rooted, the cuttings are potted separately in 3-in. pots and subsequently in larger ones. To obtain bushy plants the tips of the main shoots are pinched off, and the resulting side branches are similarly treated.

Kinds. P. prolifera bears rosy-purple flowers. The variety Barnesii is more compact in growth and the flowers are larger and of deeper coloring.

PHAIO-CALANTHE. Orchids which have been raised by crossbreeding between Phaius and Calanthe.

PHAIUS or PHAJUS (Pha'ius), (Pha'jus). Orchids which are found wild in warm parts of Asia, Madagascar, Ceylon, Australia and the Philippines. Most of them are terrestrial; all have evergreen leaves and erect flower spikes, produced from or near the base of the pseudobulbs. The pseudobulbs are usually short, are cone-like, and set close together, but in a few they are cylindrical, tapered and placed at intervals on a creeping, often branched rhizome. In others the pseudobulbs are almost stemlike. Practically all bloom in early spring and summer, from February to June, and have large, handsome flowers.

Several beautiful hybrids have been obtained by crossing the best of the Asiatic kinds with the smaller but more brightly flowered kinds from Madagascar. Phaius, sometimes spelt Phajus, is by some authorities said to mean "shining," but is probably derived from the Greek *phaios,* dusky, on account of the dusky reddish-brown coloring of many of the flowers.

Orchids for a Hothouse. Most kinds, and particularly those from India, Burma and China, are not difficult to grow. The popular P. grandifolius, from India and Burma, may be taken as typical. A greenhouse with a tropical or semitropical temperature in summer is required, and in winter the temperature should not fall below 55 degrees.

The leaves often become shabby in the winter, but though water should be given infrequently then, it must not be entirely withheld. The hard-bulbed kinds—P. flavus, for example—require very little watering in winter. In summer, when growing freely, abundance of water may be given, provided the drainage is free. Water must not be allowed to remain on the leaves, hence great care must be exercised if syringing is done.

Summer and Winter Management. The compost should consist largely of loam fiber with sufficient osmunda fiber, sphagnum moss and fine crocks to admit of a free passage of water. As P. grandifolius and its near allies have large fleshy roots, they need large pots.

Repotting should be done early in the year, when fresh growth begins; a higher temperature, one of not less than 60 degrees, is then necessary. Generally, repotting is needed every second year. Shading is required during bright weather, but may be removed in early autumn, when exposure to full light should be given.

This treatment is suitable for P. Blumei assamicus, P. Wallichii, P. flavus and P. maculatus; but P. callosus, P. Sanderianus, P. philippinensis, P. Bernaysii, P. Cooperi and P. bicolor should have a minimum winter temperature of 60 degrees.

The kinds from Madagascar need a tropical temperature throughout the summer and a winter temperature of 65-70 degrees by night. They are more delicate than those from Asia and care must be taken to avoid drafts; they need a compost of two parts of osmunda fiber and two parts of sphagnum moss, and drainage must be free.

P. simulans is an epiphytal Orchid and does best on a piece of tree fern stem, or on an Orchid raft, with a little compost placed behind the plant. This and P. tuberculosus often give better results when grown beneath a bell jar.

P. Humboldtii, like the preceding, is very susceptible to attacks from thrips and dislikes being disturbed, hence the compost should be renovated from time to time; completely renew it only when necessary, and then in the early spring. The flowers usually open in May and early summer.

The most popular kind is P. Tankervilliae (grandifolius), the spikes of which reach a height of 3-4 ft.; the flowers are reddish-brown, shaded with yellow and rose, silvery behind; they generally open in February.

P. Wallichii has larger, more richly colored flowers and taller spikes than P. Tankervilliae, while P. Blumei variety Sanderianus, May-flowering, has spikes 8 ft. or more in height and dark red flowers. P. flavus and P. maculatus have smaller, yellow flowers.

Phaius Tankervilliae is an easy-to-grow Orchid of majestic appearance.

P. simulans and P. tuberculosus bear comparatively few flowers on a spike and resemble each other in floral coloring; they have light rose-colored sepals and petals and deeper rose lips. P. Humboldtii has a much deeper-colored crimson lip.

P. Bernaysii has tall spikes with large yellowish flowers which unfortunately do not always expand properly.

PHALAENOPSIS—*Moth Orchid* (Phalaenop'-sis). A most beautiful group of Orchids, which are found wild chiefly in the Philippines, Java, the Malay Archipelago, but also extending to Burma. All are epiphytal, with evergreen leaves.

Orchids for a Hothouse. Most kinds, and particularly those from India and Burma, have no pseudobulbs; the large leathery leaves are

Phalaenopsis Schilleriana, a native of the Philippines, is one of the loveliest of winter-flowering Orchids.

arranged on a short, thick stem, and the flower spikes are often long, arching, branched and many flowered. The flowers vary greatly; most of them are brightly colored. The name Phalaenopsis is derived from *phalaina,* moth, and *opsis,* like.

Beautiful Winter- and Spring-flowering Orchids. All these Orchids require a warm moist atmosphere free from drafts; a well-heated greenhouse is necessary. During winter the temperature should never be less than 65 degrees, and in summer tropical warmth must be maintained. Ventilation must be carefully regulated, for drafts are very harmful to these plants.

From spring to autumn the plants require liberal supplies of water. The floor, walls and benches must be kept damp, but the leaves must be syringed sparingly or they will be disfigured by spots. Shading is required early in the year. In early autumn, after September, the shading should be removed. The temperature throughout the summer should not fall below 70 degrees at night.

Winter Treatment. These Orchids need a moist atmosphere, even in the winter; the day temperature should be about 70 degrees, and on sunny days may rise higher. The compost must not be allowed to get really dry, but the plants should not be syringed.

They are most frequently in bloom in late autumn, winter and spring; many flower too freely, and it is wise to pinch out those flower spikes which appear after the first spikes are over.

Suitable Potting Compost. The compost should consist of two parts of osmunda fiber and two parts of sphagnum moss well mixed. Wooden Orchid cylinders or baskets are often used. Cylinders should be three parts filled with crocks or broken brick; baskets should have a thick layer of these materials.

As the roots cling to the wooden cylinders and baskets, and thus are liable to be broken when the plants have to be removed, some growers prefer to use flower pans; when repotting is necessary, these are easily broken and the pieces, with roots attached, can be placed in the new pans. Repotting should be carried out in late February or early March; often it is sufficient to remove some of the old compost and insert fresh.

Towards the end of April, and as may be necessary during the summer, fresh sphagnum moss should be inserted in the compost.

The Chief Kinds. P. Schilleriana, from the Philippines, has long, branching, many-flowered stems bearing rose-colored blooms; it usually flowers in winter. P. Stuartiana, like P. Schilleriana, has mottled leaves and branching stems with white flowers, the lower sepals being yellow, densely spotted with red. It usually flowers later than P. Schilleriana.

P. amabilis and P. amabilis Aphrodite have large white flowers.

P. Lueddemanniana has short stems with five to seven flowers. P. Cornu-cervii, the Stag's Horn Phalaenopsis, has yellowish flowers marked with red-brown. P. Sanderiana resembles P. Schilleriana, but the flowers are larger.

PHALARIS—*Ribbon Grass, Canary Grass,* (Pha'laris; Phala'ris). Hardy annual and perennial ornamental grasses which are found wild in most countries of the North Temperate regions, and belong to the Grass family, Gramineae.

The principal perennial kind, P. arundinacea, grows abundantly in marshy places and shallow water in North America. It is 3-6 ft. in height, has linear (long, narrow), smooth, green leaves, half an inch in width, and bears terminal feathery plumes of flowers in summer. A variety of this, named picta (variegata), sometimes known as Ribbon Grass, has attractive green and white leaves.

The Canary Grass. P. canariensis, the Canary Grass, is an annual which grows 15 in. in height, has green leaves and bears variegated flowering spikes which are very ornamental. It is, however, chiefly grown for its seeds, which are used for cage-birds' food. It is naturalized in North America.

For Planting by the Waterside. P. arundinacea is not widely cultivated in gardens, but is sometimes planted on the margins of ponds. Planting may be done in October or spring. Pieces of the rhizome are planted in irregular groups in the mud. After planting, no further attention is needed, except to prevent them from spreading beyond their allotted space. Propagation is by dividing the rhizomes at planting time.

With Colored Leaves. The variegated kind, P. arundinacea picta (variegata), is planted in perennial borders for the beauty of its variegated foliage. It will flourish in ordinary garden soil and does equally well in a sunny or semi-shaded position. Planting is done in spring or fall, small clumps being set at intervals along the border. The leaves are particularly attractive in the early summer, when their colors are most vivid. (They may be used for mixing with cut flowers.)

After a few years the clumps become unwieldy and they should then be lifted, divided and replanted. The outer portions of the clumps are selected for planting; the inner parts, being worn out, are discarded. This method of division is the only means of propagation.

A Hardy Annual. P. canariensis may be grown in small clumps in the border for the beauty of its small, compact spikes of variegated flowers. Seeds are sown in April in a sunny position where the plants are to grow. They are scattered thinly on the surface of the soil and then raked in. The seedlings are afterwards thinned out to 4 in. apart. The flower spikes, when fully expanded, are cut and dried and used for mixing with everlasting flowers in winter.

The Chief Kinds. P. arundinacea, 3-6 ft.; P. arundinacea picta (variegata), 3-4 ft., green and white variegated leaves; and P. canariensis, 15 in., variegated flower spikes.

PHASEOLUS (Phase'olus; Phaseo'lus). A group of mostly twining, climbing plants that are natives of the warm regions of both hemispheres and that include many important food plants such as the Mung Bean, Scarlet Runner Bean, Lima Bean, Sieva Bean, Kidney or String Bean and others. It also includes a few species that are grown for ornament. Phaseolus belongs to the Pea family, Leguminosae. Its name is an ancient Latin one.

The cultivation of the kinds that are important as vegetables is discussed under Beans, which see. The kinds most commonly cultivated for their decorative blooms are P. coccineus, the Scarlet Runner, and P. Caracalla, the Snailflower.

The Scarlet Runner, which produces edible pods, is cultivated in the same way as Lima Beans. It needs strings, brushwood or other supports up which it can climb. There is a white-flowered as well as the usual scarlet-flowered kind. It prefers a rich, well-drained, mellow soil, full sunshine and, during its growing season, should be given abundant water. It is raised from seeds each year as an annual. See also Beans.

The Snailflower is a tropical, perennial vine with curiously coiled lavender and yellowish fragrant flowers. It grows to a height of 20 ft. and is adapted for cultivating in greenhouses or outdoors in warm regions. It is easily raised from seeds and needs a well-drained, rich soil and supports up which it can twine. Under good conditions it attains a height of 20 ft.

PHEASANT BERRY. See Leycesteria.

PHEASANT'S-EYE. Adonis, which see.

PHEASANT'S-EYE NARCISSUS. Another name for the Poet's Narcissus. See Narcissus poeticus.

PHEGOPTERIS (Phegop'teris). Hothouse ferns, from tropical America, now included in Dryopteris, which see.

PHELLODENDRON—*Cork Tree* (Phelloden'-dron). Handsome, leaf-losing (deciduous) trees of moderate size with short trunks and widely spreading branches. The large leaves are made up of 5-15 leaflets and they are decorative in character. Male and female flowers are borne by different trees in summer. They are in large clusters at the ends of the branches, but are not very showy, being small and greenish-yellow. The fruits, which are ripened in abundance where male and female trees grow together, are black.

Phellodendron belongs to the Rue family, Rutaceae, and the several kinds have the aromatic odor peculiar to various other members of the same family. The name is taken from the Greek *phellos,* cork, and *dendron,* tree, and refers to the corky bark of several kinds. They are natives of eastern Asia.

Raising Seedlings. Young plants may easily be raised from seeds which have been washed free of the fleshy matter which surrounds them. Seeds should be sown in a cold frame or in a sheltered

Phellodendrons produce an abundance of black berries that contain seeds which germinate freely.

place outdoors in fall or in light sandy soil in a greenhouse about the end of January or February. The young plants are potted singly as soon as they are large enough to handle. They should later be planted in a nursery border.

Planting and Pruning. Some difficulty may be experienced in procuring a definite leading shoot, for there is a decided tendency for the various kinds to form dual leaders. It is, however, wise to train young trees to form definite trunks even though the trunks may be short. This can be done by pruning in summer.

A splendid specimen of Phellodendron Lavallei at The New York Botanical Garden.

The Phellodendrons thrive in loamy soil and are good trees for prominent positions where they need not compete with more vigorous kinds. Any one of the several kinds in cultivation is worth planting to form a lawn specimen, and they form excellent shade trees for use with low, modern houses where trees of great height would be out of place. Both wood and roots are yellow and bitter, characteristics that are very pronounced in the Rue family.

The Amur Cork Tree. Phellodendron amurense, the Amur Cork tree, is one of the kinds with corky bark. It may grow 30-40 ft. high. The leaves are often 9-15 in. long and are composed of five to eleven leaflets. As in other kinds, the swollen base of the stalk covers the bud in the leaf axil. It is a widely distributed tree in Manchuria, northern China, Korea and Japan. Two closely allied trees, which are sometimes included as varieties of P. amurense or even given rank as species, are P. sachalinense, from Saghalien and Korea, and P. Lavallei, which is found in Japan.

P. chinense is from western China. It has longer leaflets than P. japonicum and smaller clusters of fruits. It may grow 40 ft. high in China.

PHELLOSPERMA (Phellosperm'a). One small Cactus that is a native of western America and belongs in the Cactus family, Cactaceae. Its name is derived from *phellos,* cork, and *sperma,* seed, and directly refers to the corky base of the seed.

Phellospherma tetrancistra grows not more than 1 ft. high and has purple flowers. For its culture, see Cacti.

PHILADELPHUS or MOCK ORANGE
Very Decorative Shrubs for Late Spring Bloom

Philadelphus (Philadel'phus). Mostly hardy, leaf-losing shrubs that vary in size from small dense bushes 2-3 ft. high to large ones 15-20 ft. high and equally wide in diameter. They are found wild in North America, in southern Europe, and in Asia from the Caucasus to the Himalayas and west, central and northern China and Korea. Some have been in cultivation for a long period, others are of comparatively recent introduction. There are also numerous hybrids. The flowers of many kinds are very fragrant, and a large bush in full flower can be detected from a considerable distance. The flowering time is May to July.

These Shrubs Are Sometimes Called Syringa. In addition to the common name of Mock Orange, the name Syringa is also used for these shrubs. This is unfortunate, for Syringa is the scientific name for the Lilac. Philadelphus belongs to the Saxifrage family, Saxifragaceae. The name is of Greek origin, and was originally applied to a sweet-flowering shrub.

When to Take Cuttings. Seeds sown in sandy soil in a frame in spring germinate quite freely, but cuttings root so readily that there is no need to adopt any other means of propagation. Cuttings may be made of soft shoots 4-5 in. long, in late June or early July; they are planted in a bed of sand in a greenhouse or cold frame and are shaded from bright sun. Roots will be formed in from 2-3 weeks, and if the weather is showery the young plants may be planted in a nursery border as soon as they have been hardened. A little shade will be necessary until they are established. The tips of the shoots should be removed in order to ensure bushy plants.

Hardwood cuttings also root readily if they are made 9-12 in. long and planted in a sheltered border in late autumn or winter. Or, at that time, they may be buried in sand outdoors, and dug up and planted in regular nursery rows in the garden in spring.

Preparing the Ground and Planting. The various kinds of Philadelphus give the best results when planted in an open position in loamy soil. If the soil is rather poor it should be enriched before the plants are set out. All well-established plants benefit by a surface dressing of compost or manure every second year, or by an occasional application of fertilizer. The

The hybrid Philadelphus nivalis.

vigorous kinds form excellent isolated specimens, and they may also be used in groups; the less vigorous sorts are at their best in groups or beds. Some are excellent for lawn beds.

How to Prune the Vigorous Kinds. Two types of pruning are necessary where the very vigorous and the smaller kinds are grown. Vigorous kinds, of which the common Mock Orange, P. coronarius, may be taken as an example, may be allowed to grow for many years without any general pruning. Should a bush appear to be too dense, some of the older branches may be cut out to the ground line; or, if it is badly balanced, a few branches may be shortened. Too much shortening is not recommended.

In the event of a plant becoming too large for its position it may be cut well back, leaving only a few of the younger branches. All such work should be done as soon as the flowers fade.

Pruning the Smaller Kinds. The small-growing kinds may also be left unpruned, but if that is done they do not flower so freely as when they

The single-flowered Mock Oranges or Philadelphus are easy-to-grow shrubs that are attractive in bloom.

are pruned regularly. P. Lemoinei may be taken as a representative of this group. Left unpruned, it grows 4-5 ft. high and forms a dense mass of short shoots. Regularly pruned, it can be kept to a height of 2½-3 ft. and then forms long arching branches that flower almost from end to end.

Pruning should be carried out as soon as the flowers fade, in order to take advantage of the longest possible growing season. All old wood must be cut out to the point where young shoots are appearing from near the base. If there seem to be too many new shoots, cut a few of the old shoots to the ground line. Shoots up to 2½ ft. long will be produced in the course of two months.

As this method of cultivation is an exhaustive one, care must be taken to feed the plants as and when necessary. When plants show serious signs of deterioration, they should be destroyed, the bed made up with new soil, and fresh plants put out. One of the great advantages of shrubs that are easily rooted from cuttings is that a new stock can be raised without trouble.

The Chief Kinds of Mock Orange. In the following notes on the best kinds to choose, the flowers are white except when otherwise stated.

P. cordifolius, a dense bush 6-7 ft. high, bears large clusters of flowers in June and July. It is a native of California.

P. californicus is another California bush with very large clusters of flowers; each cluster may bear as many as 20 flowers each 1 in. across. The more vigorous the plants, the larger are the flower clusters. This bush grows at least 10 ft. high and as wide in diameter.

The Common Sweet-scented Mock Orange. P. coronarius is the commonest kind and one to which the names of Mock Orange and Syringa are most often applied. It is widely distributed as a wild plant in southeastern Europe and Asia Minor. For more than 300 years it has been prominent in gardens, popular alike for its free flowering and its fragrance. It grows 12-15 ft. high and may be almost as wide. The flowering time is late May and June, and the creamy white flowers are produced freely every year, each 1-1¼ in. across, in clusters of from five to nine.

Several varieties have been given distinct names, notably aureus, with golden leaves, the color being best in spring; variegatus, with cream-margined flowers; duplex, a dwarf kind with double flowers; dianthiflorus, with large double flowers; nanus, of very dwarf habit; and salicifolius, with narrow leaves.

The flowers of the common Mock Orange are very strongly scented, and although they are delightful in the garden, their scent is found to be too strong indoors by many people. The double-flowered varieties are less strongly scented than the common kind, and are more useful and last longer as cut flowers.

P. nivalis is a good hybrid of P. coronarius and P. pubescens.

P. Delavayi, introduced from China, grows 15-16 ft. high and bears large clusters of pure white, fragrant flowers in June–July.

Useful for Cutting for Indoor Decoration. P. Gordonianus is a large bush which occurs as a native from California to British Columbia. It grows 12-15 ft. high and as far through, bearing large flowers, several together, during June–July. The flowers are only slightly fragrant.

P. grandiflorus is another large kind. It is a native of the southeastern United States and grows 15 or more feet high with a wide spread. The flowers are up to 2 in. across, pure white and scentless, and are produced freely in June-July.

P. Magdalenae is a Chinese shrub, 6-12 ft.

high, introduced in 1894 to France. The flowers are ¾-1 in. across and produced several together in clusters all over the plants.

For Mild Sections Only. P. mexicanus is more tender than most other kinds and can only be grown successfully in the milder parts of the country. The flowers are more or less cup-shaped and often produced singly, instead of in clusters, as in most other kinds. They are very fragrant, 1½-2 in. across. P. Coulteri is remarkable in that each petal is blotched with purple at the base. Both are natives of Mexico.

The Smallest Mock Orange. P. microphyllus is the most dwarf kind known. It is a low bush, 3-4 ft. high, of dense habit, with a profusion of wiry shoots clothed with small, gray-green leaves, and bears quantities of pure white, fragrant flowers in June. This is a very charming shrub for small gardens, for it is easily kept within bounds. It grows wild from Colorado to New Mexico and Arizona.

Between it and P. coronarius a number of hybrids have been raised, two of the oldest and best known being P. Lemoinei and P. Lemoinei erectus. These belong to the group that requires severe pruning after flowering to procure the best results; both have fragrant, white flowers.

Some Beautiful Double-flowered Varieties. Other very attractive shrubs of the same type are Avalanche, white, very free flowering; Albatre and Boule d'Argent, double flowers; Bouquet Blanc, flowers white, fragrant, double and large; Belle Etoile, very large white flowers flushed with purple at the base of the petals; Manteau d'Hermione, compact dwarf habit, flowers cream-colored, double; Norma, flowers white, single; purpureo-maculatus, flowers white, stained with purple at the base; Rosace, very large, semi-double, fragrant, white flowers; Virginal, one of the finest of all the double-flowered kinds, with very large, fragrant, pure white flowers.

PHILAGERIA VEITCHII (Philager'ia). This rare hybrid plant was raised by the English firm of Veitch in 1872, by crossing Lapageria rosea with Philesia magellanica (buxifolia), both belonging to the family Liliaceae. It is a loose-habited shrub with dark-green, leathery, evergreen leaves 1½ in. long and ½ in. wide, and pendulous, rosy-purple flowers about 2 in. long and ½-¾ in. wide. The flower segments are fleshy, the three outer ones being shorter and darker colored than the three inner ones. It is hardy in mild parts of North America and requires treatment similar to that given to Philesia. Philageria is a combination of the names Philesia and Lapageria.

PHILESIA MAGELLANICA (Phile'sia). A tender, flowering shrub, more familiarly known as Philesia buxifolia, which may be grown outdoors in California and similar mild climates, or in the greenhouse. It is a native of Chile and belongs to the Lily family, Liliaceae.

Philesia forms a bushy shrub, 4 ft. in height. It has short-jointed shoots clothed with alternate, linear, leathery leaves which are evergreen, smooth above and glaucous (blue-gray) beneath, and 1 in. in length. In June it bears trumpet-shaped red flowers, 2 in. in length, which closely resemble those of the Lapageria. The name Philesia is from the Greek *phileo,* to love, and refers to the beauty of the flowers.

As a Greenhouse Shrub. Philesia requires a minimum winter temperature of 45 degrees and a soil compost of equal parts of peat, turfy loam and sand. Repotting is done in March. The new, slightly larger pots must be well drained with crocks, and these are covered with coarse leaves. The plants are then taken out of their old pots and the crocks removed from the roots. The balls of soil are not disturbed, but a few of the root tips are loosened with a pointed stick so that they may more readily enter the new soil. The plants are set in the new pots, and the compost is made firm with a potting stick.

Summer and Winter Management. Careful attention to watering is needed after repotting. It

Philesia magellanica (buxifolia), a charming tender shrub with red flowers of waxy texture.

is best to allow the soil to become moderately dry first, then give it a thorough soaking and continue this treatment until the plants are well established in the fresh compost. The leaves must be syringed underneath, as well as on top, several times a day during the summer, and once a day on mild days during the winter. Syringing must be done forcibly and a moist atmosphere maintained, as these plants are subject to the attacks of red spider mites.

During the winter months less watering is required, although the soil must not be allowed to become very dry.

Pruning, which consists of shortening extravigorous shoots, is done immediately after flowering.

Suitable for Planting Out of Doors in Mild Regions. In mild localities, Philesia can be grown out of doors. The soil preferred is a sandy, peaty one. Planting should be done in spring, and the soil must be made very firm. Growth is slow; therefore very little pruning is required. The soil must be kept moist in dry weather.

Propagation by Cuttings. Propagation is by cuttings or layers. Cuttings are made from firm young shoots in July. They should be taken off about 2 in. in length, the leaves trimmed off with a sharp knife from the lower half of the stem, and a cut made below the bottom joint. The cuttings are inserted in a mixture of sand and peat moss in a greenhouse or frame and covered with a bell jar. The latter is removed daily, and the condensed moisture is wiped from the inside. It is replaced immediately and this treatment is continued until roots are formed. The roots are slow in forming so that the soil must be kept uniformly moist all the time.

Rooted plants are potted separately in 3-in. pots, and subsequently in larger ones. Plants well established in 5-in. pots are best for planting out of doors.

Propagation by Layering. Shrubs growing out of doors are layered in summer. A shoot from the lower part is bent downwards, and where it touches the soil a notch is cut just below a joint. The "tongue" thus formed is pegged down in the soil, which is kept moist until roots are formed. The branch is then detached and potted in a 5-in. pot. When well rooted, it is planted in its permanent position. Air layering is also a satisfactory means of increase.

PHILLYREA (Phillyr'ea). Evergreen trees or shrubs found wild in the Mediterranean region and in the southeastern region of the Black Sea. In a wild state they withstand a good deal of drought, remaining green and healthy through several rainless months, even when growing in crevices of rock. They have thick, leathery, opposite leaves and rather small, clear white, dull white, or greenish-white flowers produced in late spring. The flowers are followed by small fruits which are almost black when ripe.

Phillyrea is closely related to the Privets and belongs to the Olive family, Oleaceae. The name is said to be the old Greek name for the plants.

These plants are generally suitable only for regions where winters are not very severe, although P. decora lives in sheltered places outdoors in New York City.

Propagation by Seeds and Cuttings. The advantage of seeds over cuttings is that seedlings are more likely to assume a treelike habit than plants raised from cuttings. That advantage, however, can only be claimed for the taller kinds. Seedlings may be longer lived than plants raised from cuttings. Seeds should be sown in a cold frame as soon as ripe, using sandy soil.

Cuttings of short shoots, 4-5 in. long, should be taken in July and inserted in a sand bed in a frame kept close. The rooted cuttings should be potted singly and kept in a cold frame during winter, and planted out of doors in a nursery border the following May.

Layering can be practiced if desired. Simply peg down the lower branches into sandy soil in spring.

Summer Pruning. When plants are young, a little summer pruning may be necessary to induce them to grow into a good shape, or to form a leader in the case of the taller kinds; otherwise regular pruning is unnecessary. If the bushes are becoming too large, you can reduce their size by cutting them back in early spring. Very severe pruning is not recommended.

Good Seaside Shrubs. The Phillyreas thrive in various kinds of garden soil, and are at their best in well-drained loam. They also thrive in limy soil and in exposed places near the sea.

The Tallest Kind. P. latifolia is the tallest kind. Under favorable conditions it may reach a height of 30-35 ft., or it may be a bush 12-15 ft. high. At its best it forms a definite trunk 12 or more inches in diameter. Its leathery, dark green leaves may be 2-2½ in. long and 1-1½ in. wide. It is, however, very variable in character and the leaves vary a good deal in size.

In the variety ilicifolia the margins of the leaves have very definite teeth, and in the variety media the leaves are smaller than in the type. The flowers in each case are dull white and not attractive. The shrub might well be tried for hedges. **P.** latifolia and its varieties are widely distributed in the Mediterranean region.

P. augustifolia, also from the Mediterranean region differs by reason of its very narrow leaves which are usually from 1-2½ in. long and less than ¼ in. wide. They rarely reach a width of ½ in. This large bush grows 10-12 ft. high.

P. decora, sometimes called P. Vilmoriniana, is a native of Lazistan. It has much larger leaves than the other kinds and the flowers are clear white and fragrant. The leaves are oblong-lanceolate or oblong, up to 5 in. long and 1¾ in. wide, dark green above, paler beneath. It forms a spreading bush 6-10 ft. high, and if there is only room for one kind this should be chosen. There is a variety with much narrower leaves than the type.

PHILODENDRON

Decorative Foliage Plants for Homes and Greenhouses

Philodendron (Philoden'dron). Evergreen, mostly climbing plants, Philodendrons are grown in greenhouses, as house plants and, in the far South, outdoors, for their ornamental foliage. Under favorable conditions they bear interesting inflorescences ("flowers") that resemble in shape those of Calla Lilies. Philodendrons belong to the Arum family, Araceae, and are found wild in the West Indies and tropical America. The name Philodendron is derived from *phileo,* to love, and *dendron,* a tree, and refers to the plants' tree-climbing habit.

These plants, many of which twine their slender stems high among the branches of trees in tropical forests, have long aerial roots and handsome leaves. These leaves exhibit great diversity in size and shape. Some species have cordate (heart-shaped) leaves, in others they are lanceolate (long and narrow), sagittate (arrow-shaped), ovate, oblong or deeply lobed. They vary from 3 in. to 3 ft. in length. They are mostly rich green, but in some kinds they are coppery red beneath. The young leaves of a few kinds are red, but these become green when they reach maturity, and the veins of others are red.

The inflorescences ("flowers") have spathes, which are of various shades of purple, red, pink or greenish-white, and spadices (central columns which bear the tiny flowers) which are either cream, yellow or white.

Outdoors in the Far South. In frostless regions Philodendrons may be cultivated outdoors in

Philodendron oxycardium is a great favorite as a house plant.

Philodendron erubescens has coppery undersides to its leaves.

shady places. They revel in rich soil that contains a plentiful supply of organic matter and that is moderately moist.

As House Plants. Philodendrons are popular as house plants. They succeed with less light than most plants and thrive in temperatures between 60 and 72 degrees. Best success is had when they are grown in pots of soil but some, especially P. oxycardium, will live for a long time in water alone or in water to which a few pieces of charcoal have been added. The leaves of Philodendrons grown as house plants should be sponged occasionally with soapy water or an insecticide to remove dust and to control insects.

Well-rooted specimens that are grown in soil benefit from feeding with dilute liquid fertilizer every week or two weeks. During the summer they may be plunged (buried to the rims of their pots) in sand or ashes in a shaded place outdoors or be kept on a shaded porch.

As Greenhouse Plants. Philodendrons thrive in moist, tropical greenhouses. The minimum night temperature should be 60 degrees, the minimum day temperature 5-10 degrees higher. Humid conditions should be maintained by frequently damping the floor and benches of the green-

house and by syringing the foliage several times a day in summer. During the winter less syringing and damping are required, but the atmosphere must not be allowed to become very dry. Shade from direct sun is needed from mid-February to mid-November.

The plants may be grown in greenhouses in pots or in beds of soil. When the soil in which they grow is well filled with healthy roots, the plants benefit from feeding regularly with dilute liquid fertilizers.

Cultivation in Pots and Tubs. When grown either as house plants or greenhouse plants, Philodendrons thrive in pots and tubs provided they are well drained and are not excessively large for the size of the plants. They succeed best when their roots are slightly crowded in the container but not so densely packed that they form a tight ball of roots.

A soil consisting of equal parts of turfy loam, sand and peat moss, with some chopped charcoal and broken crocks or broken brick added, forms a good potting medium. Potting should be done in late winter or spring. The pots should be filled to one quarter their depth with crocks, which should be covered with turf or coarse leaves to prevent the drainage from becoming clogged. Sufficient soil is then placed in the pot, so that when the plant is set in position the top of the ball of soil is 1-2 in. below the rim of the pot. More soil is then placed around the ball and is packed moderately

Philodendron radiatum is often grown under the name P. dubium.

[8—14]
Summer Phlox
(Phlox paniculata variety)

[8—14a]
Mock Orange
(Philadelphus coronarius)

[8—15]

Lavender-flowered Phlox divaricata

Philodendron hastatum is one of the most popular Philodendrons. If planted against a piece of rough bark or against a stick wrapped with moss, the roots from the stem will grow into the support and derive moisture from it.

each having at least two joints, are inserted as cuttings in pots of sandy peat or in a mixture of sand and peat moss in a greenhouse propagating bench in spring or summer. The pots are plunged in a propagating case having a bottom heat of 70-75 degrees or are kept under a bell jar or in a terrarium in a warm room. They are shaded from direct sunshine during their rooting period.

When roots are formed, the cuttings are potted separately in 3-in. pots and subsequently in 5-in. pots. When well rooted in these, they may be potted into larger pots or be planted in a prepared bed of soil in a greenhouse or outdoors in the far South.

An alternative method of rooting stem cuttings (especially useful in the case of trailing or vining kinds, such as P. oxycardium) is to place them with their lower parts in containers of water or, better still, water to which a few lumps of charcoal have been added. In a

firmly, leaving space at the top for watering.

Newly potted Philodendrons must be watered with care, the soil being allowed to become nearly dry before each watering. This system should be followed until the roots have taken possession of the new soil, after which the soil should be kept more evenly moist. Syringing the foliage 2-3 times a day is especially beneficial for newly potted Philodendrons.

Planting in Greenhouse Beds. To prepare a bed in the greenhouse in which to plant Philodendrons, dig a hole 18-24 in. deep. Into its bottom put 6 in. of broken bricks or coarse cinders. Cover these with turfy loam or rough leaves. Then fill with a soil mixture of the kind recommended as suitable for potting Philodendrons. Make this firm and allow it a few days to settle. Then take the specimen to be planted out of its pot and, after the crocks and loose soil have been removed from the roots, set it in the prepared bed, make the soil moderately firm around its ball of roots and water it thoroughly.

Supports. Most kinds of Philodendrons need supports to which they can cling. Pieces of rough tree bark serve admirably, or stakes wrapped with a thick layer of sphagnum moss will do.

Propagation by Stem Cuttings. Pieces of stem,

Philodendron panduraeforme, because of the shape of its leaves, is sometimes called the Horse Head Philodendron.

This hybrid between Philodendron squamiferum and Philodendron laciniatum is called Philodendron Florida compactum. It is an attractive pot plant.

temperature of 65-72 degrees rooting will ordinarily take place in 4-8 weeks.

Propagation by Air Layering. Philodendrons are very easily increased by the technique called air layering. This, in fact, is the surest method of multiplying many kinds and is an especially useful method when it is desired to lower a plant that has become too tall or is devoid of leaves on its lower parts. See Air Layering.

Propagation by Seeds. Seeds of Philodendrons germinate readily if they are sown in sphagnum moss, in a mixture of peat moss and sand or in some similar rooting medium as soon as they are ripe. They should not be allowed to dry after they are removed from the fleshy covering

Philodendron Wendlandii is a non-climbing kind with short-stemmed paddle-shaped spreading leaves.

that surrounds them. The seeds germinate best in a temperature of 75-80 degrees and must be kept moist at all times. When the young plants are large enough to handle easily, they should be potted singly in small pots filled with a coarse, porous soil mixture.

The Chief Kinds. In recent years there has developed a very great interest in Philodendrons as subjects for growing in pots and tubs. These are used in great variety for the decoration of homes, offices, stores, public buildings, etc. To a very large extent they have replaced Palms, which at one time were very popular for these purposes.

Not only do people grow a large number of natural species (kinds that occur natively in the wild in some parts of the world), but American hybridizers have originated many new and, often, improved kinds. These include both climbing or vining plants and varieties that form compact, nonvining specimens. These last are sometimes called self-heading varieties. Some of the best Philodendrons are described below. First, in alphabetical sequence, are listed a selection of species and, immediately following, a selection of hybrid kinds.

P. Andreanum is a native of Colombia. A climbing plant, it has 3-ft.-long leaves of dark green suffused with brown, and with ivory-colored veins.

P. bipinnatifidum, from southern Brazil, has a short, erect stem and leaves about 2 ft. long that are twice-lobed and are dark green with prominent veins. This kind grows slowly.

P. calophyllum, a native of Brazil, has a short stem and pointed, heart-shaped leaves that are bright green and shiny.

P. cannifolium, a Brazilian, is a nonclimber with paddle-like leaves with wavy margins.

P. cordatum (the plant often sold and grown under this name is P. oxycardium, which is described below) is a trailing or climbing plant from Brazil with small or medium-sized leaves. The leaves are green, long, heart-shaped, and firmer in texture and glossier than those of P. oxycardium.

P. dubium. See P. radiatum.

P. erubescens, a native of Colombia, is a free-growing climber that has medium-sized arrow-shaped leaves that have coppery undersides.

P. giganteum, from the West Indies, is an upright grower with its stem joints close together. The broad ovate-heart-shaped, shining leaves are rich green and have lighter, depressed veins.

P. gloriosum, a Colombian native, has large, heart-shaped leaves that have a silky sheen when young. They are dark green with reddish margins and ivory-colored veins. This kind climbs.

P. hastatum is a Brazilian with bright green, arrow-shaped leaves, a climber. P. hastatum variegatum is similar, except that the leaves are beautifully variegated with white.

P. Imbe is a stout climber from Rio de Janeiro. It has pointed, lance-shaped leaves that are green above and red beneath. P. Imbe variety variegatum has its leaves handsomely and irregularly marked with creamy-white and light green.

P. lacerum hails from the West Indies. It has large, heart-shaped, light green leaves that are deeply lobed at their margins. This climber is recorded as being the first Philodendron introduced into Florida by the Spaniards.

P. laciniatum, from Brazil, is a climber that has deeply lobed or fingered light green leaves.

P. Mamei is a nonclimbing kind from Ecuador that has large, heart-shaped, green leaves beautifully variegated with white.

P. micans is a climber from Colombia. Its leaves are small and heart-shaped, green with a silky sheen above, reddish beneath.

P. nobile, from Venezuela and Guiana is self-heading. It has broad, oblanceolate leaves.

P. oxycardium, a native of the West Indies, is the kind popularly grown and usually sold as P. cordatum and P. scandens, although these names properly belong to other kinds. It has trailing or climbing slender stems and small, broad, heart-shaped, deep green leaves. P. oxycardium variety variegatum has its leaves marbled with ivory-white and gray-green.

P. panduraeforme is a popular kind that is sometimes called Horsehead Philodendron because of the fanciful resemblance of the shape of its leaves to the shape of a horse's head. The leaves are roughly fiddle-shaped and are dull, dark green in color. The plant is a climber and is well suited for use as a house plant. It is a

native of the more southern sections of Brazil.

P. pertusum, or rather the plant grown under this name, is properly named Monstera deliciosa (see Monstera).

P. radiatum is often cultivated under the name P. dubium. It is a native of Guatemala, a climbing kind with deeply lobed, rich green leaves.

P. sagittifolium is an erect, climbing kind of vigorous growth. Its leaves are arrowhead-shaped, light green and shining.

P. Selloum is stemless or has but a short stem. It is a native of Paraguay and Brazil and bears large, long-stalked, deeply lobed, deep green leaves.

P. Sodiroi is a climber from Colombia that has heart-shaped leaves of leaden-silver coloring.

P. squamiferum comes from Guiana. It has bold, five-lobed leaves that are a shiny, rich green. The leafstalks have a thick, furlike covering of long, red hairs.

P. tripartitum, from tropical America, has narrow, three-lobed green leaves. It is a climber.

P. verrucosum, from Ecuador, is one of the most beautiful kinds. It is a climber and has heart-shaped leaves that are satiny green shaded with an iridescent olive hue. Its leafstalks are furnished with conspicuous red hairs.

P. Wendlandii, a Costa Rican kind, does not climb but forms a "bird's nest" type of plant, with its short-stemmed, paddle-shaped, green leaves spreading upwards and outwards from a common center.

Hybrid Philodendrons. The following are some of the more outstanding kinds of hybrid Philodendrons. Most of these have been developed by American breeders.

P. Alleni, a self-heading type with glossy green, lobed leaves.

P. Barryi, a decorative, self-heading Philodendron with glossy, deeply lobed leaves.

P. borinquensis has large, heart-shaped, shallowly lobed, green leaves which are reddish on the veins on the under leaf surfaces.

P. Evansii is a handsome, scarcely climbing kind with huge, glossy leaves that are lobed and undulate.

P. Florida compactum is a fine hybrid that climbs slowly. It has lobed leaves which have petioles (stems of a distinctively reddish hue).

P. Lynette forms a very attractive "bird's nest" or self-heading specimen. Its leaves are bright green with strongly depressed veins.

P. Mandaianum is a splendid hybrid that climbs vigorously. It has bronzy or reddish arrowhead-shaped leaves and red leafstalks.

P. McNeilianum is self-heading and has handsome, triangular, quite deeply lobed, wavy leaves.

P. Orlando has broad paddle-shaped leaves. It is a semi-self-heading kind.

P. rubescens has arrowhead-shaped leaves that are bronze-green and on their undersides show red veins. It is a climber.

P. rubrum is a climbing hybrid that has pointed heart-shaped leaves with coppery-colored or whitish veins. Its leafstalks are red.

P. tricolor is semi-self-heading and forms a large rosette of long arrowhead-shaped green leaves which are irregularly splashed with cream and white markings.

P. wendatum climbs slowly. It has thick, oblong leaves and is semi-self-heading. Its foliage is dark green with some red on the under leaf surfaces.

P. wend-imbe has leaves that are broader and more oval than those of P. Wendatum. It is semi-self-heading and the undersides of its leaves are pink.

P. Wilsonii is a slow-growing climber with large, glossy, coarsely toothed, bright green leaves which are broad-heart-shaped in outline.

PHLOMIS—*Jerusalem Sage* (Phlo'mis). Herbaceous plants and evergreen subshrubs, some of which are attractive in foliage and flowers. They are peculiar because of their square branches, which are very noticeable in the herbaceous kinds, and also because of the flower clusters of the shrubs. In some instances branches and leaves are covered by a very dense, grayish felt which gives the whole plant a distinct and characteristic appearance. This is very apparent in the shrubby kinds.

The flowers are borne in early summer in dense whorls at intervals on long stems, and the prevailing color is yellow; there are, however, some with lilac and purplish flowers. For general interest the subshrubby kinds are to be preferred to those of herbaceous growth.

These plants are closely allied to the Sage and belong to the same family, Labiatae. Phlomis is taken from the Greek *phlomos*, a Mullein, the woolly character of the leaves having been thought to resemble that of some of the Mulleins or Verbascums. The various kinds are natives of Europe, Asia and North Africa.

Propagation by Seeds and Cuttings. Propagation of the shrubby kinds can be effected by means of cuttings placed in a close frame in July, or by seeds, when obtainable, sown in light soil in a cold frame in spring.

The herbaceous kinds can be increased by seeds or by division of the clumps in autumn or early spring. The shrubby kinds are generally tender; the hardiest, P. fruticosa, will grow outdoors in sheltered places about at Philadelphia.

Suitable for Poor Soil. The plants should be given a sunny position in well-drained, light, loamy soil that is rather poor, for it is better to produce sturdy plants with short-jointed shoots rather than those with soft, vigorous branches. They can be planted with equal success in a sunny border or in the rockery. The herbaceous kinds should be given richer soil and should be transplanted every two or three years. As soon as the flowers have faded, they should be removed if seeds are not wanted.

The best-known shrubby kind is Phlomis fruticosa, called the Jerusalem Sage. It forms a bush at least 3 ft. high with a wide spread, and bears gray-green leaves, rather like those of Sage, but much larger, up to 5 in. long and 1¾ in. wide. The yellow flowers are about 1¼ in. long and are in dense, circular clusters in July. It is a native of southern Europe.

Another shrubby kind with very woolly shoots and leaves is P. floccosa, a tender kind from Egypt. P. Bovei is a curious subshrub with stout, erect, densely felted stems crowned with sage-green leaves, which are white beneath.

The Best Herbaceous Kinds. Some useful kinds of herbaceous habit of growth are P. cashmeriana, a Himalayan plant, 2 ft. high, bearing lilac flowers; P. viscosa, 2 ft. high, yellow flowers, a native of the Levant; P. samia, a native of northern Africa, 2½-3 ft. high, yellow, purple-marked flowers; and P. tuberosa, a Chinese and European plant, 3 ft. high, purple flowers.

PHLOX: ANNUAL AND PERENNIAL

Showy Flowering Plants for Borders, Rock Gardens and Greenhouses

The Phloxes are a most important group of garden plants. Some kinds are hardy, others are more tender. They are invaluable for planting in perennial borders, rock gardens and flower beds, and the annual kinds may be grown for winter and spring bloom in greenhouses. They provide useful cut flowers. Phloxes are chiefly natives of North America, and belong to the Phlox family, the Polemoniaceae. The name Phlox, meaning flame, alludes to the brilliant coloring of the flowers.

The Annual Phlox

Phlox Drummondii is a beautiful Texas an-

nual which blooms throughout a long summer season. The flowers are of various colors—rose, crimson, scarlet, pink, pale yellow and violet as well as white. A packet of mixed seeds will furnish plants with flowers in which all or most of these colors are represented, or packets of seeds of distinct varieties can be purchased.

These annual Phloxes are admirable plants for filling summer flower beds, for, if well grown, they bear many flowers, and the plants last in bloom longer than many annuals.

When to Sow Seeds. Seeds should be sown in March, in a pan or flat of a sifted soil mixture consisting of two parts of loam and one part of leaf mold or peat moss, with a free scattering of

Phlox Drummondii, a native of Texas, is one of the most colorful of summer-flowering annuals.

Phlox Drummondii "Apricot," a good variety of the annual Phlox.

50 degrees and the daytime temperature is 5-10 degrees higher. Water frequently enough to keep the soil evenly moist but not constantly saturated and, when the pots are well filled with healthy roots, apply dilute liquid fertilizer at weekly intervals. The plants should be staked and tied neatly before they are tall enough to topple over.

Perennial Summer-flowering Kinds

The tall herbaceous perennial Phloxes, which provide such an imposing display of bloom from July to September, are varieties of Phlox paniculata, which is found wild from New York to Georgia and Arkansas, and Phlox carolina, which is native from Ohio to Florida. During their season of bloom they are of unsurpassed splendor, for the different varieties show a wide range of flower color: from white through blush to rose, crimson and scarlet, and through lavender to purple.

These Phloxes thrive in full sun or in part-day shade, provided the soil is deep and remains moist during hot, dry weather, but they are not a success in poor, sandy soil which dries out in summer.

If the soil of the garden is light it is wise to plant Phloxes in a partially shaded border. But,

sand, and lightly covered with the sifted mixture. A pane of glass is placed over the flat, which is set in a greenhouse having a temperature of 50-60 degrees.

The seedlings will soon appear, and before they become overcrowded they should be transplanted to other flats of similar though coarser soil, in which they are set 2 in. apart. A week or two afterwards, the flats should be placed in a cold frame so that the plants will be well hardened off when the time comes to plant them out of doors—that is, as soon as danger of frost has passed. An alternative method is to sow the seeds directly outdoors in early spring where the plants are to bloom and thin the seedlings to 4-5 in. apart.

Phlox Drummondii may be used as a ground cover in flower beds filled with taller plants; it is one of the most useful annuals for this purpose. The plants, when raised indoors and planted from flats, should be set 6 or 8 in. apart.

Greenhouse Cultivation. The many colorful varieties of Phlox Drummondii make charming pot plants for late winter, spring and early summer bloom in cool greenhouses. To obtain good plants, sow the seeds in pots or flats of sandy soil from August to February in a cool, airy greenhouse. When the seedlings are large enough to handle, prick them off (transplant them) to pots of 4- or 5-in. diameter, filled with good fertile soil. Space the seedlings about 3 in. apart.

Keep the young plants growing in a sunny greenhouse where the night temperature is 45-

Phlox Drummondii is attractive when grown in pots to bloom in a cool greenhouse in winter, spring and early summer.

Summer-blooming perennial Phloxes are excellent for the sunny or partly-shaded border. Plant them in groups rather than singly.

in the average garden, which consists of loamy or well-cultivated clay ground, they may be set in a sunny location. Partial shade is, however, an advantage even then, for the plants will last longer in full beauty during hot, dry weather.

When to Plant. Phloxes provide such a splendid display that it is worth while taking pains with their cultivation. The soil should be deeply dug, and plenty of decayed manure mixed with the lower layer. The best times to plant are early fall and early spring.

Phloxes are surface-rooting plants, therefore they must be kept moist; this is done by mulching the soil around them with compost, peat moss or decayed manure.

Copious waterings are required during pro-longed dry weather. When they are growing freely it is wise to look them over for the purpose of pulling up all thin, weak shoots, for these will not flower, and merely hinder the proper development of better and stronger shoots.

As a rule Phloxes need little staking, but it may be necessary to support vigorous plants of the taller varieties by a few stakes encircled by string. This support should be given if it is required to keep the stems upright.

Protection from Soil Pests. When fresh growth begins in spring, slugs may damage the tender shoots. A scattering of sifted ashes placed around the bases of the plants tends to keep these damaging pests away. Nematodes can also severely damage Phlox. Soil sterilization is effective against these.

When the leaves have fallen in autumn the stems should be cut down to within about 2 in. of the ground. It is a good plan at that time to place sand or ashes around the plants; these not only help to keep away slugs, but they afford some protection to the roots which are near the surface of the ground.

In the course of two or three years Phlox develops into a splendid clump if planted in deep, rich soil and left undisturbed.

Plants, each with one stem bearing a large head of bloom, are obtained by growing them fresh from cuttings annually; if grouped several together in the flower border, they make a first-rate display. But the average amateur will probably prefer to leave the old plants undisturbed until they begin to deteriorate.

Summer-flowering Phloxes should be fertilized with a complete fertilizer (see Fertilizers) each spring just before new growth begins. By pinching the shoots when the plants are about 6 in. tall, more compact plants are obtained, but the flower clusters are then of inferior size.

Propagation. The perennial summer-flowering Phloxes are very easily propagated by cuttings, which may be inserted at any time during the late spring and summer months. The cuttings are made from the fresh shoots of the current year's growth. It is advisable to choose flowerless

Phlox subulata is an excellent kind for planting in crevices between flagstones.

shoots for this purpose, but even the tops of shoots which have flowered may be used as cuttings if necessary.

A large percentage of the cuttings will form roots if they are planted in a sand bed in a frame which is kept close and shaded for a few weeks, or they may be placed in sandy soil on a shady border out of doors and covered with a bell jar.

Cuttings must not be overwatered or they may damp off; if the sand is watered as soon as the cuttings are inserted, they can be kept sufficiently moist until rooted by means of syringing.

Phloxes of this type can also be increased by root cuttings taken in early fall.

Division. The simplest method of propagating perennial Phloxes is by separating large clumps into several rooted pieces in October or in early spring and replanting these at once. Care should be taken to discard the central portions of the plants and to use only the younger outside pieces for replanting. This method, however, is not so satisfactory as raising fresh plants from cuttings.

Raising Perennial Phloxes from Seeds. If seeds of perennial Phloxes are sown as soon as they are mature (ripe) and ready to fall from the parent plant, they will germinate freely in spring. The seeds may be sown in a cold frame or in a sheltered place outdoors. The seedlings are transplanted to flats or to a bed in a cold frame and are grown on in a frame until they are big enough to plant in a nursery border. By autumn they will be large enough to set in their permanent locations. Plants raised from seeds are apt to include a high proportion of inferior colors.

The Best Varieties. There are innumerable varieties of the summer-flowering perennial Phloxes. The following are among the most attractive:

Augusta, rich medium red; Duchess of Gloucester, salmon-pink; Charles H. Curtis, orange-scarlet; Cheerfulness, salmon-scarlet; Columbia, light pink; Count Zeppelin, white, red eye; Daily Sketch, salmon-pink, crimson eye; Katrein, light lavender; Leo Schlageter, red; White Admiral, white; Mrs. Flanders, white; Progress, light blue; Amethyst, dark lilac; Sir John Falstaff, rich

The many beautiful varieties of Phlox subulata are easy to grow and are among the most charming of spring-flowering plants for rock gardens and perennial gardens.

salmon-pink; Starlight, violet, white center.

Perennial Spring-blooming Phloxes

The dwarf, hardy perennial Phloxes that bloom in spring form one of the finest groups of native American plants for rock gardens and wild gardens; some kinds, such as P. amoena, P. bifida, P. divaricata, P. pilosa, P. procumbens, P. stolonifera and P. subulata, are also extremely fine plants for setting at the front of perennial borders. Unfortunately, though, most of the western American ones are not easy to grow well in eastern American gardens.

Phlox adsurgens is one of the most beautiful of this group. It comes from Oregon and northern California. The plant is of prostrate growth, with broad leaves, and the large flowers are in loose heads on 4-5 in. stems in May and June. The flowers are of an exquisite pink, with a band of deeper pink down the center of each petal. Growing wild, as it does, in thin woodland, it seems to appreciate a cool or partially shaded position in the rock garden, and it especially responds to loam to which

has been added an abundance of leaf mold.

An occasional top-dressing of light, rich soil worked in among the trailing stems will greatly benefit the plant, and assist the stems to produce fresh roots.

This kind may be increased by seeds sown in pots in a cold frame in spring, or by soft cuttings of nonflowering shoots taken in early summer, and rooted in a bed of sand in a cold frame; or by simple division of the roots in

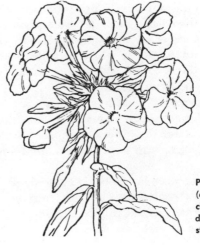

Phlox divaricata (canadensis) bears clusters of lavender flowers on 9-in. stems.

Phlox amoena, 6-9 in. tall, has flowers of deep rose-pink in May-June.

the spring time or during the early summer.

Phlox amoena, which occurs wild from Kentucky to Florida, forms compact clumps and grows about 6-9 in. high. The heads of rather large flowers are deep rose in color. It is an easy and attractive rock plant, and flowers in May. It should be planted in light loam in the wider and more level parts of the rock garden or woodland garden, or as a ground cover in light shade. It is easily increased by division of the roots in spring; or, in the same season, soft cuttings may be rooted in sand in a cold frame.

Lavender-blue Flowers. Phlox divaricata, Wild Sweet William, which is also known as P. canadensis, is a woodland plant of eastern North America; the leaves are broad and the habit of growth is erect. The large, handsome flowers, in loose heads, on 6-9-in. stems, in May and June, are a beautiful lavender-blue color and slightly fragrant. Of easy cultivation in light loam, P. divaricata is a most desirable plant for wide, open pockets on the more level parts of the rock garden. It is also valuable when grouped in the front of the flower border or used in the woodland garden.

The color varies considerably, and several good color forms are in cultivation, including alba, white; Laphamii, deep lavender-purple; and Violet Queen, with rich, violet-colored flowers.

P. divaricata may be raised from seeds sown in spring in a cold frame, by soft cuttings in spring, or perhaps most easily by division of the roots in spring or early summer.

Grows Wild on Extinct Volcanoes. Phlox diffusa, which grows in Oregon on many of the extinct volcanoes such as Mount Hood, and in British Columbia, Washington and California, is a beautiful mat-forming plant of prostrate growth, somewhat woody at the base. In the volcanic sands of Mount Hood it grows in the utmost profusion, and in endless variety of color, from pure white to lavender, mauve, lilac and pink. In cultivation, this lovely plant is at present rare.

Phlox Douglasii is a most desirable plant, but there seems to be some doubt as to its correct name. In effect it is very like some of the lavender-colored forms of P. diffusa as seen on Mount Hood and elsewhere. P. Douglasii (of gardens) is a neat, compact, mat-forming plant, spreading, under favorable conditions, in a rich green, mosslike carpet a foot or more in extent, which in May and June becomes covered with a mass of almost stemless, almond-scented blossoms of clear lavender-blue. It grows best in a light soil, and prefers an open, sunny, well-drained position.

A variety of this fine plant with lilac-colored flowers, P. Douglasii lilacina, is in cultivation and, although not quite so pleasing as the original type, is nevertheless a very desirable acquisition. Snow Queen, with pure white flowers, is usually classed as a variety of P. Douglasii, but is probably a hybrid.

P. Douglasii is propagated by soft cuttings in early summer, rooted in a cold frame in sand.

Phlox pilosa is not unlike P. divaricata but has narrower leaves which are rough with short hairs. It grows 12-18 in. tall, and bears heads of lavender-pink to deep rose-carmine flowers. It enjoys the same treatment as P. divaricata and responds to the same methods of propagation. It is a native of eastern North America.

Phlox procumbens is reputed to be, and probably is, a hybrid between P. amoena and P. subulata. It is prostrate in habit and in May and June bears handsome heads of flowers of light violet color. It is increased by division of the roots or by cuttings rooted in sand in a cold frame in spring.

One of the Earliest to Flower. P. stolonifera, which is also known as P. reptans, is a distinct and very beautiful plant from Pennsylvania to Georgia. It has roundish leaves and 6-in. stems carrying loose heads of large flowers of deep-rose or rose-purple color. It is easily grown in light loam. As to propagation, the plant itself gives the matter attention by sending out numerous stolons or runners in the manner of a Strawberry. These root where they touch the ground, each tip providing a young plant. Phlox stolonfera is one of the earliest to flower, and is in full beauty in early spring.

With Starlike Flowers. Phlox bifida belongs to the mossy or mat-forming section. It is a free grower, with long, narrow leaves and countless heads of rather large blossoms; each of the five petals is deeply cleft, giving the flower a starry appearance. The color of the flowers is the palest blue-white. This is a showy and desirable plant which may be grown with ease in any sunny spot and light soil in the rock garden, and is equally at home in the wall garden. A single plant will soon cover a foot or more of ground. It grows 6-9 in. high and blooms in May and June. It is propagated by soft cuttings taken in spring or early summer and rooted in sand in a cold frame.

The Moss Pink. Phlox subulata, the Moss Pink, is without doubt the most widely grown and generally useful and beautiful of all the rock garden Phloxes. It is a native of eastern North America, from New York to North Carolina. It forms a prostrate mat of wiry stems clothed in loose heads, on stems 3-5 in. high, in April and May; a plant will cover itself with such a profusion of blossom as practically to hide all the foliage.

There are numerous varieties in cultivation and it is possible that some of the named forms of P. subulata are of hybrid origin.

P. subulata and its varieties are of the easiest possible cultivation, thriving in loamy soil in an open, sunny, well-drained position. They are most effective when massed among rocks on a slope of the rock garden, down which they will cascade in brilliant splendor, a blaze of solid color when in flower and a handsome rug of rich green for the rest of the year. They are excellent as ground covers and for planting dry walls.

Propagation is easy. Soft cuttings taken in spring or early summer may be rooted in sand in a cold frame. Plants are also easily raised from seeds but the color of the flowers of seedlings may vary considerably, with poorer colors predominating.

Noteworthy varieties of the Moss Pink, Phlox subulata, are the following: alba, white; Appleblossom, soft-pink; Blue Hills, pale blue; Camalaensis, a strong grower with large, handsome flowers of rich rose-pink; G. F. Wilson, a strong grower producing masses of lovely lavender-blue flowers in wild profusion; Lilac Queen, deep lavender-blue with dark eye; Admiration, deep rose-red; Alexander's Pink, clear pink; Alexander's Surprise, salmon-pink; Cory Louis, clear pink; Eventide, pale blue; Scarlet Flame, red; Starglow, pale blue; White Delight, pure white; Vivid, bright pink with dark pink eye.

For Rock Walls. Apart from their great usefulness and charm in the rock garden, the various forms of P. subulata are admirable for planting in the wall garden, where they quickly make themselves at home and produce cascades of pink, lavender or white. They are, moreover, invaluable for planting in bold drifts in the forefront of the herbaceous border, where

Phlox adsurgens, a native of the Pacific Northwest, is a good rock-garden plant for a lightly shaded location.

they can make a brave show of massed color.

It is worth while planting among them some of the smaller bulbs which bloom later in order to provide a succession of flowers to follow those of the Phloxes.

PHLOX, NIGHT. Zaluzianskya capensis, which see.

PHOENIX—*Date Palm* (Phoe'nix). Palms which are cultivated for their ornamental foliage. They are found growing wild in various parts of the world, including North Africa, India, China, and the Canary Islands. They belong to the Palm family, Palmaceae. Phoenix is the old Greek name for Date.

These plants form stout, cylindrical trunks, 5-100 ft. in height, which are covered with the stumps of dead leaves. The leaves, which are formed in clusters at the tops of the stems, are 3-14 ft. in length, recurving gracefully downwards towards the ground. They are pinnate (feather-like), the leaflets being arranged at short intervals along each side of the midrib. The leaflets are linear (long and narrow), leathery, and sharp-pointed, and the edges are folded inwards. The flowers, which are not ornamental, are in large pendulous clusters, and these give rise to fleshy drupes (fruits). The well-known dates of commerce are produced by P. dactylifera.

As these Palms are tender and do not bear fruits until they attain large dimensions, they are often cultivated for their ornamental foliage only. P. dactylifera is not the most popular plant for the purpose, although easily raised from the "stones," because it is less graceful and not so compact as some of the other kinds.

Outdoor Culture. The Date Palm, P. dactylifera will fruit satisfactorily only where high temperatures and a dry, desert atmosphere prevail during critical periods of the year. Fruits are produced in parts of Arizona, California and Texas. In other warm parts of the country it, and other kinds of Phoenix, may be grown outdoors as ornamentals without any special difficulty. They prefer a moderately moist soil and light shade while young. Among the hardiest kinds are P. canariensis and P. sylvestris. P. Roebelenii is one of the most tender.

Palms for a Warm Greenhouse. Although

some of the Phoenix Palms do best in a tropical greenhouse, the majority can be successfully cultivated in a greenhouse where the minimum winter temperature is 50 degrees. They may be used for house decoration and large specimens may be stood on terraces or patios or plunged out of doors in summer to produce a subtropical effect.

The best compost for potting consists of three parts of loam, and equal parts of leaf mold (or peat moss) and well-decayed manure, with coarse sand freely added. Repotting is done in March. The plants are taken out of their pots, the crocks and loose soil are removed from their roots, and then the plants are set in pots two sizes larger. The new pots must be clean and well drained with crocks, and the compost made firm. After potting, the plants are frequently syringed and the atmosphere is maintained in a moist condition by frequently damping the floor and benches. This assists root action, and helps the plants to recover quickly from the move.

Summer and Winter Management. The soil is not watered until it becomes moderately dry, then it is thoroughly moistened. This system of

A fine specimen of Phoenix growing in Florida.

watering is continued until the roots have freely penetrated the new soil, after which the compost is kept moist throughout the summer.

On the approach of autumn, less watering is needed, and throughout the winter the compost is only moistened when it becomes fairly dry. Less syringing and damping are required in winter, but neither the compost nor the atmosphere must be allowed to remain long in a dry state.

Plants which are growing in large pots or tubs are kept vigorous for many years without an annual repotting. They are top-dressed in spring with rich compost and watered once a week in summer with dilute liquid fertilizer.

The leaves of these plants should be sponged occasionally with insecticide to keep them clean and free from scale insects.

Raising Date Palms from Seeds. Trees intended for fruit production are usually raised from suckers; for other purposes propagation is principally by stones (seeds). They are first soaked in tepid water for two days to soften them. Deep seed pans are used for sowing. These are well drained with crocks on which is laid a layer of rough leaves. The remainder of the space is filled with a compost consisting of equal parts of finely sifted loam and coarse sand. The seeds are sown 1 in. apart and 1 in. deep, and the soil is well moistened.

A pane of glass is laid over the seed pan, which is placed in a propagating case with a bottom heat of 70-80 degrees. When the seedlings, which are slow in germinating, are 2-3 in. high, they are potted separately in 3-in. pots and subsequently in larger pots.

Seedlings of the common Date Palm are easily raised by sowing seeds in pots on a window sill, or even in the open ground.

P. Roebelenii is increased by offsets in spring or summer. These are taken off and inserted singly near the edge of small pots which are plunged in a propagating case, provided with bottom heat, until well rooted. They are then treated as advised for the seedlings.

Phoenix dactylifera, in addition to producing the edible Date fruits, has other economic uses. Baskets are made of the leafstalks, and ropes and mats are made from the fiber of the leaves.

The principal kinds are P. reclinata, 20-40 ft.; P. Roebelenii, 5 ft.; P. rupicola, 20 ft.; P. canariensis, 12 ft.; P. acaulis, 12 ft.; P. sylvestris, 40 ft.; and P. dactylifera, the Date Palm.

PHOLIDOTA—*Rattlesnake Orchid* (Pholido'-ta). Curious but not showy Orchids, found wild through the East, from India to Australia. There are two types, both epiphytal (tree-growing), one with subglobose pseudobulbs and dark green, leathery leaves, the other with ascending jointed stems. The greater number flower in summer. Pholidota is derived from *pholis,* a scale, and *ous,* an ear, and alludes to the earlike appearance of the bracts.

Those with very hard pseudobulbs—for example, P. imbricata—must have a rest in winter, water being almost entirely withheld; the other kinds must be watered occasionally during that season. All require a warm greenhouse with a semitropical atmosphere during summer, and a winter temperature of 55 degrees by night. Water should be given freely when the plants are in full growth. Flowerpots or flower pans may be used, according to the size of the plant. Repotting, if required, is done in March or April, using a compost of three parts of osmunda fiber and two parts of sphagnum moss.

P. ventricosa, P. imbricata and P. articulata are the chief kinds. All have yellowish-white flowers.

PHORADENDRON — *Mistletoe* (Phoraden'-dron). A group of semiparasitic plants, natives of the Americas, that are related to the genus Viscum, which includes the European Mistletoe. Phoradendron belongs to the Mistletoe family, Loranthaceae. Its name is derived from *phor,* a thief, and *dendron,* a tree.

Phoradendron flavescens is the common Mistletoe of the eastern United States, where it occurs as a native, chiefly parasitic on Oak trees. It is not cultivated.

PHORMIUM—*New Zealand Flax* (Phor'-mium). A group of plants of vigorous growth with iris-like leaves, 5-6 ft. long, which are very ornamental. They are natives of New Zealand and belong to the Lily family, Liliaceae. The word Phormium is derived from *phormos,* a basket, and refers to the use of the leaf fiber for basket making; this fiber is also used in the

A handsome specimen of Phormium
tenax, the New Zealand Flax.

commercial manufacture of ropes and twine.

These plants are grown in gardens chiefly for
the value of their handsome leaves. They bloom
when established, the small, reddish-yellow flowers being produced on stems 8-10 ft. high in
summer.

A Striking Plant with Ornamental Leaves.
The kind chiefly found in gardens is Phormium
tenax, the common New Zealand Flax. It is a
noble plant when well developed and adds distinction to the garden. Unfortunately, it is not
hardy and is suitable for planting out of doors
only in southern gardens or in other comparatively mild places.

A Good Plant for the Waterside. The New
Zealand Flax thrives best in deep, moist, loamy
soil, and is an excellent plant for the waterside.
In places where climatic conditions are suitable
but the soil is clayey or sandy, the plant will do
well if set in a hole 2 ft. deep and 2-3 ft.
across, filled with rich, loamy soil.

When to Plant. Planting should be done in
spring. During prolonged hot, dry weather in
summer this plant must be watered abundantly
to ensure vigorous growth, and occasional applications of liquid fertilizer will assist the development of the leaves.

Propagation. It is unwise to disturb the New
Zealand Flax unnecessarily, but if the plants
outgrow their positions, or if an increased
stock is wanted, propagation by division of the
rootstocks should be practiced in March. It is an
advantage to place the rooted pieces in large
pots of loamy soil and keep them in a cold
frame for a few weeks, planting them out of
doors when they are well rooted.

Propagation can also be easily effected by
means of seeds sown in sandy, peaty soil indoors in a temperature of about 60 degrees in
January or February. Plants from such a sowing
make sizable specimens the first year.

Varieties with Colored Leaves. The typical
Phormium tenax has green leaves, but there are
several varieties in which the leaves are colored.

In variegatum they are green with white or pale yellow stripes; in atropurpureum the leaves have a bronze-purple tinge; in the variety Veitchianum, which is probably the most handsome of the New Zealand Flaxes with colored leaves, the leaves are green with a central band of pale yellow. One kind, named alpinum, which has green leaves, is less vigorous than the typical kind. The varieties with colored leaves are less hardy than the others.

Phormium Colensoi is another species from New Zealand; the leaves are not so long as those of P. tenax and the flowers are yellow.

Cultivation in Tubs or Large Pots. The New Zealand Flaxes are sometimes grown in tubs or large flowerpots in places where they cannot be safely wintered out of doors. They are potted in a compost consisting of turfy loam, two thirds, and leaf mold or peat moss and decayed manure, one third, with a scattering of sand. Rooted pieces should be potted in 8-in. pots in March, just before the plants start into fresh growth, and kept in a frostproof greenhouse or frame. When they are well rooted in these pots, they must be repotted in larger pots or tubs.

During the summer months they may be placed out of doors for the ornamentation of porches, terraces and patios, or by the side of garden steps. The varieties with colored leaves are especially worth growing in this way. Great care must be taken that the roots are well supplied with water during the summer months; that is the secret of success in keeping them healthy and vigorous.

Late in September or early in October, before there is danger of sharp frost at night, the plants should be taken indoors. They will pass through the winter safely in a greenhouse which is heated sufficiently to exclude frost, or even in a cellar which is light and frostproof.

PHOTINIA (Photi'nia). Evergreen and leaf-losing (deciduous) ornamental foliage and flowering shrubs with berry-like fruits. They are found wild in China, Japan and other parts of Asia and belong to the Rose family, Rosaceae. They form branching shrubs up to 20 ft. in height.

These shrubs have ovate, obovate or oblong leaves, which are smooth or tomentose (hairy),

Photinia serrulata growing in the United States National Arboretum at Washington, D. C.

2-7 in. long; serrate (saw-edged), and acute (pointed at the tips). The flowers, which are produced in small clusters in July, are white, ¼ in. in diameter, and are succeeded by small red fruits. The name Photinia is derived from the Greek *photeinos*, shining, and refers to the

Fruiting twig of Photinia serrulata, a handsome evergreen shrub from China.

Photinia Beauverdiana is an attractive flowering tree. This specimen is growing in The New York Botanical Garden.

The flowers of Photinia Beauverdiana are white, grow in clusters and closely resemble those of the Hawthorn.

conspicuously shining leaves of some of the species.

Shrubs for a Sunny Position. The leaf-losing kinds are mostly hardy in the North; the evergreen kinds will live outdoors over winter only where the climate is relatively mild. Ordinary garden soil is suitable. If it is badly drained or consists of heavy clay, it should be removed to the depth of 2 ft. and be replaced with light garden soil, or sandy loam. Planting is done in spring, the soil being made firm around the roots, and afterwards soaked with water.

Very little further attention is required, except to shorten extra long shoots in spring.

Propagation is by cuttings, layering or grafting. Cuttings are taken in July. Firm, well-ripened shoots, 9 in. in length, are selected. The lower leaves are removed and a cut is made just below the bottom node (joint). The shoots are then inserted in a bed of sand or sand and peat moss in a cold frame, which is kept close until roots are formed. When sufficiently well rooted, the shoots are potted separately in 5-in. pots and, when well rooted in these, are planted out in their permanent positions.

Layering is done in summer. A low branch is bent down to the soil. Then, at a point some 12 in. or so from the tip, a slit is made in the stem, just beneath a joint. The knife is then turned upwards and the cut continued through the joint to ½ in. above it. The tongue thus

formed is buried 2 in. below the soil and the end of the shoot is tied to a short stake. During dry weather the soil must be kept moist; when sufficient roots have formed, the rooted shoot is severed from the branch and potted or planted in its permanent position.

Air layering (which see) may also be employed as a method of propagation.

Grafting is done in early spring and the Quince stock is used. The stock, which should

Photinia serrulata is a tender evergreen. It has clusters of creamy white flowers in summer.

be about ½ in. in diameter and well rooted in a pot, is cut down to just above the soil level. Either the splice or cleft system of grafting may be used (see Grafting). The grafted plants must remain in the greenhouse or cold frame until the tissues have united, and the atmosphere is kept moist so that the foliage will stay fresh. Afterwards the plants are treated as described for rooted cuttings or layers.

The principal kinds are P. serrulata, leaves evergreen, smooth, flowers white, berries red; P. Davidsoniae, leaves evergreen, dark, glossy green, flowers white, fruit orange-red; P. villosa, deciduous, flowers white, fruit bright red; P. parvifolia, deciduous, a shrub with white flowers and scarlet fruit; and P. Beauverdiana, flowers white, fruit bright red.

PHOTOSYNTHESIS. This is the process by which plants produce sugars and starches, or carbohydrates—plant foods which are essential sources of energy. Photosynthesis is carried on exclusively by green (chlorophyll-containing) plants. As its name suggests (*photo,* light, and *synthesis,* putting together), it is a construction process which takes place in the presence of light. The process is so important that, should it suddenly be halted, the result would sooner or later be fatal to all life. Not only would plants disappear from this globe, but also all the animals, including man, that depend on them for food.

In the process of photosynthesis, green plants (the green color is sometimes completely or partly obscured by red or yellow pigments, as in some Coleus, Crotons and Dracaenas) combine carbon dioxide and water, through the energy of light, to produce a simple sugar, glucose. A most important material involved in the process of photosynthesis is chlorophyll. This is a mixture of pigments which has the amazing ability of being able to absorb energy from sunlight.

Under normal conditions, particles of chlorophyll are constantly being broken down and other particles are being formed, but this continues only as long as the plant is in light. A familiar example illustrates the need for light for the formation of chlorophyll: when a board which has been laid across a grassy spot for a few days is lifted, the grass beneath is no longer green, but will be noticed to have turned yellow.

Chlorophyll does not occur free in the plant cells but is contained in minute, more or less spherical bodies called chloroplasts which lie in the syrupy contents of the cells. They are present in many above-ground parts, but in varying numbers, from the largest number in the leaves to few or none in most mature stems. Underground parts may also develop chloroplasts when these parts are exposed to sunlight, as is observed in the greening of potatoes left a few days on the soil surface.

The raw materials used in the process of photosynthesis are carbon dioxide and water. Carbon dioxide is a gas which normally forms only about three hundredths of 1 per cent of the atmosphere.

While some of the carbon dioxide enters the plant by passing directly through the outermost layer of cells (the epidermis), most of it enters through large numbers of minute pores, especially through those located on the lower surfaces of the leaves. These pores (or stomata) are opened and closed by means of special cells which line the mouth of the opening to control the flow of gases into and from the leaf. They are regularly closed in darkness and also when there is an insufficient supply of water available, but ordinarily they gradually open as light becomes increasingly intense toward noon, and then close again slowly in the afternoon hours as the light intensity decreases.

The water used in photosynthesis is practically all obtained through the roots and passes from them to the leaves and green stems, where photosynthesis takes place. Without an adequate supply of water, photosynthesis is slowed down or halted.

Light Essential. It can be easily demonstrated that light is essential for the manufacture of carbohydrates in photosynthesis. A plant which has been kept in a dark closet for several days may be placed for a few hours in the light with part of one leaf covered by a piece of tinfoil or a similar shield. When this partly covered leaf is removed from the plant and tested with an iodine solution, it will be found that starch has formed only in areas of the leaf exposed to the light.

Lack of sufficient light is often the cause of less-than-peak production by plants growing out of doors. Sometimes, however, leaves in direct, full sunlight are not able to photosynthesize as rapidly as they otherwise might because the carbon dioxide supply or the supply of water is not ample enough. Thus, either the lack of sufficient light-energy or insufficient supplies of raw materials may limit the rate at which photosynthesis can produce plant foods.

In nature each species of plant has adapted itself to a certain range of light intensities at which it carries on the process most efficiently. Some species thrive only with large amounts of direct sunlight (sun plants, as most of our crop plants are), while others thrive best in the dim, leaf-filtered light of the forest floor (shade plants). Many common house plants, such as African Violets, Episcias, and many Aroids, are typical shade plants and consequently prosper in dimly lighted interiors of buildings.

Artificial Light. Many plants that thrive in dim light can be grown quite successfully in artificial light alone, in a basement or attic. The well-being of plants grown indoors can often be improved with the help of artificial light. Daylight-type fluorescent tubes may be used for this purpose—they are especially satisfactory because the amount of heat they give off is not likely to be harmful. The best results may usually be obtained by using both fluorescent and ordinary incandescent bulbs to supplement the natural light received by the plants. Whether a plant receives the necessary light from bulbs or from the sun, the course of photosynthesis is exactly the same.

The Process, Step by Step. In light, the tiny pores (stomata) in the leaf surfaces open and carbon dioxide flows into the spaces between loosely fitting cells in the interior of the leaf. Here the gas is dissolved in the film of water surrounding the cell walls and eventually passes to the chloroplasts (chlorophyll-bearing bodies). The chlorophyll absorbs light-energy, and this is used immediately to decompose some of the water into its components, oxygen and hydrogen. The oxygen thus freed passes out of the leaf and becomes part of the atmospheric oxygen. The hydrogen combines with the carbon dioxide within the leaf cells to form carbohydrates, the first of which is the simple sugar called glucose.

During the early morning hours of an ordinary day, there is a gradual increase in the total amount of sugars, resulting from photosynthesis, present in the leaf. By noon, the sugars begin to be changed into starch, which is stored in the form of small granules in either chloroplasts or in special chloroplast-like bodies. In the afternoon the amount of starch begins to decrease and, by sunrise the following morning, little, if any, of the previous day's production is left.

The explanation of this is that there is a continual movement of sugars in solution, out of the leaves where they are produced and into other, non-green parts of the plant. When the rate of photosynthesis of sugars is greater than the rate of their movement out of the leaves, as is the case in intense sunlight, the surplus is stored as starch. Then, when photosynthesis slows with diminishing light of the sun, the starch in storage is gradually changed back to sugars. These pass in solution to other parts of the plant which need energy or in which food materials are being stored.

Products of Photosynthesis. All living organisms need energy for carrying on the activities of life, although it may be more difficult to see the necessity for large quantities in plants than in animals. However, plants do use significant amounts of energy in the construction of new cells in the growth of stems, roots, flowers, fruits, etc. Rather large amounts are also used regularly in the formation of such complicated materials in the plant as proteins, fats, chlorophyll and various enzymes. All this energy is released from the carbohydrates formed in photosynthesis, by the transformation of these foods, in the presence of oxygen, into carbon dioxide and water. A large proportion of this stored energy is never used by the plant but becomes a source of energy for animals when they consume the plant. Thus, the cycle is complete; the energy of the sun, trapped in the products of photosynthesis, is released sooner or later for the maintenance and reproduction of the plant or for the nutrition of animals which feed upon it.

Many plants, such as fungi and bacteria, do

not contain chlorophyll and, being unable to synthesize food materials from simple elements, are obliged to obtain their food in much the same way as animals do—that is, they depend either directly or indirectly upon green plants for it; they feed upon the tissues, living or dead, of other plants or animals.

Ordinarily, plants get enough carbon dioxide from the normal amounts in the air for photosynthesis to take place at a satisfactory rate, but it has been shown experimentally that the rate of food manufacture in plants can be increased several hundred per cent by increasing the amount of the carbon dioxide in the atmosphere to about 1 per cent, provided there is sufficient light and water to support the higher rate of production. Unfortunately, it is not generally practicable or economical to increase the percentage of carbon dioxide in the atmosphere about plants.

PHRAGMIPEDIUM. A name that is correctly applied to a group of Orchids that, in gardens, are most usually known by the older name Cypripedium. In this book they are treated under Cypripedium, which see.

PHRAGMITES MAXIMA—*Common Reed Grass* (Phragmi'tes). A tall marsh Grass, of the family Gramineae, that is a native of North America and many other parts of the world. Its name is from the Greek, *phragma,* a fence or screen; it frequently grows along ditches in the form of a hedge.

Although too rampant to be admitted to small gardens or small pools, this is a handsome plant for selected use in landscape planting. A native of marshes with either brackish (salty) or sweet water, it will thrive in any fairly moist soil. Once established in a marshy area, it is difficult to eliminate.

Phragmites maxima (communis) grows 10-15 ft. tall and bears plumed flower heads that may be dried for use in winter flower arrangements. It is propagated by division of the rootstocks and by seeds. In addition to the green-leaved form, a variety called variegata, with leaves striped with white, has been named.

PHRYNIUM. Another name for a number of tropical, ornamental-leaved plants, which are dealt with under Ctenanthe, which see.

PHYGELIUS CAPENSIS — *Cape Fuchsia* (Phyge'lius). An herbaceous native of South Africa, which belongs to the Snapdragon family, Scrophulariaceae. The name is derived from *phyga,* flight, and *helios,* sun, and refers to the plant's liking for shady places in its native country.

Only one kind is in cultivation, Phygelius capensis. This is an attractive plant which reaches a height of about 3 ft. and bears narrow, tube-shaped, scarlet or orange-scarlet flowers in July and August chiefly.

For a Sunny, Sheltered Location. As it is not very hardy, Phygelius is only suitable for planting out of doors in comparatively mild districts. In sheltered places it survives outdoors as far north as Philadelphia. It thrives best in a sunny place, and needs well-drained soil; it is most successful in light, loamy ground. Heavy clayey land can be made suitable by adding compost or other organic material and sand. Planting should be done in spring.

Propagation. It is unwise to disturb the plants while they continue to flourish, unless it is wished to increase the stock by division. That is done by lifting them in spring and separating them into rooted pieces; the latter should be potted and grown in a cold frame until they are sufficiently well rooted to be planted out of doors.

Another method of propagation, and the one to be preferred, is to detach small shoots when fresh growth begins in spring. The lowest leaves are removed from these shoots, which are cut beneath a joint and inserted as cuttings in a propagating case in a slightly heated greenhouse. Or seeds may be sown under glass in spring.

PHYLICA ERICOIDES (Phyl'ica). A shrub from South Africa, suitable for cultivation in a sunny greenhouse with a minimum temperature of 45 degrees and outdoors in mild climates such as that of California. It belongs to the family Rhamnaceae. The name is from *phyllikos,* leafy. Phylica should be potted in a compost of sandy peat, and is increased by cuttings in July. The plant grows 2-3 ft. high and bears white flowers in summer.

PHYLLAGATHIS ROTUNDIFOLIA (Phyllag'athis). A warm-greenhouse shrub with ornamental flowers and leaves. It is a native of

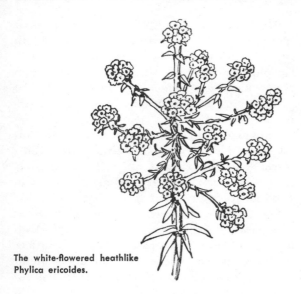

The white-flowered heathlike Phylica ericoides.

Sumatra and belongs to the family Melastomaceae. This plant grows 1-2 ft. in height and has quadrangular (four-sided) stems. The leaves are very ornamental; they are opposite, almost round, 6-9 in. in diameter, and heart-shaped at the base. The upper surface is deep metallic-green flushed with red, and the undersides are deep red. The flowers, which are small, four-petaled, and reddish, are produced in terminal clusters in summer. The name is from *phyllon,* leaf, and *agatheos,* divine, and refers to the beauty of the foliage.

Ornamental-leaved Plant for a Hothouse. This plant requires a minimum winter temperature of 55 degrees. The best potting compost consists of two parts of fibrous loam, one part of peat, and a little well-decayed manure, with sand added freely.

Repotting is done in February. After potting, the soil is not watered until it approaches dryness, when it is thoroughly saturated. This method of watering is continued until the plants are well established, when the compost is kept moist. During the winter it is only moistened when it becomes quite dry.

From the time growth commences until early autumn, the atmosphere is kept continually moist by frequently damping the floor and benches. During the autumn and winter much less atmospheric moisture is required. In spring and summer the foliage must be shaded from strong sunlight, but for the rest of the year no shading is required.

Propagation is chiefly by cuttings in March or April. They are placed in a propagating case in the hothouse. When roots are formed the plants are potted separately in 3-in. pots and subsequently in larger pots.

Leaves may also be used as cuttings. They are detached with the leafstalk intact and are inserted in pots of sandy soil and treated as advised for the cuttings.

PHYLLANTHUS—*Otaheite Gooseberry* (Phyllanth'us). Tropical, shrubby plants which are cultivated for the beauty of their leaves and, in some cases, for their edible fruits. They are found wild in many parts of the world, including the West Indies, tropical Asia, South America, South Africa, and Australia, and belong to the Euphorbia family, Euphorbiaceae.

These plants are light and graceful in habit and form shrubs or small trees 20-30 ft. in height. The side branches are slender, in some kinds horizontal and the small, ovate or oblong leaves are arranged along each side, giving the branchlets the appearance of large pinnate leaves.

Decorative Plants. The apetalous (without petals) flowers are small, and greenish or yellow. Although individually they are inconspicuous, they are produced so abundantly that they form a striking feature of the plants, hanging singly or in clusters on long, slender stalks from the undersides of the branches. The name Phyllanthus is derived from *phyllon,* a leaf, and *anthos,* a flower, and refers to the flowers' being borne apparently on the leaves.

Cultivation. In southern Florida the Otaheite Gooseberry, or Star Gooseberry as it is sometimes called, is occasionally cultivated for its edible fruit and it also occurs spontaneously as an escape (a plant that has escaped from cultivation). It attains a height of about 20 ft. and needs no special cultural care.

When grown in greenhouses, Phyllanthus requires a minimum winter temperature of 55 degrees and a soil compost of equal parts of loam, leaf mold and peat, with sand added freely. Repotting is done in March. The plants are taken out of the old pots and after the crocks and loose soil have been removed from the roots, are set in slightly larger pots. These are filled to one quarter of their depth with crocks which are covered with a layer of rough leaves. The soil must be made firm, and sufficient space left at the top of the pot for watering. The plants are shaded from sunlight until established, and the atmosphere is kept moist by damping the floor and benches.

No water is given until the soil becomes moderately dry, when it is thoroughly moistened. This system of watering is continued until the plants are well rooted, then the soil is kept moist throughout the summer. When growth is finished, less water is given, and during the winter the soil is only watered when it becomes nearly dry.

Although these plants can be grown year after year to form large specimens, they are most useful and ornamental for greenhouse purposes, in small pots. Therefore, it is usual to grow them only for two or three years and then to discard them and replace them by young plants grown from cuttings.

When to Take Cuttings. Tips of the shoots, about 3 in. in length, are taken off, and prepared by removing the leaves from the lower half and making a cut below the bottom joint. They are then inserted in a mixture of equal parts of peat moss and sand in a propagating case. The case is kept close, except for a few minutes each morning when the top is raised and the moisture is wiped from the underside of the glass. Unless attention is paid to this detail, the propagating case becomes so charged with moisture that the cuttings are liable to decay before they have formed roots.

When roots are formed, the plants are potted separately in 3-in. pots and subsequently into larger pots. Plants with a single stem, 12 in. in height, are very effective where small specimens are desired. Bushy plants are obtained by removing the tip of the main stem when it is a few inches high and treating the side branches similarly.

The Chief Kinds. P. acidus, Otaheite Gooseberry; P. Chantrieri, P. mimosoides, P. salviifolius, and P. pulcher (Reidia glaucescens). Plants grown as P. nivosus are Breynia nivosa.

PHYLLITIS (SCOLOPENDRIUM) — *Hart's-*

Tongue Fern (Phyllit'is). Hardy and tender evergreen Ferns which are found growing wild in Brazil, China, North America and Europe. Most of these Ferns have strap-shaped or tongue-like fronds; hence the common name, Hart's-Tongue Fern. The Latin name, Phyllitis, is derived from *phyllon,* a leaf, and refers to the fact that the fronds are undivided. P. Scolopendrium was formerly called Scolopendrium vulgare.

Beautiful Hardy Ferns. The common Hart's-Tongue Fern, Phyllitis Scolopendrium, grows abundantly in Europe and in a few places in North America. It may be found in moist shady woods, by the sides of streams and waterfalls, in the crevices of old walls, between the forking branches of trees, or in almost any position which is shaded, and where the roots are able to obtain sufficient moisture. In dense, shaded woods, the fronds attain their maximum length of 12 in., but in the crevices of walls, where the light is more intense and the atmosphere less humid, they are often not more than 2 in. in length.

Varieties of the Hart's-Tongue Fern. There are numerous varieties with crested or tessellated fronds. Some of the best of these are crispum, cristatum fimbriatum, grandiceps, marginatum undulatum and multipedum. These Ferns are ideal for decorating dull, sunless spots and, being evergreen, they are ornamental throughout the year.

Planting the Hardy Kinds. When preparing the site, the soil, if unsuitable, is excavated to the depth of 2 ft. and the hole or bed filled with a compost of two parts of leaf mold and one part of sandy loam.

The plants show to best advantage if the bed is slightly raised, with a gentle slope towards the front. Irregular boulders, preferably of sandstone, should be partly sunk, to provide a rocky effect, and the plants set between them.

Planting should be done in April or October, and the soil thoroughly moistened after the plants are inserted. When they are established, they need very little attention beyond watering in dry weather. The dead fronds should not be removed until April, as they form a protection to the young fronds. A light mulching with well-decayed leaf mold each spring is beneficial, as it provides additional nourishment and keeps the roots cool and moist in summer.

Ferns for a Cool Greenhouse. The crested and tessellated forms of the Hart's-Tongue Fern make very ornamental pot plants; they can be grown in a cool greenhouse, provided they are shaded from strong sunlight and the atmosphere is kept moist. They can also be grown in a cool, shady window.

Repotting should be done in April, or as soon as new fronds commence to uncurl. Well-drained pots are necessary and a soil compost of two parts of leaf mold and one part of sandy loam, with sufficient sand to keep it porous, should be used. The soil must be kept moist throughout the year, although less frequent watering is necessary during the winter.

Ferns for a Warm Greenhouse. The warm greenhouse kinds require a minimum winter temperature of 55 degrees. They must be shaded from strong sunlight, and the atmosphere must be kept moist by frequently damping the floor and benches; no syringing is necessary.

Every spring, in February or March, the plants should be examined to see if repotting is necessary. Those which have filled their pots with roots should be repotted in larger pots. The others can be left until a later date or, in some cases, repotting may not be necessary until the following spring. If, however, the soil is sour and the plants have made little root, then all the old soil must be washed away from the roots and the plants repotted in pots of the same size or even smaller. A compost of two parts of leaf mold and one part of sandy loam, with a small quantity of sand, is most suitable.

The principal kind for the warm greenhouse is P. brasiliensis, fronds 9 in. long.

Potting and General Management. When used for potting, the compost must contain sufficient moisture. To test it, squeeze a handful. If moisture exudes, it is too wet; if, when the hand is opened, the soil trickles out, it is too dry. When a handful of soil is squeezed and the hand opened, the soil should fall apart at the lightest touch. When repotting, the soil must be pressed firmly with the fingers, not rammed with a potting stick.

After potting, no water is applied to the soil until it approaches dryness, and then it is thoroughly moistened. Care must be taken to avoid overwatering the Ferns until the pots are filled with roots. Afterwards the soil should be kept moist throughout the year; but during the winter months less frequent watering is necessary, about once a week being enough.

Raising the Hart's-Tongue Fern from Spores. Most kinds are raised by sowing spores as soon as they are ripe. Generally they are of a deep brown color and, when the frond is shaken, they fly off in the form of a fine powder. They are sown in well-drained pots or pans, filled with finely sifted compost. This should be sterilized, if possible, to prevent the development of mosses. For further details, see Ferns.

Other Methods of Propagation. Both the hardy and greenhouse kinds are easily increased by division. They are lifted from the open ground, or taken out of their pots at planting or potting time, and separated into smaller sections.

The hardy kinds are replanted in the garden and the greenhouse kinds potted in small pots.

A few kinds, such as P. Scolopendrium crispum, which do not produce spores freely, may be increased by inserting the stipes (frond stalks) as cuttings in pots of sand. Bulbils eventually form at the base of the stipes; from these bulbils young Ferns will develop.

One or two kinds form small bulbils on their fronds. These, if taken off and pressed into the surface of the soil, will eventually form new plants.

PHYLLOCACTUS. A name previously used for the showy genus of Cacti now called Epiphyllum, which see.

PHYLLOCLADUS—*Celery-topped Pine* (Phyllo'cladus; Phyllocla'dus). Evergreen trees and shrubs, natives of Tasmania, New Zealand, the Philippine Islands and Borneo, in which the true leaves are reduced to small, narrow, scalelike bodies in seedling plants; they are followed by green, leaflike branches (cladodes) that function as leaves. Those on the lateral branches, or those laterally placed on the shoots, are spirally arranged and look like simple leaves, but those near the points of the shoots, particularly the main shoots, are deeply lobed, sometimes pinnate, and arranged in whorls. It is on the edges of these leaflike structures that the flowers, and subsequently the seeds, are borne.

The male flowers are in slender cylindrical catkins, the female flowers are very small and solitary. A single nutlike seed develops on a scale which become fleshy as the seed matures. Phyllocladus belongs to the Yew family, Taxaceae. The name is taken from the words *phyllon*, leaf, and *klados*, branch, and alludes to the leaflike branchlets.

Propagation may be carried out by seeds sown, as soon as received, in a sandy compost of fibrous loam, peat and sand, in a warm greenhouse. Cuttings of short side shoots may be inserted in a warm propagating frame during spring or summer. All the kinds are tender and are only suitable for cultivation out of doors in the mild parts of North America. They require moist soil fairly free from lime and should be given a position sheltered from cold winds.

In their native countries the larger kinds are useful timber trees, the timber being rather like that of Yew. It works to a fine surface and with age takes on a rich color. Among other uses, it is popular for furniture and cabinetwork. The bark is rich in tannin.

The Chief Kinds. P. alpinus, commonly called Alpine Celery-topped Pine, is a bush or tree, 5-25 ft. high, with many branches. It is found in both the North and South Islands of New Zealand and, when stunted, bears some resemblance to Gaultheria. It is too small to have any timber value. P. glaucus is a tree 20-40 ft. high, known as Toatoa in the Auckland district of New Zealand; it forms a distinct tree but has little commercial value. P. hypophyllus is a bush or small tree, up to 35 ft. high, native to the Philippine Islands, New Guinea and Borneo. It is one of the most tender kinds.

P. rhomboidalis is a Tasmanian tree, growing 60 ft. in height, with a trunk girth of 6-9 ft., or on high mountains it may be a stunted bush. The wood is valuable in Tasmania for many purposes, but is too scarce for export. It is commonly called Celery-topped Pine.

P. trichomanoides is the Tanekaha of New Zealand. It grows into a tree 30-60 ft. high, with a trunk girth of 3-9 ft. The timber is of good quality and is much used in New Zealand.

Where these trees and bushes cannot be grown out of doors they form interesting pot plants for a cool greenhouse, for they are quite unlike other members of the Coniferae.

PHYLLODOCE (Phyllo'doce; Phyllodo'ce). Very attractive, dwarf evergreen shrubs allied to the Heathers and of heathlike habit, but with stiffer branchlets and larger leaves. The flowers are also larger than those of the Heathers, produced singly or several together, and they are bell- or pitcher-shaped. These shrubs are natives of North America, northern Europe and northern Asia; some of the kinds were at one time named Bryanthus. Phyllodoce belongs to the Heath family, Ericaceae, and the name is taken from Phyllodoce, the sea nymph of the classics.

For Moist Acid Soil in the Rock Garden. These shrubs are excellent for a moist position in the rock garden where the soil is acid, and they may also be used in masses in the Heath garden.

Seeds form a satisfactory means of propagation. Sow them on the surface of a flat or pan of sandy peat in a frame in autumn or spring and shade from sun until the young plants appear. As soon as they can be handled, transplant them, an inch apart, to flats of sandy peat; when the young plants meet, plant them in a nursery border.

Taking Cuttings. Cuttings of half-ripe shoots, an inch long, can be inserted in sandy peat under a bell jar or in a cold frame that is kept close in July; they are more difficult to root than the Heaths and do not grow so freely as seedling plants. As soon as the cuttings are rooted, they should be potted singly in small pots and kept in a cold frame until thoroughly well rooted before planting out.

Branches can be rooted by layering them (see Layering), and leaving them for two years, but plants raised by layers are often difficult to establish. When seeds can be procured, they should be preferred to cuttings or layers.

The only pruning necessary is the removal of flower heads as soon as the flowers fade.

The Chief Kinds. P. nipponica, a Japanese shrub, 6-8 in. high, bearing bell-shaped, white, pink-tinged flowers in May; P. Breweri, a California shrub, 6-12 in. high, with rosy-purple flowers in May; P. caerulea, a low shrub 6-9 in. high, widely distributed through the northerly parts of the Northern Hemisphere—its pitcher-shaped flowers are bluish-purple to reddish-purple and usually appear in June and July.

P. empetriformis is a western North American plant, 6-9 in. high, bearing reddish-purple, pitcher-shaped flowers in May and June. There are also P. glanduliflora from Alaska, and P. aleutica from Alaska and northern Asia.

PHYLLOSTACHYS—Bamboo (Phyllo'stachys; Phyllostach'ys). A group of Bamboos with long, elegant wandlike branches, natives of eastern Asia and the Himalayas; many kinds are suitable for cultivation out of doors in the milder parts of the United States.

The Phyllostachys can be distinguished from Arundinaria, the other large group of comparatively hardy Bamboos, by the way in which the side shoots are produced. In Phyllostachys the side shoots are in threes, two large, one small. In Arundinaria the side shoots are indefinite in number, but numerous and very mixed in size. Furthermore, in Arundinaria the sheaths on the stems are retained for a long while, whereas in Phyllostachys they fall very early in life.

Phyllostachys belongs to the Grass family, Gramineae. The name is taken from the Greek *phyllon,* leaf, and *stachys,* spike, and alludes to the leafy character of the flowering shoots.

These Bamboos Die After Flowering. As with many other groups of Bamboos, all the Phyllostachys die after flowering; therefore, when a plant shows signs of flowering, an effort should be made to save seeds. It may be necessary to net the plants, for the seeds are much sought after by birds. Fortunately the flowering cycle is only once in 30-40 years, but at that time, or within a year or two, the whole of the plants grown from one lot of seed flower, no matter where they may be growing. When seeds are not available the best means of propagation is by division of the clumps or masses of canes, which all spring from a common base, in spring.

Propagation by Division. If moderately large pieces are taken off they may be set out directly in the open ground; small pieces, with few roots attached, should be placed in flowerpots in a compost of loam, peat moss and sand and kept in a greenhouse until the new roots are active.

It is also possible to get young plants by laying long shoots in moist peat moss and sand or in sand under glass, to encourage young plants to appear from dormant buds near the base of the stems. This method is not very satisfactory.

Plants for a Moist Soil and a Sheltered Place. Like other Bamboos, the Phyllostachys may be expected to give the most satisfactory results when planted in rich, moist soil on the light rather than the heavy side. They should be in the vicinity of water or in such a place that they can be given plenty of water during dry weather, for they soon suffer from excessive drought. They must be sheltered from cold winds and, as they may be brown and ragged from February until early summer, they should be planted in a position away from spring-flowering shrubs. From July to February they are very charming evergreens, but they are often of drab appearance in spring.

Planting or transplanting is best carried out when the new shoots are an inch or two long. Plants moved at this time usually re-establish themselves at once, but those moved in fall or very early spring may grow very poorly for a year or two.

Pruning should be carried out once a year and should take the form of removing the oldest shoots to the ground line. The gardener can easily see which shoots to remove—those whose tips are beginning to die. This work should be done before the young shoots begin to grow. On no account should the ends of the shoots be cut off and lower parts left; they look ugly and do not grow again. At the time of pruning it is a good plan to wash the plants thoroughly with water from a hose in order to remove dust and grime.

If no transplanting is to be done, follow up the pruning and washing by lightly forking the ground beneath the shoots and applying a surface dressing of well-decayed manure, or apply a complete fertilizer and a mulch of compost or peat moss. If the ground is not very good an application of liquid fertilizer now and then, between April and August, will do good. Should the plants become very dry, make a basin of soil around the stems and allow water to trickle in from a spray hose for several hours at a time.

A large quantity of water given at once may run around the plants and fail to penetrate the dense mass of roots.

The Chief Kinds. The kinds described below are suitable for planting out of doors. As all form large plants, they should be given plenty of space.

Phyllostachys aurea, a Japanese plant known as Golden Bamboo, grows 10-15 ft. high; the stems are yellowish, erect and densely crowded.

P. bambusoides variety Castilloni, from Japan, is a graceful plant 10-12 ft. high, on which some of the leaves are variegated; the stems are yellow, with the flattened section of each joint green. It is a very attractive kind and one of the most vigorous.

The Black-Joint Bamboo. P. niger grows 12-25 ft. high. It is distinct by reason of its dark brown or sometimes almost black canes and small, bright green leaves. The variety Boryana has purple-spotted stems. In variety Henonis the stems are greenish to yellowish.

P. flexuosa forms a shapely plant with gracefully arching shoots. It is a native of China and grows about 18 ft. high.

P. sulphurea, the Moso Bamboo, is another vigorous kind. It forms stout stems that are yellow when mature, and may reach a length of 20 ft. A native of Japan, it has been grown in Western gardens since 1890.

Economic Uses. Many of the Phyllostachys are grown in Japan for plant stakes, and ripened stems are also used for building purposes, and in the manufacture of furniture.

PHYSALIS—*Husk Tomato, Chinese Lantern Plant* (Phy'salis). A group of annuals and perennials, some of which are grown for their edible fruits, and others for the ornamental value of their large, highly colored swollen calyces, which resemble miniature "Chinese lanterns." They grow wild in Asia, Europe and America and belong to the Potato family, Solanaceae. The name Physalis is derived from *physa,* a bladder, and alludes to the large calyx.

Kinds with Edible Fruits. The best-known Physalis that produces edible fruit is the Husk Tomato or Strawberry Tomato, P. pruinosa, which occurs naturally from Massachusetts to

The rich orange-colored "fruits" of Physalis Alkekengi are valuable for home decorations in winter.

Florida and westward. It is very easily cultivated in a sunny location in well-drained soil. The seeds may be sown directly outdoors in spring or young plants may be raised indoors and planted out when danger of frost has passed. The plants are of sprawling habit of growth and require spacing at least 4 ft. apart each way. The fruits are useful for making into preserves.

Two other species that require approximately the same culture but are more tender and need a longer season of growth are P. ixocarpa, the Tomatillo, a Mexican native that produces purplish berries and grows about 4 ft. tall, and P. peruviana, the Cape Gooseberry, which has yellow berries, grows 3 ft. tall and is a native of tropical South America.

The Chinese Lantern Plant. P. Alkekengii and its varieties are known by the common names of Alkekengi, Chinese Lantern Plant and Winter Cherry. These are perennials which spread by means of underground stems. In gardens they are sometimes grown as annuals.

There is nothing difficult in the cultivation of these plants. They are hardy and will thrive in well-drained soil in a sunny border; they are not a success in shady places or in heavy, ill-drained land. Light soil suits them well; heavy ground can be made suitable by deep digging and by mixing in compost and sand. Planting may be done in early fall or spring.

The simplest method of propagation is to lift and separate the plants into rooted pieces in spring and replant them. They may also be raised from seeds sown in a flat of sandy soil placed in a greenhouse in March, or in a cold frame in April. Seedlings may also be raised by sowing seeds in a nursery border out of doors in spring. Those raised indoors should be planted in a nursery border for the summer, and be set in their final positions in autumn or spring. Those raised by sowing seeds out of doors must be transplanted 6 in. apart, before they become crowded.

In soil which suits them, these kinds of Physalis soon spread, and care must be taken to lift and separate the clumps before they become overcrowded, or they may cease to bloom and fruit freely.

Useful for Indoor Decoration. The Chinese Lantern Plant and its varieties are very attractive in the garden in the late summer months, and the stems, bearing the large orange-colored "fruits," are invaluable to cut for use indoors during the autumn and winter; they last a long time and fill a large vase attractively.

The "fruits," as they are commonly called, are the swollen calyces of the white flowers which open in early summer. The stems, bearing the lantern-like calyces, should be cut as soon as they have developed their full coloring. The plants are grown in considerable numbers to supply the demand of florists.

Physalis Alkekengii has several distinct varieties. The one known as Franchetii is most robust, Bunyardii is compact and free-flowering, and major has exceptionally large "fruits," while those of the form called monstrosa are curiously contorted. The variety nana grows only 6 in. high.

PHYSOCARPUS — *Ninebark* (Physocar'pus). Hardy, leaf-losing (deciduous) shrubs, a few of which are deserving of cultivation in gardens. They are closely allied to Spiraea, and were previously included in the genus Neillia.

Thirteen kinds of Physocarpus grow natively in North America and one in northeastern Asia. They are distinguished from Neillia by their flowers, which are borne in corymb-like clusters, whereas those of Neillia are in racemes. The name Physocarpus is from the Greek *physa*, a bladder, and *karpos*, a fruit, and refers to the inflated fruits.

The best-known kind is Physocarpus opulifolius, a native of eastern North America. It grows 6-9 or 10 ft. high and may form a bush 15-20 ft. or more across, but this is not always an advantage; smaller clumps which have been grown in good soil are usually more vigorous in growth, with larger inflorescences. The broadly ovate leaves are lobed and doubly toothed. The corymbose inflorescences of white, pink-tinged flowers are showy during June. They are followed by attractive fruits. The variety luteus has yellow foliage which is attractive in early summer, but the rich coloring fades later in the season.

Another attractive kind is P. monogynus, which grows 3-3½ ft. tall and is native from Wyoming to South Dakota, Texas and New Mexico. Other kinds are sometimes grown.

PHYSOSIPHON TUBATUS (Physosi'phon; Physos'iphon). A small epiphytal Orchid, found wild in Mexico: it is of tufted growth and has slender stems, each with one evergreen leaf. The spikes, 6 in. or more high, bear numerous flowers in summer or autumn; these are orange-brown and greenish. The name, which refers to the shape of the flowers, is derived from *physa*, a bladder, and *siphon*, a tube; the tube of the flower is somewhat inflated.

A greenhouse with a moist atmosphere, a minimum winter temperature of 50 degrees, and as near 60 degrees as possible for the remainder of the year, suits this Orchid. Shading must be given in bright weather and the plants kept moist throughout the year. They are repotted in March, using a compost of three parts of cut osmunda fiber and two parts of sphagnum moss. If large enough, they may then be divided. Water must be given throughout the year.

PHYSOSTEGIA—*Obedient Plant, False Dragonhead* (Physosteg'ia). A small group of hardy, herbaceous plants of North America, which belong to the Mint family, Labiatae. The principal kind, P. virginiana, grows 3-5 ft. in height, has smooth green stems, clothed with lanceolate (lance-shaped) leaves, 3-5 in. in length, with serrate edges. The flowers, which are produced

Pink flower spikes of the autumn-blooming Physostegia virginiana, the Obedient Plant.

Vivid, 1½ ft., which has bright rose-red flowers.

PHYTEUMA—*Horned Rampion* (Phyteu'ma). An interesting group of mountain plants belonging to the Bellflower family, Campanulaceae, only a few of which are in cultivation. Phyteuma is an old Greek name meaning "the plant."

These are hardy perennial herbs, natives of Europe, the Mediterranean region and temperate Asia. They are mostly of easy cultivation in light, well-drained, loamy soil, and may readily be increased by seeds sown in pots of light, sandy soil in a cold frame in spring.

The flowers are arranged in spherical heads, or in spikes several inches long, and each flower is curiously tube-shaped and often inflated at the base, with threadlike stigmas protruding from the top of the tube.

The Best Kind. Phyteuma comosum is the choicest and the most curious of all. It is a cliff-dwelling plant, native to Dalmatia, Carniola, southern Tyrol, etc., where it inhabits the hardest limestone rock, its fleshy roots being packed tightly into the minutest cracks and crevices. It is chiefly adaptable for cultivation in regions such as the Pacific Northwest, where fairly cool summers prevail.

Phyteuma comosum is a dwarf plant, never rising above two or three inches in height, though an old specimen may spread to six inches or even a foot across. The leaves are holly-shaped, dark, glossy green, and the flower heads are strangely large for the height and size of the plant. Each bottle-shaped blossom, swollen at

in large, terminal spikes, are two-lipped, rose-colored and in a bell-shaped calyx. The name Physostegia is derived from *physa,* a bladder, and *stege,* a casing, and refers to the shape of the calyx. It is called the Obedient Plant because if the individual flowers are moved sideways they remain where placed.

A Showy, Hardy Border Plant. These plants spread rapidly by means of long, white, underground stolons, and soon form large clumps. They produce their showy flowers throughout the later part of the summer. They do best in a partially shaded position, but can be grown in full sunlight. Ordinary soil is suitable. If the ground is very sandy or clayey, a liberal dressing of organic matter should be dug in. Planting may be done in fall or spring, the plants being set 12 in. apart in irregularly shaped clumps. They appreciate watering in dry weather.

The chief kind is P. virginiana, 4 ft., pink. There are several varieties of this: speciosa has larger spikes of bloom, alba has white flowers, nana is of dwarf growth, but the best of all is

Flower head of the blue, 18-in.-tall Phyteuma orbiculare.

The charming rock-garden plant named Phyteuma comosum. The bottle-shaped flowers are soft violet.

the base, is an inch or more in length and violet or amethyst in color. A well-developed head of these odd flowers is one of the most striking and curious things the rock garden has to offer in June and July.

This plant's cultivation is in no way difficult. In the rock garden in the open it delights in loam to which has been added lime rubble or lime in some other form. It prefers an open, well-drained position with rocks closely surrounding it. A deep, soil-filled rock crevice is an ideal home for the plant, though crevice planting is not absolutely essential, despite its strictly saxatile (rock-loving) habits in nature. It will flourish, too, in the limestone moraine garden. Phyteuma comosum is, moreover, a first-rate subject for cultivation in a pot or pan in the alpine house. A sharp lookout must be kept for slugs.

One of the best of all ways of growing this plant is in a large piece of tufa. If a deep hole is cut with a chisel in the soft tufa, an inch or two in diameter and five or six inches deep, and filled with soil, and the Phyteuma planted in this, it will flourish.

Raising Seedlings. Seed is the best and almost only means of propagation, but is not easily obtained. It is extremely small, and should be sown in a pot of fine sandy soil in a cold frame in spring, kept shaded, and very carefully watered. Leave the seedlings undisturbed until large enough to pot off into tiny pots, and keep them for planting out the following year.

Phyteuma humile is an attractive dwarf plant from Switzerland, with globular heads of blue flowers on 2-3 in. stems.

P. hemisphaericum is a choice dwarf kind, only an inch or two tall, with heads of blue or violet flowers, and small roundish leaves.

Phyteuma Scheuchzeri grows about 12 in. high, with spherical heads of blue flowers. It is a very pretty plant and is easy to cultivate.

Phyteuma orbiculare grows 6-18 in. tall, with attractive heads of blue flowers. It is found wild in England and other parts of Europe.

PHYTOLACCA — *Pokeweed* (Phytolac'ca). This genus consists of various types of plants, including hardy and tender herbaceous plants, trees, and shrubs. Phytolacca belongs to the family Phytolaccaceae, and is found wild in North America. South America, Africa and Asia. The name Phytolacca is derived from *phyton,* a plant, and *lacca,* lake, and refers to the color of the juice of the berries. Very few kinds are in cultivation.

The common Pokeweed, P. americana (decandra), is found wild from Maine to Florida and Mexico. It is a coarse herbaceous plant which under favorable circumstances attains a height of 10 ft. or more, but is often lower. In summer and fall it produces racemes of rich, reddish-purple berries. It is of little value as a garden plant, but may occasionally have a place in wild gardens.

The roots of P. americana are extremely poisonous and care should be exercised not to use them in error for Horse-radish, which they resemble. The young shoots of this plant are sometimes cooked and eaten in spring as greens.

Phytolacca dioica, the Umbra, is a quick-growing handsome tree that is a native of South America and is planted for ornament in California and in other mild climates. It is an evergreen and grows to a height of about 60 ft. Its flowers are white.

PICEA or SPRUCE
Ornamental Conifers for Garden Planting

Picea (Pi'cea). Evergreen trees of very considerable importance from a decorative and utilitarian point of view. They are widely distributed in temperate countries, in the Northern Hemisphere, being found as far north as any trees and in alpine altitudes in mountainous regions. The same kind or species may occur as a tree of the largest size or as a stunted bush, owing to exposure. Although perfectly hardy so far as winter cold is concerned, many Spruces are tender when young, and small trees, particularly when they are growing at a low altitude, sometimes suffer from wind burn in winter. As they advance in height they become hardier, and the young growths are less liable to injury.

Differences Between Spruce and Fir. The Piceas have been confused with the Abies or Firs, and the names of the two genera have been badly mixed. Careful examination of shoots and cones reveals a number of distinguishing features. When the leaves fall from the shoots of Picea a small peglike base is left on the stem, which gives the bark a roughened character almost like a nutmeg grater, but when the leaves fall from Abies no such peg is left—there is simply a disclike scar. Moreover, the base of the leafstalk of Abies is slightly swollen, but no such swelling occurs in Picea.

In Picea, the cones are pendulous from the branches, except when very young, and they remain intact on the branches for several months after the seeds are ripe. In Abies, the cones are erect on the branches and they break up as soon as the seeds are ripe, leaving only a central core on the shoot.

The Norway Spruce, Picea Abies, is a favorite kind.

When planted in fairly moist soil and given room to develop, the Blue Spruce, Picea pungens, forms a handsome specimen.

In both instances cones are more common on the higher parts of trees than lower down, and good cone years may be followed by one or more years when few cones are produced. In very cold regions, even though cones may be formed, good seed is produced at infrequent intervals.

Picea pungens variety glauca "R. H. Montgomery." This dwarf spruce is in the Montgomery Conifer Collection at The New York Botanical Garden.

Although some of the Spruces are important timber-producing trees, certain varieties of the same species may be so dwarf as never to grow more than 2 ft. high. These kinds are valued for planting in rock gardens, where they associate well with alpine plants because they grow no taller than high mountain Spruces that have been stunted by cold and exposure.

The various Spruces are very widely distributed through Europe, in Asia, from the Himalayas northwards, and from the extreme East through Japan; they are also found in many parts of North America. Picea belongs to the Pine family, Pinaceae; the name is taken from the Latin *pix*, pitch, and refers to the resin or pitch obtained from the common European kind.

Where to Plant. The Spruces should not be planted in places where there are considerable atmosphere impurities. They rarely thrive where soot and other impurities are deposited on the leaves, and though they sometimes grow fairly well on dry soils, they give much better results in places where the soil never gets very dry. They are among the best of all Conifers for planting

Picea Omorika, the Serbian Spruce, a quick-growing tree of graceful habit.

others are at their best when planted in small groups or as isolated trees on lawns.

When to Plant. Spruces planted under forest conditions are put out when quite small, often 9-15 in. high, and are planted in very small holes or even in slits made in the ground. A few ounces of superphosphate is sometimes mixed with the soil for each plant.

When Spruces are planted in gardens it is usual to set out larger plants, specimens 3-4 ft. tall being generally preferred. Even much larger trees can be transplanted safely by skilled gardeners and nurserymen because Spruces form compact balls of fibrous roots which make transplanting them with minimum shock to the trees possible.

Planting is best done in early spring before new growth begins, or from late August until mid-fall. Late autumn planting is not recommended because the roots do not have time to re-establish themselves before the beginning of winter. Except for very small plants, Spruce trees should be moved only when balled and burlapped (see Ball)—with a good, unbroken ball of soil attached to the roots of the tree.

How to Plant. For trees that are to be grown as decorative specimens, holes 2 ft. or more deep, and at least a foot wider all around than the balls of soil, should be prepared. If the

on moist ground. Two of the commoner kinds, P. Abies (P. excelsa) and P. pungens, are planted a good deal as decorative trees, and several others are also cultivated for the same purpose. Some kinds make good shelter belts,

The tree in the foreground is Picea pungens Kosteriana. The dark tree immediately behind it is Picea orientalis. The trees further back are Firs.

Although Spruces usually thrive much better in the country than in cities this group is prospering at The New York Botanical Garden in New York City. Spruces do not tolerate dry soils well.

natural soil is poor, make larger holes and bring in good soil.

Set the ball so that the roots are about an inch deeper than they previously were, pack good soil mixed with a generous amount of compost or other organic matter about it, soak the soil thoroughly with water, and mulch the soil surface with peat moss, leaf mold, compost or other suitable material.

Aftercare. For the first year or two following planting—until the newly moved trees have established themselves in their new locations—it is important to soak the soil thoroughly with water at such intervals during periods of dry weather as will ensure that the roots never suffer for lack of moisture. The maintenance of a mulch about the trees is excellent practice; in any case the ground about them should be kept free of weeds.

How to Raise Seedlings. Species or wild types are usually increased by seeds; varieties may be propagated by cuttings or by grafting upon stocks of their respective types that have pre-

viously been established in pots. When trees have to be raised in large numbers for forest planting, it is usual to sow the seeds in well-prepared beds out of doors after mixing the seeds with red lead as a protection against vermin. The ground for seed beds must be well worked to provide friable (crumbly) soil.

Sowing time is in spring. The seed may take from two to four weeks to germinate, and sowing should be so arranged that danger from spring frost will have passed before the seedlings appear. Upon no account should seed beds be made upon ground where water accumulates in wet weather. After reducing the ground to a fine, crumbly condition, mark out beds 3-4 ft. wide, separated by paths 12-15 in. wide. Make a moderately firm seedbed, rake off a little of the surface soil and sow the seeds thinly. They may be lightly rolled if the weather is dry and covered by a quarter of an inch of soil or coarse sand. It is advantageous to protect the seedbeds from the effects of direct sun and excessive frost by covering them with slat shades.